INVESTIGATING HUMAN ERROR: INCIDE
AND COMPLEX SYSTEMS

This book is dedicated to the memory of my father, Samuel Strauch

Investigating Human Error: Incidents, Accidents, and Complex Systems

BARRY STRAUCH

ASHGATE

Published by
Ashgate Publishing Limited
Gower House
Croft Road
Aldershot
Hants GU11 3HR
England

Ashgate Publishing Company
Suite 420
101 Cherry Street
Burlington, VT 05401-4405
USA

Ashgate website: http://www.ashgate.com

First published in hardback 2002.

British Library Cataloguing in Publication Data
Strauch, Barry
    Investigating human error : incidents, accidents, and
    complex systems
    1.Accident investigation 2.Aircraft accidents - Human
    factors 3.Aircraft accidents - Investigation 4.Errors
    I.Title
    363.1'2065

Library of Congress Control Number: 2002103117

ISBN 1 84014 931 0 (Hbk)
ISBN 0 7546 4122 8 (Pbk)

Printed and bound in Great Britain by MPG Books Ltd, Bodmin, Cornwall

Contents

List of Figures

List of Tables

Foreword

Like the rest of the modern world, I owe an enormous debt to the skills of professional accident investigators. As a traveller and a consumer, I am extremely grateful for what they have done to make complex technologies significantly safer; but as an academic I have also been especially dependent on their published findings. Although, mercifully, I have had very little first hand experience of the real thing, this has not prevented me from writing, lecturing and theorizing about the human contribution to the breakdown of complex systems for the past thirty years or so. There are perhaps two reasons why I have so far been able to pull this off. The first is that the ivory tower provided the time and resources to look for recurrent patterns in a large number of adverse events over a wide range of hazardous technologies, a luxury that few 'real world' people could enjoy. The second has been the high quality of most major accident reports. If such accounts had later been shown to lack accuracy, insight, analytical depth or practical value, then my reliance upon them would have been foolish or worse. But while many have challenged the theories, very few have questioned the credibility of the sources.

So, you might ask, if accident investigators are doing so well, why do they need this book? The most obvious answer is that human, organisational and systemic factors, rather than technical or operational issues, now dominate the risks to most hazardous industries—yet the large majority of accident investigators are technical and operational specialists. Erik Hollnagel (1993) carried out a survey of the human factors literature over three decades to track the increasing prominence of the 'human error' problem. In the 1960s, erroneous actions of one kind or another were estimated as contributing around 20 per cent of the causal contributions to major accidents. By the 1990s, however, this figure had increased fourfold. One obvious explanation is that the reliability of mechanical and electronic components has increased markedly over this period, while complex systems are still being managed, controlled and maintained by Mark I human beings.

In addition, this period has seen some subtle changes in the way we perceive the 'human error' problem and its contribution to accidents. For the most part, 'human error' is no longer viewed as a single portmanteau category, a default bin into which otherwise unexplained factors can be dumped. We now recognise that erroneous actions come in a variety of forms and have different origins, both in regard to the underlying psychological mechanisms and their external shaping factors. It is also appreciated that frontline operators do not possess a monopoly on error. Slips, lapses, mistakes and violations can occur at all levels of the system. We are now able to view errors as consequences rather than sole causes, and see frontline operators more as the inheritors rather than the instigators of accidents in complex systems.

System complexity derives in large part from the existence of diverse and redundant layers of defences, barriers and safeguards that are designed to prevent the operational hazards from coming into damaging contact with people, assets and the environment. The nuclear industry calls them 'defences-in-depth.' Such characteristics make it highly unlikely that accidents in complex systems can arise from any single factor, be it human, technical or environmental. The apparently diabolical conjunction of several different factors is usually needed to breach all of these defences-in-depth at the same time. This makes such events less frequent, but the causes more complex. Some of the latent contributions have often lain dormant in the system for many years prior to the accident. Given the increasing recognition that contributing factors can have both a wide scope and a long history, it is almost inevitable that investigators will net larger numbers of human and organizational shortcomings.

Another associated change–at least within the human factors and investigative communities–has been a shift away from the 'person model' of human error, in which the search for causes and their counter-measures is focused almost exclusively upon the psychology of individuals. Instead, there has been an increasing willingness to take a systems view of accident causation in which the important question is not 'Who blundered?' but 'How and why did the defences fail?' Unfortunately, the person model is still deeply embedded in the human psyche, and is especially pernicious in its moral (or legal) form. This is the widespread belief that responsible and highly trained professionals (pilots, surgeons, ships' officers, control room operators, and the like) *should not* make errors. However, when such erroneous actions do occur, it is assumed that they are *sufficient* to cause bad accidents. The reality, of course, is quite different. Highly trained, responsible professionals make frequent errors, but most are inconsequential, or else they are detected and recovered (see, for example, Amalberti and Wioland, 1997). Moreover, these errors are only occasionally *necessary* to add the final touches to an accident-in-waiting, a potential scenario that may have been lurking within a complex system for a long time.

The achievements of accident investigators are all the more remarkable when one considers the snares, traps and pitfalls that lie in their path. Aside from the emotional shock of arriving at often inaccessible and hostile locations to confront the horrors of an accident site, investigators are required to track backwards—sometimes for many years—in order to create a coherent, accurate and evidence-based account of how and why the disaster occurred, and to make recommendations to prevent the recurrence of other tragedies. The first and most obvious problem is that the principal witnesses to the accident are often dead or incapacitated. But this, as most investigators would acknowledge, goes with the territory. Other difficulties are less apparent and have to do with unconscious cognitive biases that influence the way people arrive at judgements about blame and responsibility and cause and effect. While human factors specialists have focused mainly upon the error tendencies of the operators of complex systems, there has also been considerable interest in how people trying to make sense of past events can go astray. Let me briefly review some of these investigative error types. They fall into two related groups: those that can bias attributions of blame and responsibility, and those that can distort perceptions of cause and effect.

Here are some of the reasons why the urge to blame individuals is so strong. When looking for an explanation of an occurrence, we are biased to find it among human actions that are close in time and place to the event, particularly if one or more of them are considered discrepant. This leads to what has been termed the *counterfactual fallacy* (Miller and Turnbull, 1990) where we confuse what might have been with what ought to have been, particularly in the case of bad outcomes. The fallacy goes as follows: had things been otherwise (i.e., had this act not happened), there would have been no adverse result; therefore, the person who committed the act is responsible for the outcome.

Another factor that leads to blaming is the *fundamental attribution error* (Fiske and Taylor, 1984). This is the universal human tendency to resort to dispositional rather than to situational influences when explaining people's actions, particularly if they are regarded as unwise or unsafe. We say that the person was stupid or careless; but, if the individual in question were asked, he or she is most likely to point to the local constraints. The truth usually lies somewhere in between.

The *just world hypothesis* (Lerner, 1970)–the view that bad things happen to bad people, and conversely–comes into play when there is an especially unhappy outcome. Such a belief is common among children, but it can often last into adulthood. A close variant is the *representativeness heuristic* (Tversky and Kahneman, 1974) or the tendency to presume a symmetrical relationship between cause and effect–thus bad consequences must be caused by horrendous blunders, while particularly good events are seen as miracles.

Yet another reason why people are so quick to assign blame is the *illusion of free will* (Lefcourt, 1973). People, particularly in western cultures, place great value in the belief that they are the controllers of their own fate. They can even become mentally ill when deprived of this sense of personal freedom. Feeling themselves to be capable of choice naturally leads them to assume that other people are the same. They are also seen as free agents, able to choose between right and wrong, and between correct and erroneous actions. But our actions are often more constrained by circumstances than we are willing to admit or understand.

All accident investigators are faced with the task of *digitising* an essentially analogue occurrence; in other words, they have to chop up continuous and interacting sequences of prior events into discrete words, paragraphs, conclusions and recommendations. If one regards each sequence as a piece of string (though it is a poor analogy), then it is the investigator's task to tie knots at those points marking what appear to be significant stages in the development of the accident. Such partitioning is essential for simplifying the causal complexity, but it also distorts the nature of the reality (Woods, 1993). If this parsing of events correctly identifies proper areas for remediation, then the problem is a small one; but it is important for those who rely on accident reports to recognise that they are–even the best of them–only a highly selected version of the actuality, and not the whole truth. It is also a very subjective exercise. Over the years, I have given students the task of translating these accident narratives into event trees. Starting with the accident itself, they were required to track back in time, asking themselves at each stage what factors were necessary to bring about the subsequent events–or, to put it another way, which elements, if removed, would have thwarted the accident sequence. Even simple narratives produced a wide variety of event trees, with different nodes and different factors represented at each node. While some versions were simply inaccurate, most were perfectly acceptable accounts. The moral was clear: the causal features of an accident are to the analyst what a Rorschach test (inkblot test) is to the psychologist's client—something that is open to many interpretations. The test of a good accident report is not so much its fidelity to the often-irrecoverable reality, but the extent to which it directs those who regulate, manage and operate hazardous technologies towards appropriate and workable countermeasures.

A further problem in determining cause and effect arises from the human tendency to confuse the present reality with that facing those who were directly involved in the accident sequence. A well-studied manifestation of this is *hindsight bias* or the *knew-it-all-along effect* (Fischhoff, 1975; Woods, et al., 1994). Retrospective observers, who know the outcome, tend to exaggerate what the people on the spot should have appreciated. Those looking back on an event see all the causal sequences homing in on that point in time at which the accident occurred; but those involved in the prior events, armed only with limited foresight, see no such convergence. With hindsight, we can easily spot the indications and warning signs that should have alerted those involved to the imminent danger. But most 'warning' signs are only effective if you know in advance what kind of accident you are going to have.

Sydney Decker (2001) has added two further phenomena to this catalogue of investigative pitfalls: he termed them *micro-matching* and *cherry-picking*. Both arise, he argues, from the investigator's tendency to treat actions in isolation. He calls this 'the disembodiment of human factors data.' *Micro-matching* is a form of hindsight bias in which investigators evaluate discrete performance fragments against standards that seem applicable from their after-the-fact perspective. It often involves comparing human actions against written guidance or data that was accessible at the time and should have indicated the true situation. As Decker puts it: 'Knowledge of the 'critical' data comes only with the omniscience of hindsight, but if data can be shown to have been physically available, it is assumed that it should have been picked up by the practitioners in the situation.' The problem, he asserts, is that such judgements do not explain why this did not happen at the time. *Cherry-picking*, another variant of hindsight bias, involves identifying patterns of isolated behavioural fragments on the basis of post-event knowledge. This grouping is not a feature of the reality, but an artefact introduced by the investigator. Such tendencies, he maintains, derive from the investigator's excessive reliance upon inadequate folk models of behaviour, and upon human reactions to failure. Fortunately, he outlines a possible remedy 'in the form of steps investigators can take to reconstruct the unfolding mindset of the people they are investigating, in parallel and tight connection with how the world was evolving around these people at the time.'

Clearly, accident investigators need help in making sense of human factors data. But I am not sure that Olympian pronouncements (or even Sinaian tablets) are the way to provide it, nor am I convinced that investigators can ever 'reconstruct the unfolding mindset of the people they are investigating'–I can't even construct my present mindset with any confidence. This book, on the other hand, delivers the goods in a way that is both useful and meaningful to hard-pressed accident investigators with limited resources. It is well written, well researched, extremely well informed and offers its guidance in a down-to-earth, practical and modular form (i.e., it can be read via the contents page and index rather than from cover to cover). It is just the thing, in fact, to assist real people doing a vital job. And, as far as I know, there is nothing else like it in the bookshops.

James Reason

References

Amalberti, R & Wioland, L. (1997). Human error in aviation. In H. M. Soekkha (Ed.), *Aviation Safety*. Utrecht: VSP.

Decker, S. W. A. (2001). The disembodiment of data in the analysis of human factors accidents. *Human Factors and Aerospace Safety*, 1: 39-58.

Fischhoff, B. (1975). Hindsight is not foresight: The effect of outcome knowledge on judgement under uncertainty. *Journal of Experimental Psychology: Human Perception and Performance*, 1: 288-299.

Fiske, S. T. & Taylor, S. E, (1984). *Social Cognition*, Reading, Massachusetts: Addison-Wesley.

Hollnagel, E. (1993). *Human Reliability Analysis*: Context and Control. London: Academic Press.

Lefcourt, H. M. (1973). The function of illusions of control and freedom. *American Psychologist*, May, 417-225.

Lerner, M. J. (1971). The desire for justice and the reaction to victims. In J. McCauley & I. Berkowitz (Eds.), *Altruism and Helping Behavior*. New York: Academic Press.

Miller, M. W., & Turnbull, W. (1990). The counterfactual fallacy. Confusing what might have been with what ought to have been. *Social Justice Research*, 4: 1-9.

Tversky, A. & Kahneman, D. (1974). Judgment under uncertainty: Heuristics and biases. *Science*, 185: 1124-1131.

Woods, D. D. (1993). Process tracing methods for the study of cognition outside of the experimental laboratory. In G. A. Klein, J. Orasunu, R. Calderwood & C. E Zsambok (Eds.), *Decision Making in Action. Models and Methods*. Norwood, NJ: Ablex.

Woods, D. D., Johannesen, L. J., Cook, R. I. & Sarter, N. B. (1994). *Behind Human Error: Cognitive Systems, Computers and Hindsight*. Dayton OH: CSERIAC.

Preface

From the time I was a boy growing up in Brooklyn I have been fascinated with New York's subway system. When I was 11, I began a tradition that lasted three years. To celebrate the last day of school, I would ride at the head end of a subway train on a route that I had not taken before. I never told my parents. I doubt they would have understood. I loved the subways and riding at the very front of the train allowed me to see not only the track ahead but also to watch the operator, then called the motorman, as well. I would stand there for hours, fascinated watching the train's movements and the train operator as he would move the train forward and then slow it down and stop it at each station.

From these beginnings, my interest in complex systems and especially transportation systems has grown. I later became fascinated with another system, aviation, and I tried to learn as much as I could about that field. After completing graduate school I indulged myself by learning to fly. I became hooked. All of my free time and disposable income went to pay for lessons and flight time. After several years I was fortunate that I could afford to acquire several pilot ratings. I even briefly considered trying to become an airline pilot. However, the airlines weren't hiring many pilots in those days and I had to enter the field another way. I became an accident investigator with the National Transportation Safety Board (NTSB).

I joined the NTSB as a human performance investigator in 1983, with several other young human factors professionals. We were among the first at the agency, or anywhere for that matter, to systematically examine the role of operator error in accidents in complex systems. They wanted us to provide more insight into the cause of an accident than to attribute it solely to operator error, the standard practice of the day.

The NTSB was, and is, a special place. Its investigators are thoroughly dedicated to its mission–to learn what causes an accident in order to prevent future accidents. Often at considerable personal sacrifice, they travel to often-inhospitable locales and work under great stress, to get to the bottom of terrible tragedies.

In those days there wasn't much to guide us beyond the standard human factors design texts. Researchers at NASA Ames had been actively engaged studying team errors and crew resource management for several years, but the fruits of their efforts would still be several years away. The Danish researcher Jens Rasmussen, and the British James Reason, Neville Moray, and their colleagues in Europe were just beginning to examine error as a systems construct, after the nuclear accident at Three Mile Island. Elsewhere, the field of human error was only just beginning to emerge as a field worthy of extensive study in and of itself.

Much has happened to the field of human error since 1983, and to me as well. I have held a variety of positions at the NTSB, all related to either investigating or training others to investigate error, in both the United States and abroad. I have met many involved in transportation safety, all as dedicated and committed as my colleagues at the NTSB. But many have asked the same question—given the prominence of human error in the cause of accidents, is there anything written on how to investigate error? Unfortunately, I would have to answer that, although there was much written on error, little was available to explain how to investigate it.

I wrote this text to remedy that situation. I have based it not on any formal method that the NTSB has adopted, but on my own reading, experience, and belief in what works. It is intended for those who are interested in human error and for those who investigate errors in the course of an incident or accident investigation.[1]

I am indebted to many people who have helped me along the way and without whose help this text would not have been possible. Although I cannot name them all, I would like to thank several whose assistance was invaluable. Dr. Michael Walker, of the Australian Transportation Safety Bureau, commented on the organization of the text when it was still in its formative stage. Drs. Evan Byrne and Bart Elias of the National Transportation Safety Board provided beneficial comments and suggestions on an early draft. Dr. Douglas Wiegmann, of the University of Illinois, took time out from his schedule to review a draft and his comments are greatly appreciated. The questions that Dr. John Stoop, of the Delft University of Technology in the Netherlands, raised were incisive and helped guide my thinking on subsequent drafts. Dr. Mitchell Garber, the medical officer of the National Transportation Safety Board, meticulously read and offered suggestions on several drafts. His guidance went well beyond medical and human factors issues and greatly improved both the content and structure of

---

[1] The text reflects my views and opinions, and not necessarily those of the National Transportation Safety Board.

the text. My editor, Ms. Joanne Sanders-Reio, worked with me to arrange my thoughts and more important, helped to refine and organize the text. Ms. Carol Horgan reviewed the final draft for clarity. My publisher, John Hindley provided ongoing support from the beginning. Prof. James Reason of the University of Manchester, encouraged my efforts at all stages of my work.

I am especially indebted to my wife Maureen, my son Sean, and my daughter Tracy. They have put up with the over three and half years that I have spent on this project, with the attendant absences from their lives and frustrations these efforts produced. Without their patience and encouragement, this book would not have been possible.

Finally, although he passed away over two decades ago, my father, Samuel A. Strauch, encouraged and supported a quest for learning that has remained with me to this day. This book is dedicated to his memory.

Barry Strauch
Annandale, Virginia

Part I
Errors and Complex Systems

1 Introduction

The ValuJet accident continues to raise troubling questions—no longer about what happened but about why it happened, and what is to keep something similar from happening in the future. As these questions lead into the complicated and human core of flight safety, they become increasingly difficult to answer. (Langewiesche, 1998)

The Atlantic Monthly

Introduction

"To err is human" it is said, and people make mistakes–it is part of the human condition. When people err they may be embarrassed or angry with themselves, but often the errors are minor and they pay little attention to the consequences. However, sometimes the errors lead to more serious consequences. Occasionally people in settings such as hospitals, airlines, power stations, or refineries commit errors–errors that lead to accidents with catastrophic consequences to those who played no part in the error. These settings establish high standards of employment and performance, and those who committed the errors may have gained highly responsible positions in these domains.

These settings, known as "complex systems" (Perrow, 1999), generate electricity, refine crude oil, manage air traffic, transport products and people, and treat the sick, to name a few. They have brought substantial benefits to our way of life, and permitted a standard of living to which many have become accustomed, but when someone who works in these systems makes an error, the consequences may be severe.

A new catastrophe seems to occur somewhere in the world with regularity, one that is later attributed to someone doing something wrong. Whether it is an airplane accident, a train derailment, a tanker grounding, or any of the myriad events that seem to occur regularly, the tendency of often-simple errors to wreak havoc continues. Despite the progress made in advancing technology, systems have not yet been developed that are immune to the errors of those who operate them. The genetic structure has been mapped and the Internet developed, but human error has not yet been eliminated.

The Crash of ValuJet Flight 592

To illustrate how even simple errors can lead to a catastrophic accident, let us look at an event in one of the safest systems–commercial air transportation. Despite numerous measures that had been developed to prevent the very types of errors that occurred, several people, including some who were not even involved in the conduct of the flight, committed critical errors that led to the accident.

On May 11, 1996, just minutes after it had taken off from nearby Miami, Florida, a McDonnell Douglas DC-9 crashed into the Florida Everglades (NTSB, 1997a). Investigators determined that the cause of this crash was relatively simple and straightforward; an intense fire broke out in the airplane's cargo compartment and within minutes burned through the compartment into the cabin. The pilots were unable to land before the fire raged through the cabin. All who were onboard were killed in the crash.

The investigation led to considerable worldwide media attention that increased over time. As with any large-scale event that is accompanied by a substantial loss of life, this was understandable. But other factors played a part as well. The airline had been operating for less than three years, and it had employed non-traditional airline practices. It had expanded rapidly, and in the months before the accident, had experienced two non-fatal accidents. After the accident of flight 592, many criticized the airline, questioning its management practices and its safety record. Government officials initially defended the airline's practices, but then reversed themselves. Just over one month after the accident, government regulators, citing deficiencies in the airline's operations, forced it to cease operations until it could satisfy their demands for reform. This led to even more media attention.

As details about the crash emerged and more was learned, the scope of the tragedy increased. Minutes after takeoff, the pilots had declared an emergency, describing smoke in the cockpit. Within days of the accident, investigators learned that despite strict prohibitions, canisters of chemical oxygen generators had been loaded onto the aircraft. It was believed that the canisters, the report of smoke in the cockpit, and the accident were related.

Oxygen generators are harmless when properly installed in protective housings in aircraft cabins. However, if the canisters are not packaged properly or without locks to prevent oxygen generation, they could begin to generate oxygen inadvertently. The process also creates heat as a byproduct, bringing the surface temperature of the canisters to as high as 500° F (250° C). Investigators believed that boxes of canisters were placed into the airplane's cargo hold, and that the canisters began generating oxygen. This heated the canisters to the point that they ignited adjacent material in the cargo compartment. The canisters then fed pure oxygen to the fire, producing one of extraordinary intensity.

Because of the potential danger that unprotected oxygen generators pose, they are considered hazardous and airlines are prohibited from loading unexpended and unprotected canisters of oxygen generators onto an aircraft. Yet, after the accident it was clear that someone had placed the canisters on the airplane. As a result, a major focus of the investigation emerged, to determine how the canisters were loaded onto the airplane.

Investigators learned that no single error led to loading the canisters onto the aircraft. To the contrary, several individuals had committed relatively insignificant errors, in a particular sequence, errors that had been committed about two months before the accident. Each error, in itself, was seemingly minor–the type that people may commit when rushed, for example. Rarely do these types of errors cause catastrophic consequences. However in this accident, despite government-approved standards and procedures designed and implemented to prevent them, people still committed the errors.

However, although the errors may have appeared insignificant, a complex system such as aviation has little room for even insignificant errors. Investigators seeking to identify the errors and relate them to the cause of the accident faced multiple challenges. Many specialists had to methodically gather and examine a vast amount of information, then analyze it to identify the critical errors, the persons who committed them, and the context in which the errors occurred.

Although it took substantial effort to understand the errors that led to this accident, investigators succeeded in learning how the errors were committed. The benefits of their activities were substantial. By meticulously collecting and analyzing necessary data, investigators were able to learn what happened and why–information that managers and regulators then applied to system operations to make them safer. Many learned lessons from this accident, and they applied what they learned to their own operations. Although the tragedy of the accident cannot be diminished, it made the aviation industry a safer one. Although there have been other accidents since this accident occurred, the aviation industry has not witnessed a similar one. This is the hope that guides investigations into error, that circumstances similar to the event being investigated will not recur.

Investigating error

Today, in many industrialized countries, government agencies or commissions generally investigate major incidents and accidents. Some countries have established agencies that are dedicated to that purpose. For example, the National Transportation Safety Board (NTSB) in the U.S., the Transportation Safety Board of Canada and the Australian Transport Safety Bureau, investigate incidents and accidents across transportation modes in their respective countries. In other countries, government agencies investigate accidents in selected transportation modes, such as the Air Accidents Investigation Branch of Great Britain and the Bureau Enquetes Accidents of France, which investigate events in commercial aviation.

However, when relatively minor accidents or incidents occur, organizations with little, if any, experience may conduct the investigations, if investigations are even carried out. Without the proper understanding those investigating error may apply investigative procedures incorrectly and fail to understand how the error came about. Although researchers have extensively examined error (e.g., Reason, 1990, 1997; Woods, Johannesen, Cook, and Sarter, 1994), there is little material that is available to guide those wishing to investigate error. Despite the high proportion of accidents and incidents in complex systems that are caused by operator error, it appears that few understand how to apply a formal process of inquiry to investigate error.

This text presents a general method of investigating errors believed to have led to an event. The method can be applied to error investigations in any complex system, although most of the examples presented are aviation-related. This primarily reflects the long tradition and experience of agencies that investigate aviation accidents, and the author's experience participating in such investigations. Please consider the examples presented as tools to illustrate points made in the text and not as reflections on the susceptibility of any one complex system or transportation mode to incidents or accidents. Neither the nature of the errors nor the process of investigating errors differs substantially among systems.

This book is intended to serve as a roadmap to those with little or no experience in human factors or in conducting investigations. It is designed for practitioners and investigators, as well as for students of error. Though formal training in human factors, psychology, or ergonomics, or experience in formal investigative methodology is helpful, it is not required. The ability to understand and effectively apply an investigative discipline to the process is as important as formal training and experience.

Chapters begin with reviews of the literature and, where appropriate, follow with explicit directions on documenting data specific to the discussion in that chapter. Most chapters also end with "Helpful techniques," designed to serve as quick investigative references.

Outline of the text

The text is divided into five sections, each addressing a different aspect of error in complex systems. The first defines concepts that are basic to the text, error and complex systems, the second focuses on types of antecedents to error, the third describes data sources and analysis techniques, the fourth section discusses two contemporary issues in human error, and the final section reviews an accident in detail and presents thoughts on selected issues important to error investigations.

Chapter 2 defines error in complex systems and introduces such critical concepts as operator, incident, accident, and investigation. Contemporary error theories are discussed, with particular attention devoted to Perrow's conception of system accidents (1999) and Moray (1994) and Reason's (1990, 1997), models of error in complex systems. Changes in views of error over the years are reviewed.

Chapter 3 begins the focus on antecedents to error by examining the role of equipment in creating antecedents to error, the source of much of the early scientific work in the field of human factors. Information display and control features that affect operator performance are discussed and illustrations of their relationship to operator errors in selected accidents are presented.

Antecedents pertaining to the system operator, historically the primary focus of those investigating error, are addressed in Chapter 4. Behavioral and physiological antecedents to error are examined, and antecedents that are operator initiated or caused are differentiated from company-influenced antecedents.

Antecedents pertaining to companies that operate complex systems, and regulators that oversee the work of those companies, are examined in Chapter 5. These antecedents incorporate many that are discussed in earlier chapters, including operating procedures and company oversight of the application of those procedures to system operations. The role of regulators, who establish and approve the rules governing system operations and oversee compliance with those rules, is reviewed.

Chapter 6 reviews antecedents that are exclusive to the maintenance and inspection environment. With the exception of Reason (1997) and Drury (1998), researchers have generally paid little attention to the role of maintenance and inspection in creating antecedents to error. These antecedents include environmental factors, tool design, the tasks themselves, and other factors related to the distinctive demands of system maintenance and inspection.

Features of multi-operator systems and their role in operator error are reviewed in Chapter 7. The complexities of contemporary systems often call for teams of operators with diverse skills and backgrounds to operate the systems. System features that necessitate the use of multi-operator teams, the errors that members of these teams could commit, and their antecedents, are examined.

Chapter 8 assesses the impact of culture on error antecedents. Two types of culture, national and company-related, are examined. Although they are distinct in terms of their relationship to antecedents, they share many characteristics that influence operator performance. Several accidents, which illustrate the types of antecedents that can arise from cultural factors, are reviewed.

Chapter 9 addresses the first of the data sources investigators rely on, data that systems recorders capture and record. Types of recorders used in different systems are examined and their contribution to the investigation of error in those systems discussed. A recent accident is presented to illustrate how recorded data can provide a comprehensive view of system state and an understanding of the errors leading to an accident.

Written documentation, an additional data source for investigators, is examined in Chapter 10. These include records that companies and government agencies maintain and factors that affect the quality of their information. Several accidents are reviewed to illustrate how written documentation can help investigators understand both the errors that may have led to events in complex systems and their antecedents.

Chapter 11 focuses on a third type of data for investigators, interview data, and their use in error investigations. Memory and memory errors are reviewed, and their relationship to error investigations discussed. Types of interviewees are discussed and factors pertaining to each, such as the type of information expected, the interview location, and the time since the event, examined. Suggestions to enhance interview quality and maximize the information they can provide are offered.

Chapter 12 discusses the analysis of data obtained in a human error investigation. Different types of analyses are described and their relationship to human error explored. A hypothetical illustration of the application of the analysis methodology to an accident involving human error is presented, with the logic involved in each of the steps examined.

The fourth section of the text, the discussion of two contemporary issues in error in complex systems, begins with Chapter 13. This chapter examines situation awareness and decision making and their relationship to system safety. Factors that can influence situation awareness are discussed, many of which are also reviewed as error antecedents elsewhere in the text. The relationship of situation awareness to decision making is outlined. Two models of decision making are reviewed, classical decision making, applied to relatively static domains, and naturalistic decision making, employed in dynamic environments. A case study involving a critical decision making error is presented to illustrate the role of decision making in system safety.

Chapter 14 examines a second issues in error, automation, a subject that has received considerable attention in the literature on error and complex systems. Changes in technology have introduced antecedents that are specific to highly automated systems. Their effects on operator performance in an accident involving a marine vessel are examined.

The final part of the text reviews issues previously discussed in the text. Chapter 15 examines an accident in detail to illustrate many of the concepts and methodology presented throughout the text. The Everglades DC-9 accident, discussed in this chapter, which involved a series of errors that different operators committed well before the accident, is detailed. The role of both the company and the regulator are examined in detail.

In the final chapter, 16, goals outlined in the first chapter are reexamined. Major principles of human performance investigation, as discussed in earlier chapters are reviewed, and ways that investigations into error can be used proactively to enhance system safety suggested.

Each chapter is meant to stand alone, so that those interested in a specific issue or technique can readily refer to the section of interest. The chapters may also be read out of sequence if desired. However, although the reader may review the chapters individually or out of sequence, reading them sequentially will provide a comprehensive overview of the literature and the field itself. It is hoped that by the end of the text the reader will feel confident to effectively investigate error in a complex system.

2 Errors, Complex Systems, Accidents, and Investigations

Patient accident reconstruction reveals the banality and triviality behind most catastrophes. (Perrow, 1999, p. 9)

Normal Accidents

Operators and complex systems

There have been extraordinary changes in the machines that affect our daily lives. The equipment has become more complex, more sophisticated, and more automated than before. In commercial aviation for example, two pilots were needed to fly the first commercially successful air transport aircraft, the Douglas DC-3, an aircraft that was designed over 60 years ago. The DC-3 could carry about 30 passengers at a speed of about 150 miles an hour, several hundred miles without refueling. Today, two pilots are also needed to operate a commercially successful aircraft, the Boeing 747, but this aircraft transports over 400 passengers, several thousand miles, at speeds in excess of 500 miles an hour. Although the acquisition and operating costs of the 747 are many times those of its predecessor, the per-seat operating costs are lower. This has helped to make air transportation affordable to many more people than in the DC-3 era.

Yet, there is a cost to these technological advances. The cost of travel has gone down substantially since the DC-3, but more people travel and more are exposed to the consequences of operator errors than before. By today's standards, industrial accidents that occurred a century ago, such as factory fires, exposed relatively few people to risk. By contrast, thousands have been lost in single events, such the 1987 sinking of the ferry Dona Paz in the Philippines, or the 1984 chemical event in Bhopal, India.[2]

Complex systems

People work with machines routinely and when they do they become machine operators. Whether it be a lawn mower, automobile, word processor, or power saw, people use machines to perform tasks that they either cannot do themselves, or can perform more quickly, accurately, or economically with machines. Together the operator and the machine form a system in which each is a critical and essential system component. As Chapanis (1996) defines,

> A system is an interacting combination, at any level of complexity, of people, materials, tools, machines, software, facilities, and procedures designed to work together for some common purpose. (p. 22)

Systems support our way of life, including water and sewage treatment, electrical power generation and transmission, and international financial systems, to name but a few. These systems, considerably more sophisticated than, say a person operating a lawn mower, have become so integral to our daily activities that in the event that they fail even briefly, whole economies are threatened.

However, as Perrow (1999) notes, the complexity of many systems has increased inordinately.

> We have produced designs so complicated that we cannot anticipate all the possible interactions of the inevitable failures; we add safety devices that are deceived or avoided or defeated by hidden paths in the systems. The systems have become more complicated because either they are dealing with more deadly substances, or we demand they function in ever more hostile environments or with ever greater speed and volume. (p. 12)

As our dependence on systems increases, more is asked of them, and with their increasing technical capabilities has come increased complexity. Complex systems are more than merely operators and equipment working

---

[2] On December 29, 1987 the ferry Dona Paz sank off the coast of Manila killing 4,235 people. On December 3, 1984, a gas leak at Union Carbide's chemical processing plant in Bhopal, India, killed an estimated 3,800 people and injured thousands more.

together, they are entities that may perform numerous tasks of considerable import to both companies and individuals.

Although complex systems need not necessarily be high-risk systems, many apply the terms interchangeably. Systems that are sufficiently complex are often high-risk systems, if for no other reason than because so many have come to depend on them. However, although the focus of this text will be on complex systems, the methodology described can be readily adapted to simple systems as well–even to the system of one person operating a lawn mower.

Operators

Operators interact with and control complex systems and play a central role in system safety. Despite the diversity of skills they need, equipment used, and settings in which they operate, one term should be used to describe them. Others have used terms such as "actor," "technician," "pilot," "controller," and "worker," the term operator will be used presently. However, in reference to maintenance activities, the term technician and inspector will be used, as appropriate.

Whether it is a financial, air transport, or electrical generating system, operators essentially perform two functions: they monitor the system and they control its operations. To do so, they obtain system-related information from the system and its operating environment, and use their knowledge and experience to interpret the information and understand the system state.

Because of the potential severity of the consequences of error in complex systems, people who control the equipment are expected to be skilled and fully qualified. Operators are the first line of defense limiting the effects of system anomalies to prevent them from becoming catastrophic. However, operators sometimes precipitate rather than prevent system incidents or accidents.

Normal accidents and complex systems

The changes that have taken place in complex systems have fundamentally altered the relationship between operators and the machines they control. Once directly controlling the machines, operators now largely supervise their operations. These tasks are performed at a higher cognitive and a lower physical level than was true of operators who manually controlled the machines.

Charles Perrow (1999) suggests that complex systems have changed to the extent that "interactive complexity" and "tight coupling" have made "normal accidents" inevitable. That is, as systems have become more efficient, powerful, and diverse in the tasks they perform, the consequences of system failures have increased. In response, designers have increased the number of system defenses against malfunctions, thus increasing internal system complexity. At the same time systems have become tightly coupled, so that processes occur in strict, time-dependent sequences, with little tolerance for variability in system operation. Should a component or subsystem experience even a minor failure, little or no "slack" would be available within the system, and the entire process will be impacted. The combination of increased complexity and tight coupling has created system states that neither designers nor operators had anticipated.

Perrow suggests that unanticipated events in tightly coupled and highly complex systems will inevitably lead to accidents. As he explains,

> If interactive complexity and tight coupling–system characteristics– inevitably will produce an accident, I believe we are justified in calling it a normal accident, or a system accident. The odd term normal accident is meant to signal that, given the system characteristics, multiple and unexpected interactions of failures are inevitable. (p. 5)

It seems difficult to accept that fundamental characteristics of complex systems have made accidents the norm. Perrow, however, has greatly influenced how incidents and accidents in complex systems are considered. James Reason (1997), the British human factors researcher, expanded on Perrow's theory and suggested that two kinds of accidents occur in complex systems: those resulting from the actions of people, what he terms "individual accidents," and those resulting largely from the actions of companies, termed "organizational accidents." Reason's description of organizational accidents has much in common with Perrow's normal accidents,

> These [organizational accidents] are the comparatively rare, but often catastrophic, events that occur within complex modern technologies such as nuclear power plants, commercial aviation, the petrochemical industry, chemical process plants, marine and rail transport, banks and stadiums. Organizational accidents have multiple causes involving many people operating at different levels of their respective companies. Organizational accidents...can have devastating effects on uninvolved populations, assets and the environment. (p. 1)

Both Reason and Perrow suggest that, given changes in the nature and function of these systems, new and largely unanticipated opportunities for human error have been created.

Vicente (1999) elaborates on Reason and Perrow's work and identifies elements of what he refers to as "sociotechnical systems," that have increased the demands on the system operators. These include the social needs and different perspectives of multiple team members that often operate complex systems, the increasing distance among operators and between operators and equipment, the dynamic nature of the systems, increasing system automation, and uncertain data. By escalating the demands on operators, each element has increased the pressure on them to perform without error.

Human fallibilities being what they are, there will always be a possibility that an operator will commit an error, and that the consequences of even "minor" errors will present a threat to the safety of complex systems. Some, such as Senders and Moray (1991), Hollnagel (1993), and Reason (1997), suggest that the impossibility of eliminating operator error should be recognized, by focusing instead on minimizing the consequences of errors.

Human error

Most errors are insignificant and quickly forgotten. The relatively minor consequences that result from errors justify the relative inattention people pay to them. Some situations even call for errors, such as learning new skills. Children who learn to ride bicycles are expected to make numerous errors initially, but fewer errors as they become more proficient, until they reach the point of riding without error. Designers and training professionals, recognizing the value of errors in learning environments, have developed equipment simulators that enable operators to be trained to operate systems in realistic environments free of the consequences of error.

People require feedback after they have erred; without it, they may not even realize that they have committed errors. Someone who forgets to deposit money into a checking account may continue to write checks without recognizing that the account lacks sufficient funds. That person would not likely be considered to be committing an error each time he or she wrote a check. Rather, most would consider the person to have committed only one error–the initial failure to deposit the funds into the account.

It should be apparent that the nature of errors and the interpretation and determination of their significance are largely contextual. Turning a crank to close an automobile window the wrong way is a minor error that would probably be quickly forgotten. On the other hand, turning a knob in the control room of a nuclear power plant in the wrong direction can lead to a nuclear accident. Both errors are similar–relatively simple acts of rotating a control in the wrong direction–yet under certain conditions an otherwise minor error can cause catastrophic consequences. What ultimately differentiate errors are their contexts and the relative severity of their consequences.

Theories of error

Modern error theory suggests that in complex systems, operator errors are the logical consequences of antecedents or precursors that had been present in the systems at the time they were committed. Moreover, theorists have not always considered system antecedents to play as large a role in error causation as is considered today.

Freud

Freud and his students believe that error was a product of the unconscious drives of the person (e.g., Brenner, 1964). Those who erred were considered to be less effective and possibly more deficient than those who did not, an interpretation that has had wide influence on theories of error and on subsequent research. For example, the concept of "accident proneness, "influenced by Freud's view of error, considered certain people to be more likely to commit errors than others because of their particular traits. However, recent studies, (e.g., Rodgers and Blanchard, 1993; Lawton and Parker 1998) found serious methodological deficiencies in the initial studies upon which much of the later assumptions about error proneness had been based. For example, the failure to control the rates of exposure to risk minimized the applicability of conclusions derived. Lawton and Parker conclude, "…it proved impossible to produce an overall stable profile of the accident-prone individual or to determine whether someone had an accident-prone personality" (p. 656).

Norman

Unlike Freud, contemporary error theorists consider the setting in which errors are committed when examining error. For example, Norman (1981, 1988) studied both cognitive and motor aspects of error and differentiated between two types of errors: slips and mistakes. Slips are action errors or errors of execution that are triggered by schemas, a person's organized knowledge, memories, and experiences. Slips can result from errors in the formation of intents to act, or faulty triggering of schemas, among other factors. He categorized six types of slips, exemplified by such errors as striking the wrong key on a computer keyboard, pouring coffee into the cereal bowl instead of the cup adjacent to the bowl, and speaking a word other than the one intended.

Mistakes are errors of thought in which a person's cognitive activities lead to actions or decisions that are contrary to what was intended. To Norman, slips are errors that logically result from the combination of environmental triggers and schemas. Applying the lessons of slips to design, such as standardizing the direction of rotation of window cranks in automobiles, would reduce the number of environmental triggers and therefore the likelihood of slips.

Rasmussen

Jens Rasmussen (1983), the Danish researcher, expands the cognitive aspects of error that Norman and others described, and defines three types of operator performance and three types of associated errors: skill-based, knowledge-based, and rule-based. Skill-based performance, the simplest of the three, relies on skills that a person acquires over time and stores in memory. Skill-based performance errors are similar to Norman's slips, largely errors of execution. Rule-based performance, more advanced than skill-based, applies rules to situations that are similar to those that operators have encountered through experience and training. Rule-based performance errors result from the inability to recognize or understand the situations or circumstances encountered. This can occur when the information necessary to understand the situation is unavailable, or the operator applies the wrong rule to unfamiliar circumstances.

Rasmussen maintains that the highest level of performance is knowledge-based. Rather than applying simple motor tasks or rules to situations that are similar to those previously encountered, the operator applies previously learned information, or information obtained through previous experience, to novel situations to analyze or solve problems associated with those situations. Knowledge-based performance errors result primarily from shortcomings in operator knowledge or limitations in his or her ability to apply existing knowledge to new situations.

Reason

James Reason (1990) enlarged the focus of earlier definitions of errors and further distinguished among basic error types. He defines slips as others had–relatively minor errors of execution, but he also identifies an additional type of error, lapses, which he characterized as primarily memory errors. A lapse is less observable than a slip and occurs when a person becomes distracted when about to perform a task, or omits a step when attempting to complete the task.

Reason also distinguishes between mistakes and violations. Both are errors of intent–mistakes result from inappropriate intentions or incorrect diagnoses of situations, violations are actions that are deliberately non-standard or contrary to procedures.

Reason does not necessarily consider violations to be negative. Operators often develop violations to accomplish tasks in ways they believe would be more efficient than they could with procedures that designers and managers developed. By contrast Reason considers a deliberate act, intended to undermine the safety of the system, sabotage.

Reason's categorization of errors corresponds to Rasmussen's performance levels. Slips and lapses are action errors that involve skill-based performance and mistakes involve either rule-based or knowledge-based performance.

Reason considered the role of designers and managers, those who operate at the higher levels, what he labels the "blunt end" of a system, in committing what he terms "latent errors" (but more recently (1997) referred to as "latent conditions") within a system. Operators, located at the "sharp end" of a system, commit what he calls "active errors," errors that directly lead to accidents.

Operators' active errors are influenced, Reason argues, by latent errors that those at the blunt end have committed, errors that lie hidden within the system. Although active errors lead to consequences that are almost immediately recognized, the consequences of latent error may go unnoticed, becoming manifest only when a combination of factors weaken system defenses against active errors. Reason believes that system designers and managers place internal defenses in systems to prevent errors from leading to incidents and accidents because they recognize the potential fallibility of human performance. However, should the defenses fail when an operator commits an error, catastrophic consequences could occur.

Reason (1990) uses a medical analogy to explain how latent errors can affect complex systems,

> There appear to be similarities between latent failures in complex technological systems and resident pathogens in the human body. The resident pathogen metaphor emphasises the significance of causal factors present in the system before an accident sequence actually begins. All man-made systems contain potentially destructive agencies, like the pathogens within the human body. At any one time, each complex system will have within it a certain number of latent failures, whose effects are not immediately apparent but that can serve both to promote unsafe acts and to weaken its defence mechanisms. For the most part, these are tolerated, detected and corrected...but every now and again a set of external circumstances–called here local triggers–arise that combines with these resident pathogens in subtle and often unlikely ways to thwart the system's defences and to bring about its catastrophic breakdown. (p. 197)

Reason illustrates how company-related defenses and resident pathogens affect safety by pointing to slices of Swiss cheese that are lined up against each other (Figure 3.1). Unforeseen deficiencies within the system, including questionable managerial and design decisions, line managers actions, "psychological precursors" to operators such as reactions to stress or other aspects of the "human condition," and unsafe acts, resemble holes in the Swiss cheese. The solid parts of the cheese slices represent company-related defenses against the hazards of unsafe acts. If the Swiss cheese slices were placed one against the other, the holes or deficiencies would be unlikely to line up in sequence. Company-related defenses, portrayed as portions of the cheese, would block an error from penetrating. However, should the deficiencies (holes) line up uniquely, an active error could breach the system, much as an object could move through the holes in the slices, an unsafe act would not be prevented from affecting the system, and an accident could result.

To Reason, even though managerial and design errors are unlikely to lead directly to accidents and incidents, an examination of human error should assess the actions and decisions of the managers and designers at the blunt end at least as much, if not more, than the actions of the system operators at the sharp end. His identification of the role of both design and company-related or managerial antecedents of error has greatly influenced contemporary treatments of error. For example, the International Civil Aviation Organization (ICAO) has formally adopted Reason's model of error for its member states to facilitate their understanding of human factors issues and aviation safety (ICAO, 1993).

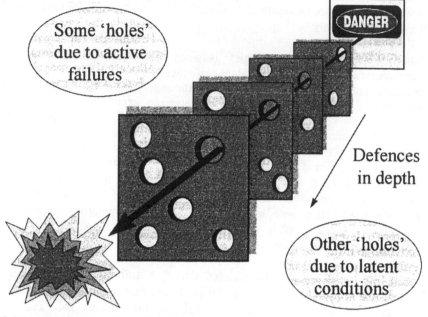

Figure 3.1 Reason's model of error (Reason, 1997)

Definitions of error

Researchers generally agree on the meaning of an error. To Senders and Moray (1991), it is "something [that] has been done which was not intended by the actor, not desired by a set of rules or an external observer, or that led the task or system outside its acceptable limits" (p. 25). Reason (1990) sees an error as "a generic term to encompass all those occasions in which a planned sequence of mental or physical activities fails to achieve its intended outcome, and when these failures cannot be attributed to the intervention of some chance agency" (p. 5). Woods, Johannesen, Cook, and Sarter (1994) define error as "a specific variety of human performance that is so clearly and significantly substandard and flawed when viewed in retrospect that there is no doubt that it should have been viewed by the practitioner as substandard *at the time the act was committed or omitted"* (emphasis in original, p. 2).

Hollnagel (1993) believes that the term "human error" is too simplistic and that "erroneous action" should be used in its place. An erroneous action, he explains, "is an action which fails to produce the expected result and which therefore leads to an unwanted consequence" (p. 67). He argues that one should not make judgments regarding the cause of the event. The term erroneous action, unlike error, implies no judgment and accounts for the context in which the action occurs.

Despite some disagreement, most agree on fundamental aspects of error, seeing it as the result of something that people do or intend to do that leads to outcomes that were different from what they had expected. Therefore, to be consistent with these views on error, error will be defined as *an action or decision that results in one or more unintended negative outcomes*. Errors that occur in learning or training environments, where they are expected, tolerated, and used to enhance and enlarge a person's repertoire of skills and knowledge, will not be considered further.

Error taxonomies

Senders and Moray (1991) developed an error taxonomy based largely on the work of Rasmussen, Reason, and others, to better understand errors and the circumstances in which people commit errors. Senders and Moray's taxonomy suggests that error results from one or more of the following factors operating alone or together: the person's "information-processing system" or cognitive processes; environmental effects; pressures on and biases of the individual; and the individual's mental, emotional, and attentional states. This taxonomy describes errors in terms of four levels; "phenomenological" or observable manifestations of error, cognitive processes, goal-directed behaviors, and external factors, such as environmental distractions or equipment design factors.

Shappell and Wiegmann (1997, 2001) propose a taxonomy to apply to the investigation of human error in aircraft accidents. Expanding on Reason's work, their taxonomy differentiates among operations that are influenced by unsafe supervision, unsafe conditions, and unsafe acts. Unsafe acts include various error categories, while unsafe conditions include both behavioral and physiological states and conditions. Unsafe supervision, which distinguishes between unsafe supervisory actions that are unforeseen and those that are foreseen, incorporates elements that Reason would likely term latent errors or latent conditions.

Sutcliffe and Rugg (1998) propose a taxonomy based on Hollnagel's (1993) differentiation between error phenotypes (the manifestation of errors) and genotypes (their underlying causes). They group the operational descriptions of errors into six categories, and divide causal factors into three groups: cognitive, social and company-related, and equipment or tool design.

O'Hare (2000) proposes a taxonomy, referred to as the "Wheel of Misfortune," to serve as a link between researchers in human error and accident investigators seeking to apply research findings to incidents or accidents. As Reason, he delineates company-related defenses that could allow operator error to affect system operations unchecked.

Incidents, accidents, and investigations

Incidents and accidents

Researchers disagree on the definition of an incident or accident in complex systems. Senders and Moray (1991) term an accident "a manifestation of the consequence of an expression of an error" (p. 104). Others suggest that accidents are events that are accompanied by injury to persons or damage to property. In this way even minor injuries can change the categorization of an incident to an accident.

Perrow (1999) distinguishes between accidents and incidents largely by the extent of the damage to property and injuries to persons. He considers incidents to be events that damage parts of the system, and accidents events that damage subsystems or the system as a whole, resulting in the immediate shutdown of the system. He suggests that although a system accident may start with a component failure, it is primarily distinguished by the occurrence of multiple failures interacting in unanticipated ways. Catastrophic system accidents may bring injury or death to bystanders uninvolved with the system, or even to those not yet born. For example, accidents in nuclear generating stations can lead to birth defects and fertility difficulties among those exposed to radiation released in the accident.

Legal definitions

The classification of an event into accident follows specific definitions in both international law and in the laws of individual nations. For example, ICAO (1970) defines an aircraft accident as,

> An occurrence associated with the operation of an aircraft which takes place between the time any person boards the aircraft with the intention of flight until such time as all such persons have disembarked, in which:
>
> a person is fatally injured…or
> the aircraft sustains damage or structural failure…or
> the aircraft is missing or is completely inaccessible. (p. 1)

ICAO also precisely defines injury and death associated with an accident. Injuries include broken bones other than fingers, toes, or noses, or any of the following: hospitalization for at least 48 hours within seven days of the event, severe lacerations, internal organ damage, second- or third-degree burns over five percent or more of the body, or exposure to infectious substances or injurious radiation. A fatal injury is defined as a death from accident-related injuries that occurred within 30 days of the accident. An incident is an event that is less serious than an accident.

Other government or international agencies use similar definitions, albeit specific to the particular domain. For example, the U.S. Coast Guard defines a marine accident as,

> Any casualty or accident involving any vessel other than public vessels if such casualty or accident occurs upon the navigable waters of the United States, its territories or possessions or any casualty or accident wherever such casualty or accident may occur involving any United States vessel which is not a public vessel…[including] any accidental grounding, or any occurrence involving a vessel which results in damage by or to the vessel, its apparel, gear, or cargo, or injury or loss of life of any person; and includes among other things, collisions, strandings, groundings, founderings, heavy weather damage, fires, explosions, failure of gear and equipment and any other damage which might affect or impair the seaworthiness of the vessel…[and] occurrences of loss of life or injury to any person while diving from a vessel and using underwater breathing apparatus (46 Code of Federal Regulations 4.03-1 (a) and (b).

The term serious marine incident includes the following events involving a vessel in commercial service: (a) Any marine casualty or accident as defined in Sec. 4.03-1…and which results in any of the following: (1) One or more deaths; (2) An injury to a crewmember, passenger, or other person which requires professional medical treatment beyond first aid, and, in the case of a person employed on board a vessel in commercial service, which renders the individual unfit to perform routine vessel duties; (3) Damage to property, as defined in Sec. 4.05-1(a)(7) of this part, in excess of $100,000; (4) Actual or constructive total loss of any vessel subject to inspection under 46 U.S.C. 3301; or (5) Actual or constructive total loss of any self-propelled vessel, not subject to inspection under 46 U.S.C. 3301, of 100 gross tons or more. (b) A discharge of oil of 10,000 gallons or more into the navigable waters of the United States, as defined in 33 U.S.C. 1321, whether or not resulting from a marine casualty. (c) A discharge of a reportable quantity of a hazardous substance into the navigable waters of the United States, or a release of a reportable quantity of a hazardous substance into the environment of the United States, whether or not resulting from a marine casualty. (46 Code of Federal Regulations 4.03-2)

To avoid confusion among the various definitions, both incidents and accidents in complex systems will be defined as: *unexpected events that cause substantial property damage or serious injuries to people*. Accidents lead to consequences that are more severe than those of incidents.

Investigations

Senders and Moray (1991) acknowledge that investigations can be conducted for a variety of purposes. "What is deemed to be the cause of an accident or error," they note, "depends on the purpose of the inquiry. *There is no absolute cause*" (emphasis in original, p. 106). For example, law enforcement personnel conduct criminal investigations to identify perpetrators of crimes and to collect sufficient evidence to prosecute and convict them. Governments investigate accidents to protect the public by ensuring that the necessary steps are taken to prevent similar occurrences, mandating necessary changes to the system or, changing the nature of its oversight of the system. Kahan (1999) notes that governments have become more involved in the investigation of transportation accidents. Whereas governments initially investigated accidents on an individual basis and assigning investigators to the investigations as they occurred, governments are establishing agencies with full-time investigative staffs exclusively to investigate accidents.

Rasmussen, Pejtersen, and Goodstein (1994) contend that investigators examine system events according to a variety of viewpoints. These include a common sense one, and those of the scientist, reliability analyst, therapist, attorney, and designer. Each influences what Rasmussen et al. refer to as an investigation's "stopping point," i.e., the point at which the investigator believes that the objectives of the investigation have been met.

For example, an investigator with a common sense perspective stops the investigation when satisfied that the explanation for the event is reasonable and familiar. The scientist concludes the investigation when the mechanisms linking the error antecedent to the operator who committed the error are identified, and the attorney concludes the investigation when the one responsible for the event, usually someone directly involved in the operation who can be punished for his or her actions or decisions, is found. The objective advocated in this text is based on suggestions of Rasmussen et al. (1994). Investigators should conduct investigations to learn what caused an incident or accident by establishing a link between antecedent and error, so that changes can be implemented to prevent future occurrences.

Human error investigations in complex systems

Assumptions

This objective requires several assumptions about operator error in complex systems, assumptions that form the foundation of this approach. These are–

- The simpler the task, the lower the likelihood that an error will be committed.
- The more people involved in performing a task, the greater the likelihood that an error will be committed.
- Errors cannot be eliminated, but opportunities for error can be reduced.

Although the first two assumptions may seem rather obvious, some assume the contrary, that by adding steps and operators to a task the chances of error decrease. In fact, with certain exceptions, the opposite is true. As a task becomes more complex and more people are needed to perform it, opportunities for error increase.

Systems that people design, manage, and operate, cannot be immune to error because of the inherent imperfections of the human designer and operator. Designers cannot design a perfect system and operators cannot ensure error-free performance. Operators of any system, irrespective of its complexity, purpose, or application, can err. Their errors can help us learn their causes so that modifications to the system can be proposed, and the circumstances that led to the errors prevented from recurring.

General model

Researchers have focused on system characteristics and how they contribute to error, views that have influenced the way investigations are conducted. Paries and Amalberti (2000) describe what they term a "safety paradigm shift" that has occurred over the past 50 years among safety specialists and investigators, as systems have become more complex and views on the nature of error have changed. They suggest that investigators have increased the period they consider to be involved in the cause of an event from the time of the immediate operator actions back to influences on those actions. The size of the system being examined and the "depth of explanation" of the cause have also increased, to include those who influence, but may not be directly involved in, system operations.

Neville Moray (1994, 2000), the British human factors researcher, contends that error in complex systems results from elements that form the systems and, to investigate system errors, one must examine the pertinent elements. He outlines these features with concentric squares that show the equipment as a core component of the system (Figure 3.2). These elements shape the system–

- Equipment
- Individual operator
- Multi-operator team
- Company and management
- Regulator
- Society and cultural factors.

Each system component affects the quality of the system operation, and can create opportunities for operator error. For example, the information operators obtain about the system affects their perception of the system state. Displayed information that is difficult to read can increase the likelihood of error. Each of these elements can lead to error in itself, or can interact with the others to create opportunities for error.

Antecedents

Because errors are unintended, one assumes that operators want to operate systems correctly. Their errors reflect internal or external influences on their performance because they wanted to perform well but did not because of system characteristics.

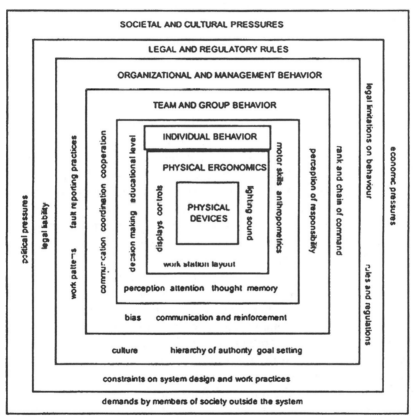

Figure 3.2   Moray's model of error (Moray, 2000)

These characteristics are referred to as precursors or antecedents to error. Antecedents may be hidden within systems, such as in the equipment design, procedures, and training, where they remain unrecognized but can still degrade the system operators' performance. The mechanisms by which each antecedent or precursor exerts its influence varies with the context and nature of both the system element and the antecedent itself. For example, an antecedent may distract an operator during a critical task, hinder his or her ability to obtain critical information, or limit his or her ability to recall or apply the proper procedure.

The presence of an antecedent is noted in two ways, by identifying an action, situation, or factor that influenced the operator's performance during the event, and more important, by obtaining evidence demonstrating that the operator's performance was affected by the antecedent. The evidence, which can take many forms, will be discussed subsequently.

Summary

Complex systems are those combinations of people, materials, tools, machines, software, facilities, and procedures designed to work together for a common purpose. Perrow argues that the interactive complexity and "tight coupling" or close interrelationships among complex system elements create conditions that make accidents and incidents "normal." When component malfunctions occur the combination of interactive complexity and tight coupling within the system can create system states that neither operators nor designers had anticipated.

Error is defined as an action or decision that results in one or more unintended negative outcomes. Perrow's work has influenced theories of error, and has changed the way the system's influence on operator performance is viewed. Where researchers had seen errors as primarily reflecting on the person committing them, contemporary views of error see it originating within the operating system. Reason likens these elements to pathogens residing within the body. As pathogens can cause illness when certain conditions are met, system-related deficiencies (latent errors or latent conditions) cause the normal defenses to fail and lead to an operator error, which causes an event. Moray delineates system elements that can lead to error in complex systems.

Error investigations can have many objectives and purposes, depending on the investigator's perspective. The objective of an investigation should be to mitigate future opportunities for error by identifying the critical errors and their antecedents, and eliminating them or reducing their influence in the system. The model of error that is proposed in the text describes six types of antecedents, each of which, alone or in combination, can adversely affect operator performance and lead to an error.

Part II
Antecedents

3 Equipment

The representation of the problem provided to a problem solver can affect his, her, or its task performance. (Woods, 1995, p. 158)

Introduction

A well-known accident involving a complex system, the March 1979 accident at the Three Mile Island nuclear generating plant (Kemeny, 1979), showed how poorly designed equipment can hurt operator performance in complex systems. Investigators found that the operators, confused by the many alarms and warnings signaling a malfunction, had difficulty interpreting the displayed data to understand the event.

In World War II, U.S. Army Air Corps and British Royal Air Force independently recognized the importance of equipment design on the safety of pilots who were in training. Both changed aspects of cockpit features to enhance flight safety, based on their studies of pilot-aircraft interactions (Meister, 1999; Nickerson, 1999). Researchers have continued to study and apply human factors and ergonomics principles to the design of equipment in both simple and complex systems to improve system safety (e.g., Corlett and Clark, 1995; Karwowski and Marras, 1999; Wickens and Hollands, 2000).

Research has shown that, although operators obtain much of the information they need about operating systems from system displays, they use other sources as well. Mumaw, Roth, Vicente, and Burns (2000) found that operators actively acquire information from other operators, maintenance and operating logs, and their own observations of operating conditions. Today, it is recognized that experienced operators obtain system information from many sources, but still rely extensively on features of the equipment itself to understand the system's state. This chapter will examine features of equipment design to understand their effects on operator performance.

Visual information

Operators acquire and use system-related information to readily understand the current and near term system states and operating environments. Operators can obtain this information through any sensory modality, although most systems present information visually and aurally. Each modality has distinct advantages and disadvantages in their effects on operator performance.

Visually-presented information has a high degree of precision and as a result, most systems information is presented visually. But visually-presented information must be displayed properly for operators to efficiently obtain critical information. These features affect the quality of visual information–

- Number of displays
- Organization and layout
- Conspicuity
- Interpretability
- Trend portrayal.

The number of displays

Visual information is presented primarily through either analog or digital displays. Analog displays are found in older systems, and generally show a one to one relationship between a component or subsystem and the corresponding information display. Systems with numerous components and subsystems may have hundreds of displays, each providing critical information about one component or subsystem. For example, the illustration of a Soviet era nuclear power plant in Figure 3.3 shows a display with dials too numerous for operators to readily monitor. Should one show information revealing an unusual or unexpected occurrence, the operator would be unlikely to notice the information without assistance. The operator would have to search the displays to identify and locate the needed information before even trying to comprehend the cause of the occurrence. During high workload periods, such as during anomalous operating conditions, numerous displays could interfere with an operator's ability to quickly locate and understand the critical data in the available time.

© Gary Knight. Reprinted with permission.

**Figure 3.3   Soviet era nuclear power plant. Note the numerous dials
and controls**

Organization and layout

Display organization can influence an operator's ability to access needed
system data, especially in a system with numerous displays. Display
groupings that do not conform to the logic that operators use to understand
the system state can prolong the time they need to find and understand the
needed data. The more readily the display organization allows operators
access, the fewer the opportunities for operator error.

Rasmussen and Vicente (1989) propose organizing information
according to what they term "ecological interface design," by matching the
organization of the displays the operator's mental model of the system
state. This will support an operator's cognitive activities during interactions
with the systems, and hopefully reduce opportunities for error.

Poorly organized displays, "cluttered" displays, or displays that do not
separate critical information from non-critical information will adversely
affect operator performance. Wickens and Carswell (1995) refer to these

adverse effects as the "information access cost" of display organization. The greater the cost, the more cognitive effort operators exert and the more time they spend accessing and interpreting the critical information.

Conspicuity

The greater the contrast between a display feature and that of other displays, the more conspicuous the displayed data will be and hence, the lower the operator's information access cost. Display conspicuity is influenced by display size, contrast, and luminance relative to adjacent displays. The larger a display, and the relatively brighter it is compared to others, the greater it will stand out against the prevailing background, and the more likely the operator will notice it (e.g., Sarter, 2000).

Interpretability

The more interpretable the data, the more readily operators can use the information to understand the system state. Consider a gauge that displays an automobile's coolant temperature. By itself the temperature has little meaning to those who are unaware of the optimum temperature range during "normal" operating conditions. But a gauge that displays a picture of an engine as a face that smiles, with the smile changing to a frown and the face color becoming a deeper red as the temperature increases, would convey considerably more interpretable information to drivers who would otherwise not understand the meaning of the temperatures.

Designers have used different methods to increase operators' ability to understand visually-presented data. Abbott (2000) describes a method of presenting of aircraft engine information that is considerably more interpretable than current displays of the same information, because the presentation more closely matches the needs of the operator. Aircraft engine-related data displays, and their effects on operator performance, will be discussed more fully in chapter 9.

Color can also quickly convey information. Parsons, Seminara, and Wogalter (1999) found that in numerous countries and cultures, the color red indicates potentially hazardous conditions. Similarly, green and yellow or amber signify normal and cautionary operating conditions, respectively. Designers have often placed colors behind a pointer or gauge on analog displays so that operators can quickly recognize the value of the component parameter as the pointer approaches the color. Automobile drivers use tachometer colors to determine when an engine "red lines" or approaches its maximum safe operating range.

Digital displays also allow substantial flexibility in presenting data. They can be designed to present pictures, smiles or frowns for example, to convey information. Some systems use flow diagrams to display the state of electrical, pneumatic, and other subsystems, enabling operators to quickly identify a flow anomaly and recognize its impact on the system as a whole.

Although digital displays offer flexibility in presenting information, the relationship of display flexibility to operator performance has not been demonstrated consistently. Miller and Penningroth (1997) conclude that digital displays may not necessarily result in superior operator performance relative to analog displays. By contrast, Abbott (2000) believes that properly designed digital displays can enhance operators' ability to interpret data.

Trend portrayal

Because of the dynamism of many complex systems, operators need to quickly detect and interpret trend information, the direction and rate in which component parameters change, in order to understand their effects on system state. Analog displays have traditionally presented direction information by the clockwise or counter-clockwise movement of an indicator or pointer, and rate of change by the rapidity of that movement. These features are often seen in airplane disaster movies, for example, in which the rapidly unwinding altimeter–the instrument that depicts an aircraft's altitude–conveys the seriousness of the situation. Some analog displays use vertical or horizontal "tapes" or lines to convey trend information. The lines move up or down or left or right to convey the direction and rapidity of system changes.

Digital displays do not necessarily present trend information better than do analog displays. A digital format that presents system parameters in Arabic numerals gives the operator precise parameter information. However, in the event of a rapid change, the numerals corresponding to the parameter would also change rapidly, and operators may not be able to quickly interpret the direction of change, i.e., whether the parameters are increasing or decreasing.

Yet, properly designed digital displays can present trend information in at least a comparable, if not superior way, to analog displays. These generally depict the nature and rate of the change pictorially to minimize operators' time spent interpreting trend data, as in the illustration of the face to portray engine coolant temperature.

Aural information

Visually-presented information has one drawback, operators must look at the information to receive it. If they are looking at displays of non-critical information, or engaged in other tasks and focusing elsewhere, they will not receive the information. Designers compensate for this shortcoming by adding aurally-presented information to the displays.

Because of the salience of aurally-presented information—even inattentive operators receive the information—designers have usually relied on aurally-presented information to rapidly communicate critical information to operators (e.g., Edworth, Loxley, and Dennis, 1991; Patterson, 1990). However, aurally-presented information also has limitations in that the conveyed information is less precise than visually-presented information, and it can quickly distract operators and hinder their performance (e.g., Banbury, Macken, Tremblay, and Jones, 2001).

The quality of aurally-presented information is primarily influenced by –

- Conspicuity
- Distractibility
- Uniqueness
- Accuracy
- Relative importance.

Conspicuity

To perceive aurally-presented information operators must distinguish the critical sound from others. Designers generally use of one of two methods to increase the conspicuity of critical sounds relative to those of other sounds, increasing volume or varying sound elements such as pitch, frequency, and rhythm. Patterson (1990) suggests increasing the volume of critical sounds by at least 15 dB over the volume of background noises, to make them clearly audible. In environments in which the ambient sounds are fairly loud, this could cause aurally-presented information to be quite loud, even approaching dangerous levels over extended periods.

Distractibility

Once aural information has been presented, continuing to present the information adds little additional information, and can distract operators and degrade their performance. The longer aural information continues to be presented and the more conspicuous the sound, the more likely the information will interfere with and degrade operator performance. On the other hand, Banbury, Macken, Tremblay, and Jones (2001) point out that after about 20 minutes of exposure the distracting effects of sounds are reduced. Unfortunately, exposure to the interfering effects of sounds for as long as 20 minutes can substantially degrade operators' ability to respond effectively.

Aurally-presented information should cease to be presented after operators have received and understood it. However, many systems cannot recognize when this has been accomplished. Too often, aural information first informs and then distracts operators.

Aural information can also distract and interfere with the work of operators who were not the targets of the initial information, especially in small operating environments such as locomotive cabs, ship bridges, or aircraft cockpits. Allowing operators to silence alerts might negate these disadvantages. However, as will be discussed shortly, systems that allow operators to silence alerts have other disadvantages.

Accuracy

Aurally-presented information that is inaccurate and inconsistently conveys useful information will lose its value over time, and will eventually fail to elicit operator attention. Yet, designers generally consider the consequences of missed alerts, where aural information is presented but operators do not respond, to be more critical to system safety than those of false alarms, where alerts are sounded but a response is unnecessary. Therefore, they set the system state threshold sufficiently low to ensure that critical events will elicit alerts, even if this results in non-critical events eliciting alerts as well. This can repeatedly expose operators to false alarms, which has been found to reduce operators' sensitivity to the alerts, and as Sorkin (1988) found, can lead to outright operator action to silence them altogether.

In a January 1987 rail accident near Baltimore, Maryland, the locomotive engineer and brakeman who were operating two freight locomotives, silenced an alarm they considered distracting, a shrill whistle that sounded when the head locomotive passed a stop signal (NTSB, 1988a). The locomotives passed the signal and entered a track section that was reserved for an approaching high-speed passenger train. Shortly thereafter, the passenger train struck the freight locomotives, killing the train's engineer and 16 of its passengers. Investigators concluded that the aural alert would have informed the freight locomotive's engineer and brakeman of their impending entry onto a prohibited track section. Investigators also found that the two operators had smoked marijuana before the accident and were impaired at the time.

Uniqueness

Designers create distinct sounds that are associated with different system elements, system states, or desired operator responses. Uniqueness characterizes the degree to which a sound is associated with specific system-related information. Operators learn to associate certain sounds with their corresponding system states so that when they are heard they will need little time to interpret them, and will be unlikely to confuse the sounds with others. Emergency vehicles use distinctive sirens to alert drivers and increase the likelihood that drivers will quickly recognize and respond to them.

Aurally-presented information can take a variety of forms. "Traditional" sounds such as bells, whistles, horns, and sirens are found on older equipment. Each sound can be readily distinguished from others and, if loud enough, could be heard over ambient sounds.

As with visually-presented information, modern equipment usually offers more flexibility in presenting aural information than does older equipment. Synthesized or recorded human voices that articulate simple voice messages can be used, in addition to traditional sounds (Stern, Mullennix, Dyson, and Wilson, 1999). Belz, Robinson, and Casali (1999) proposed using auditory icons, such as screeching tires, sounds that can be distinctly associated with particular system states with little additional operator training and experience. These are more interpretable than abstract sounds, and hence should lead to rapid operator recognition and response.

Relative importance

A single event can precipitate multiple system warnings or alerts, each reflecting the state of a single system parameter rather than the event that led to the parameter change. Certain phenomena can produce a cacophony of sounds and alarms that signify the effects of an event, rather than the precipitating event itself. When this occurs the operator must be able to effectively evaluate the individual alerts in order to understand the phenomenon that led to the alerts, rather than the effects of the phenomenon on the system.

Some systems inhibit both visual and aural alerts, which do not require immediate operator action, during critical operating cycles. This reduces the likelihood that non-critical alerts would distract operators during critical tasks, as occurred in the crash of a Boeing 757 off the coast of Lima, Peru, in October 1996. Investigators found that the pitot static system, a critical system component that measures airspeed, climb and descent speeds, and altitude, was blocked by a maintenance error, which led to its presenting erroneous information to the pilots (Accident Investigation Commission, 1996).

After takeoff numerous airspeed and altitude warnings and alerts, including low terrain, low airspeed, impending stall (the "stick shaker"), and windshear, were heard. The alerts began within five seconds of each other and continued until impact. Each signaled a specific hazardous situation, but there was no alert that corresponded to the failure that had caused the multiple alerts–the inoperative pitot static system. The pilots were unable to determine the cause of the alerts. More important, operating at night and over water they could not visually estimate the airplane's airspeed and altitude. The alerts distracted the pilots, hindered their communications, and interfered with their ability to effectively diagnose the anomaly.

Multiple warnings or alerts that sound simultaneously or in quick succession often require the highest level of operator performance. Yet, they are presented when operator workload tends to already be high because they must, 1) continue to operate the system, 2) diagnose and respond to the anomaly, and 3) avoid causing additional damage. Combined these tasks are challenging, but when multiple alerts sound simultaneously during periods of high workload they can degrade performance.

Kinesthetic/tactile alerts

Some have proposed presenting information through other sensory modalities to compensate for the limitations of both visual and aural information (e.g., Sklar and Sarter, 1999; Sarter, 2000). Transport airplane designers use both kinesthetic and aural cues to simultaneously alert pilots to a critical event, an aerodynamic stall. A stall requires immediate pilot action or the airplane may crash. Just before reaching the airspeed that would precede an aerodynamic stall, pilots hear a particular alert and feel a distinctive control column motion, sensations that are very difficult to ignore. However, as with aurally-presented information, constant presentation of kinesthetically- or tactually-presented information can distract operators and degrade their performance.

Controls

Operators use controls to modify system operations. Control design characteristics can influence operator performance and the likelihood of error, as displays can. Controls can take many shapes and forms, move in a number of directions, and be placed in a variety of locations. Automobiles, for example, employ at least three primary controls to enable drivers to direct their motion. The accelerator controls forward motion, the brake pedal slows or stops the vehicle, and the steering wheel controls lateral motion. Vehicles equipped with standard transmissions have two additional controls, a clutch and gearshift lever, for changing transmission gears as vehicle speed and engine rotation rates change. Other controls enable drivers and passengers to change window height, windshield wiper speed, audio system characteristics, headlight brightness, heat, air conditioning or ventilation levels, horns, turn signals and other, less critical components.

Investigators generally apply these criteria to assess the quality of control design–

- Accessibility and location
- Direction of movement and function
- Shape
- Standardization.

The quality of keyboard controls, which are increasingly used in complex systems, is evaluated according to other criteria.

Accessibility and location

Accessibility, the ease with which operators can reach and manipulate desired controls, can influence operator performance. In systems with relatively unlimited space, in which time to manipulate controls is not critical, accessibility will not substantially influence operator performance. However, in systems with space limitations, designers need to shape and locate controls so that operators can readily access them, with little regard to the operators' physical dimensions. Well-designed systems have controls that operators can reach and manipulate without moving far from their stations.

Inaccessible, hidden, or obscured controls can delay operator response when time is critical and thus serve as antecedents to error. Large church or concert organs illustrate well-designed controls. Organists adjust their access to the controls by moving their seats, and use both their hands and feet to operate the controls, the keys and the pedals.

Direction of movement and function

The direction in which a control moves should intuitively correspond to the direction of change in the corresponding component. Raising a control should increase an aspect of the system such as production rate, component height, or illumination level, while lowering a control should reduce it. Depressing a button should engage a component function while releasing the depressed button should disengage it. Controls that move in directions that are counterintuitive can become antecedents to error if operators actuate the control incorrectly after using similar controls that move in a "standard" direction.

Mode errors Systems with limited available space often employ multi-function controls, in which one control directs multiple system activities. Operators who are unfamiliar with or do not perceive the distinction among the various control functions may initiate a control action and an unanticipated system response, what has become known as a mode error (Norman, 1988).

Multi-function controls can be designed to reduce opportunities for mode errors by giving operators unambiguous information or feedback about the system's operating mode. The quality of the presentation of feedback is affected by the same visual, aural, and kinesthetic factors discussed previously. Visually-presented feedback should be sufficiently conspicuous to enable operators to receive the information. Aurally-presented information is likely to be the least confusing, but operators will tend to ignore aural information if presented repeatedly.

Investigators concluded that the pilots of an Airbus A-320 that crashed short of the runway at Mont St. Odile, France, in 1992, committed a mode error while preparing to land (Commission of Investigation, 1994). A single control, a knob that turned clockwise or counterclockwise to increase or decrease the rate of change in the desired mode, also controlled both the airplane's descent rate and its flight path angle. Pilots selected the mode by either depressing or pulling the knob and then turning it to establish the desired descent rate or descent angle. Incorrectly controlling the knob engaged the mode other than the one intended.

Investigators concluded that the pilots had inadvertently selected the wrong mode, and established a descent rate that was triple the typical rate, believing that they had commanded a moderate descent angle. Because of the dual purpose of the control knob, and the ambiguous information available about the mode that they had engaged, the pilots were not aware of their error and then failed to notice the rapid descent to the ground.

Shape

Controls can take a number of forms and shapes, such as knobs, buttons, wheels, switches, levers, or pedals. Designers may shape a control to resemble a distinctive task or function. In some systems regulators have mandated specific design characteristics. For example, the lever that extends or retracts airplane landing gear is required to be circular to reduce the possibility of confusion with an adjacent control. By shaping the lever to correspond to the shape of the controlled component, the aircraft wheels, pilots can recognize the control by touch alone, minimizing the possibility of control confusion.

Control shape can play an important role in operator performance. In high workload or stressful situations, operators may not have the time to visually identify a control before manipulating it. Rather, they may locate and select controls by touch alone, without visual verification. In these circumstances, operators may find similarly shaped controls to be undistinguishable, and select the wrong control.

Standardization

Operators have come to expect a certain configuration, shape, and direction of movement in the controls that they manipulate. Unfortunately, unless regulators establish rules governing the design of both displays and controls, designers may create controls and displays that suit their own rather than the operators' needs. This can lead to large differences in the shape of similar controls on comparable equipment. Those who have driven cars that are different from their own at night, and had difficulty locating and engaging the windshield wipers or headlights because the controls were located in unexpected places, have encountered these differences.

So long as operators interact with only one type of equipment, nonstandard control shapes, locations, and directions of movement will not create antecedents to errors. However, those who interact with comparable equipment that have different controls and displays could, out of habit, move a control incorrectly or direct the wrong control when alternating between the two equipment types. If operators repeatedly reach one location to access a control, or move it in a certain direction to accomplish an action, they will likely continue these movements on different equipment, even if the movements produce unintended consequences.

The NTSB found that the rate at which pilots had failed to extend the landing gear before landing was higher among pilots of aircraft that had been designed and built by one manufacturer than with pilots of comparable aircraft of other manufacturers (NTSB, 1980a). The NTSB attributed this difference to the location of the landing gear and flap controls. Controls in the cockpits of the airplanes with the higher accident rates were located differently than controls on other aircraft. Investigators concluded that pilots who had operated other aircraft would inadvertently reach for and select the "wrong" controls occasionally, actions that would have been appropriate on those aircraft.

Unfortunately, there is no short-term solution for a lack of control and display standards. Designers could reduce the role of this antecedent to error by adhering to a common control and display design standard. However, a transition period would be needed to implement a standard to prevent operators from being confused by what may be a new design. Over the long term, as manufacturers slowly introduce new equipment and companies train operators to use the new equipment, standardizing controls and displays would reduce opportunities for error.

Keyboard controls

In older systems, operators exerted considerable physical force to manipulate controls. Many modern systems use keyboard controls, either with the familiar QWERTY format derived from the typewriter keyboard, or a variant. Operators using keyboard controls are physically able to control the system without error, so long as they don't inadvertently strike the wrong key.

Highly automated systems largely rely on keyboards with well-separated keys that minimize slips when operators manipulate them by touch alone, and place the keyboards in a location that minimizes fatigue over extended use. Other characteristics of automated systems and their effects on operator performance are discussed more fully in Chapter 13.

Summary

The manner of presenting system-related information to operators can affect their understanding of the system state. Information that involves a high degree of precision is generally presented visually. The number of displays, their conspicuity, organization, and portrayal of trends in system performance, influence operators' capacity to obtain and interpret system information. Information that is difficult to access and interpret can lead to misinterpretations and errors.

Information that requires immediate attention, independent of operators' focus, is generally presented aurally. Sound volume, precision, and conspicuity influence how well operators receive and comprehend the information. Continued presentation of aural information can distract and interfere with an operator's ability to concentrate, perform other tasks, and perceive other aurally-presented information. Sounds should be distinctive and associated with system states or required operator actions to continue to be meaningful. Sounds that are inconsistently associated with system information or operator response will lose their meaning over time.

The design of controls that operators use to alter or modify system operations can affect their performance. Controls should be readily accessible and move in the direction that corresponds to the direction of change in the associated system parameter. Control shapes should be readily distinguishable from one another, particularly if adjacent. Over the long term, standardization of control and display features will reduce the potential for confusion and errors among operators who work on comparable, but non-standardized equipment.

Documenting equipment

- Photograph, videotape, audiotape, or otherwise capture a record of displays and controls in the operating environment of the equipment involved in the event. If this is not possible, refer to handbooks for operating station diagrams as necessary.
- Use comparable systems or a system simulator, noting differences between the two, if the equipment was excessively damaged as a result of the event.
- Interview designers to obtain information about the initial philosophy that guided display and control design.
- Interview designers, instructors, and operators, and refer to operating manuals, to obtain information on differences between designers' and instructors' intentions and operator practices.
- Refer to ergonomics handbooks for guidance, if necessary, when evaluating display or control design features (e.g., Ivergard, 1999; Sanders and McCormick, 1993).

Displays

- Document the number of displays and their locations, and note the displays that operators use to understand the event, compared to the total number of displays presented nearby.
- Note how closely the logic of the organization corresponds to the way operators access displays or their associated controls.
- Contrast the color, brightness, and data size in the display to comparable features in adjacent displays to determine display conspicuity.
- Identify display colors, pictures, diagrams, design, or other features that affect data interpretability and if necessary, refer to operating manuals and handbooks to understand the meaning and relevance of displayed data
- Determine the portrayal of direction and rate of changes in parameter trend information.

Aurally-presented information

- Measure sound volume, duration after initial presentation, volume of ambient sounds, and changes in features of the sounds of interest with changes in component status.
- Document features of aurally-presented information among sound elements such as volume, pitch, frequency and rhythm.
- Determine the meaning of each aural warning, alert, or other sound, and their association with specific system states.
- Identify sounds that call for a specific action or response, the information they convey, and the corresponding required or advised operator action or response.
- Measure the length of time alerts sound before they are silenced, either by the equipment or by the operators.
- Document operator actions needed to silence alerts, the system state that will resume the alert, and the length of time needed from the first sounding of the alert to its operator-initiated silencing.
- Interview operators to determine the actions they have taken to silence the alerts.

Controls

- Document the location and positions of system controls, their accessibility to operators, and obstructions to accessibility.
- Determine the direction of movement of the controls and their correspondence to the direction of change in component parameters.
- Determine the feedback operators receive concerning changes in system state.
- Assess shapes, sizes, and distances among controls.
- Determine differences among control parameters among comparable systems if operators interact with equipment of different manufacturers.
- Document the accessibility, sizes, and distances among keyboard controls.

4 The Operator

Each person–the butcher, the parent, the child–occupies a different position in the world, which leads to a unique set of experiences, assumptions, and expectations about the situations and objects she or he encounters. Everything is perceived, chosen, or rejected on the basis of this framework. (Vaughan, 1996)

The Challenger Launch Decision: Risky Technology, Culture, and Deviance at NASA

Introduction

Our uniqueness as individuals–the way we were raised and educated, our work experiences, and genetic compositions–affect the way we perceive the world and act upon it. Because of these differences two operators, encountering identical system states, could perceive them differently, even if they have had identical training and similar backgrounds.

In the past, investigations of error had largely focused on the operator, often to the exclusion of other system elements that may have contributed as much, if not more, to operator errors than factors related to the operators. For example, checklists that were developed to guide investigations of error, many of which are still widely used today, focus primarily on characteristics of the operator rather than other system elements (e.g., ICAO, 1993).

The approach to investigating error advocated here considers operator-related factors within a broad view of error. This approach does not minimize the influence of operator factors in incident and accident causation; these can, and do, affect performance and lead to error. Because of the central role of the operator in complex systems operations, it is important to understand the role of operator factors in affecting performance, within the context of other system components. This chapter will focus on operator-related antecedents to explain the effects of these factors on the operator.

Physiological factors

Operator-related antecedents can be categorized into one of two general groups: physiological or behavioral. Each includes antecedents with which most of us are familiar, having likely observed their effects in our own experiences, and each can affect operator performance over both the short- and long-term.

Physiological antecedents can temporarily or permanently degrade operator performance by leading to either general or specific impairment. The number of potential physiological antecedents that can influence operator error is sizeable, and numerous medical and physiological texts, journals, and articles have examined them. The major ways that physiological antecedents can degrade operator performance and lead to error will be reviewed, and data needed to determine if a relationship between the two exists suggested, but a full discussion of these antecedents is beyond the scope of this text.

General impairment

Illness Because operators must interpret data, recognize situations, anticipate system performance, and make decisions to effectively oversee system operations, any condition that degrades their ability to perform these tasks could serve as an antecedent to error. Physiological antecedents can increase reaction times, interfere with cognition, and limit recall ability, among other ways.

An operator is impaired when the quality of his or her performance has been degraded to a level below that needed to function effectively and safely. Operators are expected to notify their superiors and not report to work when they are ill. However, many operators do not recognize the subtle effects of illness and will report to work when they are only mildly ill. They remove themselves from system operations only when their illness or discomfort is manifestly impairing.

Researchers have found that even mild illness and discomfort, well below what many consider impairing, may still degrade performance and create antecedents to error. Smith (1990) examined the effects of two fairly minor illnesses, colds and influenza, which account for what he termed a substantial proportion of all consultations in general medical practice, on performance. He measured cognitive skills and reaction times of volunteers who had been infected with a cold or influenza virus, or had been given a placebo. Those who were infected demonstrated significantly poorer cognitive skills and reaction times than those who were not infected. Many of the infected volunteers who demonstrated degraded performance were still in the incubation periods of their illnesses and asymptomatic.

Medications The potential effects of both prescribed and over-the-counter medications on operators vary according to factors such as the potency of the drug, the amount taken, the time since taking the drug, the presence of other drugs in the operators' systems, and individual variation in susceptibility to the drugs in question. The side effects of many drugs in and of themselves may adversely affect performance.

In a retrospective study the NTSB examined fatal accidents in a variety of transportation modes in the United States, and found that many of the operators involved in the accidents had taken prescription medications beforehand (NTSB, 2000a). Prescription medications were found in the bodies of over 21 percent of the general aviation pilots killed in aircraft accidents in one year, and in many of the bodies of operators killed in accidents in other transportation modes as well. Investigators concluded that both prescription and over-the-counter medications impaired transportation operators, and that their impairment led to numerous transportation accidents.

Over-the-counter and prescribed medications can adversely affect operator performance, even hours after being consumed. One medication, sedating antihistamines, found in many over-the-counter cold and allergy medications, slows reaction time and causes drowsiness. Weiler et al. (2000) found that the performance of automobile drivers in a driving simulator was as adversely affected by an antihistamine, diphenhydramine, available in over-the-counter cold medications, as they were by alcohol.

Many over-the-counter medications carry generalized warnings on their labels about the hazards of driving or operating heavy machinery after use, but these warnings are often written in small font that users neither read nor apply to their own situations. The extensive promotion of these drugs, their widespread availability and use, and the frequent lack of operator awareness of their side effects, increase the likelihood that operators will use them without recognizing their potential to impair and degrade performance.

The adverse effects of diphenhydramine on operator performance were seen in a 1998 accident in which a commercial bus ran off of the road and struck a parked truck, after the bus drive had fallen asleep, killing the bus driver and six passengers (NTSB, 2000b). Toxicological analysis of specimens from the body of the driver revealed the presence of diphenhydramine and two other drugs, all of which were contained in an over-the-counter preparation marketed for the treatment of colds and allergies. The amount found and the rate of the drug's metabolism indicated that the driver had likely taken the medication several hours before the accident. Investigators concluded that the drug exacerbated effects of two additional antecedents, an irregular sleep-work cycle, and the time of day, to cause the driver to fall asleep while driving.

Alcohol and drugs of abuse The effects of few, if any drugs, have been studied as much as those of alcohol. Even small amounts of alcohol can impair performance in a variety of cognitive and motor tasks (e.g., Ross and Mundt, 1988; McFadden, 1997).

A direct relationship has been established between the amount of alcohol in the bloodstream, measured by blood alcohol content or BAC, and the extent of impairment. The higher the BAC, the more impaired the person. In most of the United States eight percent BAC is considered impairing for automobile drivers, and even lower levels are considered impairing for other tasks. Unusually high BAC concentrations, say 20 percent or higher in an individual who was still able to function at some level, may indicate alcohol-dependency or addiction.

Those addicted to alcohol or other substances may experience withdrawal after a period of abstinence of even a few hours, withdrawal that can also impair performance (Tiffany, 1999). For example, cocaine, a highly addictive drug (National Institute on Drug Abuse, 1999), is a stimulant. After its effects have worn off cocaine users will likely be fatigued, particularly if they had taken the drug at a time when they would ordinarily have been asleep. Because fatigue causes impairment, the effects of withdrawal from sustained use of cocaine–effects that include mood alteration in addition to sleep disruption–can create antecedents to error.

Investigators determined that the pilot of a regional aircraft that crashed on approach to Durango, Colorado, had been fatigued after consuming cocaine the night before the accident (NTSB, 1989). He and the first officer were flying a challenging flight path through the Rocky Mountains and were about to land. Postmortem toxicological analysis of specimens from the captain's body found benzoylecgonine, cocaine's principle metabolite. Given the amount of the drug and its metabolite that were present, and the rates of cocaine metabolism, investigators determined that he had consumed the drug between 12 and 18 hours before the accident. Because the accident occurred at 6:20 pm local time, he would likely have consumed the cocaine the night before, at a time when he would ordinarily have been asleep, thus disrupting his normal sleep pattern. Further, after taking the cocaine he would have had been expected to have encountered difficulty sleeping until the effects of the drug had worn off.

Investigators concluded that the captain's piloting skills "were likely degraded from his use of the drug before the accident" and that he was likely experiencing the effects of withdrawal, including, "significant mood alteration and degradation, craving for the drug, and post-cocaine-induced fatigue" (p. 29). The findings demonstrate that even hours after someone has consumed drugs, and the drugs were subsequently metabolized, performance can be degraded.

Other accidents have also shown the adverse effects of illegal drug consumption on operator performance. For example, investigators of the 1991 train accident discussed in Chapter 3, in which two freight locomotives had passed a stop signal and inappropriately entered track reserved for the passenger train, found that shortly before the accident the engineer and brakeman had consumed marijuana while operating the locomotives. Investigators concluded that they proceeded beyond the stop signal because they were impaired from their marijuana consumption.

As with alcohol, high levels of a drug or its metabolites may indicate that the operator is a drug abuser, that is, a long-term user of a drug or drug addict. If an operator is suspected of abusing medications, pharmacy records of prescribed medications may reveal a pattern of use over time. The operator may have approached several physicians and obtained prescriptions from each. The operator also may not have informed his or her employer of either the medication use, or the condition for which the medications were prescribed.

Other information, such as records of convictions for driving while under the influence of alcohol or drugs, may also suggest a pattern of substance abuse (see Chapter 10). In the United States, the FAA requires pilots to report such infractions, and reviews the driving records of all pilots to learn of such offenses, regardless of their self-reports (McFadden, 1997). A substance abuse specialist evaluates all pilots with two or more convictions, and some with one, to determine whether they are chemically dependent. Only after these specialists have reviewed the operator's history and concluded that he or she would likely refrain from future drug or chemical use, does the FAA grant the medical certificates needed to serve as pilots.

Company-maintained personnel records may contain information reflecting an operator's history of substance use. Prolonged absences, or absences at the beginning and end of work weeks or work periods, may indicate chemical use. Performance appraisals may also show marked changes in work habits or work performance–another indicator of chemical dependency (see Chapter 10).

Specific impairment

Many of the tasks that operators perform require acute vision or hearing, or subtle senses of feel and touch. Impairment in any of these sensory modalities may lead to errors. Operators in most complex systems are expected to demonstrate sufficient visual acuity to read displays from their control stations, see motion and depth, and distinguish among colors both within and outside of the immediate environment. They should also be able to demonstrate sufficient aural acuity to identify various alerts, electronic and voice communications, and other system-related sounds, and determine the direction from which the sounds originated.

Yet, operators may not always recognize their own impairment and even when they do, they may deliberately withhold that information from others if they believe that reporting the impairment could adversely affect their careers. Investigators saw this in 1996 when a passenger train operator failed to stop the train he was operating at a red stop signal and struck another train, killing him and injuring more than 150 passengers (NTSB, 1997b). Investigators learned that for almost 10 years the operator had been treated for diabetes, and that he had undergone corrective surgery for diabetic retinopathy, an eye disease brought on by diabetes. They attributed his failure to stop to impaired vision; he was unable to distinguish the signal colors. Although required to do so, he did not inform his supervisors of his medical condition, and despite the impairment, he continued to serve as a train operator.

Depending on the complex system and the sensory modality involved, impairment may be so subtle that neither operators nor their supervisors recognize it, becoming evident only in unusual or unexpected conditions. Investigators encountered this in an investigation of a 1996 air transport aircraft accident in which the captain, who was attempting to land at New York's LaGuardia Airport, lost depth perception on landing, substantially damaging the airplane, although all on board escaped serious injury (NTSB, 1997c).

The captain had been intermittently wearing monovision contact lenses for several years without incident, lenses that corrected near vision in one and distant vision in the other eye simultaneously. However, in certain visual conditions the contact lenses degraded his depth perception.

The final moments of the flight path had been over water and through fog, conditions with limited background features, until just above the runway. The reduced visual cues in the prevailing visual conditions, with the adverse effects of the monovision lenses, sufficiently reduced his depth perception to the point that he allowed the aircraft to descend too low and strike the runway.

Behavioral antecedents

Behavioral antecedents, which develop from the operator's near- or long-term experiences, can adversely affect performance. They can, for example, follow profoundly stressful events; such as the loss of an immediate family member. The grief and stress of people in these situations, and the effects of that stress on their performance, are understandable.

Many have encountered the effects of behavioral antecedents at one time or another and can attest to their adverse influence. The effects they exert on the performance of an operator in question, however, may be different from that on other's performance. Two behavioral antecedents, fatigue and stress, are of particular interest to error investigators. Others, that are company-influenced, may also be important.

The company's role

Because of the role of the company in the conduct of its operations, antecedents that may appear to be related to the operator may instead be related to the company. Operators may commit errors because of skill or knowledge deficiencies, and these deficiencies may serve as *the* antecedents to *the* errors in question. But companies that employ the operators establish minimum qualification levels, hire applicants whom they believe will meet those qualifications, and train and certify them as qualified to safely operate their systems. Consequently, because of the company's role in overseeing its operations, company antecedents and not operator antecedents may influence errors that result from a lack of operator knowledge or skills. Companies may also be considered to have influenced operator performance if company-established work schedules led to operator fatigue. If, however, operators engaged in personal activities that led to their fatigue, then the company would not be considered the source of the fatigue and the antecedent to error.

Fatigue

Fatigue and its adverse effects on human performance have been studied extensively (e.g., Costa, 1998; Gander, Rosekind and Gregory, 1998; Mitler and Miller, 1996; Rosekind, Gander, Miller, Gregory, Smith, Weldon, Co, McNally and Lebacqz, 1994). The research has consistently shown that fatigue degrades human performance and can contribute to or cause error. Dawson and Reid (1997a, b) found that those who had been awake as long as 18 to 27 hours continuously exhibited cognitive performance decrements that were equivalent to having a BAC of 5 percent or greater.

In a study of accidents in several transportation modes, the NTSB examined the role of fatigue in transportation safety (NTSB, 1999a). As investigators conclude,

> Researchers have studied factors that affect fatigue, such as duration and quality of sleep, shiftwork and work schedules, circadian rhythms, and time of day. Cumulative sleep loss and circadian disruption can lead to a physiological state characterized by impaired performance and diminished alertness. Fatigue can impair information processing and reaction time, increasing the probability of errors and ultimately leading to transportation accidents. (pp. 5 and 6)

Investigators determined that fatigue led pilots of a DC-8 cargo flight to commit critical errors in a 1993 accident at the United States Naval Air Station in Guantanamo Bay, Cuba, in which the crew allowed the airplane to turn too steeply and strike the ground just before landing (NTSB, 1994a). The three pilots had been sleep-deprived at the time of the accident. The captain had received only five hours of sleep in the previous 48 hours and had been awake for 23.5 hours at the time of the accident. The first officer had been awake for 19 hours continuously and had gotten only 10 hours of sleep in the 57 hours before the accident..

There are several causes of fatigue leading to impaired performance, including excessive sleep loss in a 24-hour period, accumulated sleep loss over several days, disrupted circadian rhythms, and time of day. Most people need about eight hours of sleep daily, give or take one to two hours. Those who receive less than six to 10 hours of sleep may be fatigued. The greater the difference between the number of hours a person generally sleeps, and the amount obtained in the 24 hours before the accident, the more likely that person will experience acute fatigue and demonstrate impaired performance.

People can also experience chronic fatigue from accumulating a sleep debt over several days. Again, assuming that most people need eight hours of sleep nightly, those who sleep only five to six hours a night for a week will likely be chronically fatigued by the end of the week, as any parent of an infant can attest.

Most people have regular schedules and they tend to get tired and hungry about the same time each day. When their schedules are disrupted, for example, by transoceanic air travel, they will have difficulty sleeping during the "new" night, but what had been the day in the "old" time zone, no matter how fatigued they are. Several hours later, during the day in the "new" time zone, they may be unable to remain alert, despite coffee, tea, exercise or other technique that had otherwise been effective in restoring some degree of alertness. Thereafter, they may experience similar sleep disturbances upon their return, when they must readjust to the "old" time zone after becoming acclimated to the "new" one.

Many physiological and behavioral functions, including sleep cycle, digestion, hormonal activity, and body temperature, are regulated in approximate 24-hour cycles. Disrupting these functions, as transoceanic airline travelers and shift workers who work days one week and nights the next find, is also fatiguing because the change in schedules is more rapid than is the body's ability to adjust. The experience is known as circadian desynchronosis, popularly referred to as "jet lag."

Circadian desynchronosis makes it difficult for people to sleep when they would otherwise be awake, and creates difficulties in concentrating or cognitive performance among those who would otherwise be asleep. Disrupted circadian rhythms lead to chronic fatigue, until the body adjusts to the new schedule and the person receives sufficient rest to compensate for the sleep deficits (e.g., Tilley, Wilkinson, Warren, Watson, and Drud, 1982). Because circadian rhythms do not adjust rapidly, a person whose circadian rhythms have been disrupted may be fatigued for days afterward, depending on the extent of the difference between the previous and current schedules. Therefore, although it may be early afternoon local time, a period in which operators would otherwise be alert, operators experiencing circadian desynchronosis may still be performing as if it were 3:00 a.m. Dawson and Fletcher (2001), and Fletcher and Dawson (2001), have studied the effects of circadian desynchronosis on employee performance., and developed a scheduling model, which considers circadian effects, to schedule duty times of shift workers or transoceanic workers to minimize their disruptive effects. They found that considering circadian factors in scheduling worker's activities can reduce the effects of circadian disruptions.

Further, the quality of sleep is not constant; people sleep most deeply between 3:00 a.m. and 5:00 a.m. in their local time zones. They also experience an equivalent decrease in alertness 12 hours later, between 3:00 p.m. and 5:00 p.m. local time. With these phased changes in sleep quality, the likelihood of committing errors also changes. Monk, Folkard, and Wedderburn (1996) found that the number of errors committed in a variety of performance measures varies with the time of day, errors that can be directly related to operator performance and to accidents. In a study of on-the job injuries in several factories, Smith, Folkard, and Poole (1994) found that night shift workers were injured on the job significantly more often than were day shift workers who performed the same tasks for the same employers. The evidence demonstrates that time of day can affect performance, and the times in which operators are most likely to commit errors occur when they would otherwise be in their deepest sleep cycles, between 3:00 and 5:00 a.m., and the afternoon correlate of those hours, between 3:00 and 5:00 pm.

Stress

The effects of stress on performance have been studied extensively. Definitions of stress vary, but Salas, Driskell, and Hughes' definition (1996) will be used presently. They define stress as, "a process by which certain environmental demands evoke an appraisal process in which perceived demand exceeds resources and results in undesirable physiological, psychological, behavioral or social outcomes" (p. 6).

The effects of individual stressors depend largely on the person and how stressful he or she perceives them. Stressors that are perceived to be moderate can enhance performance by counteracting the effects of boredom or tedium in settings in which little changes (Hancock and Warm, 1989). However, stressors considered severe can degrade performance.

Person-related stress Personal stress, influenced by circumstances unrelated to an operator's job that cause "undesirable physiological, psychological, behavioral or social outcomes," are differentiated from system-induced stress.

Operators may encounter more than one stressor simultaneously, both person- and system-related, and their performance may be affected by both.

The more stressors a person experiences, the more likely that person's performance will be degraded by their effects.

Person-related stressors include marital breakups, the illness or death of family members, or disruptions to routines such as a move or the departure of a household member. Person-related stressors may not necessarily be negative; they can result from what most consider happy occasions. Alcov, Borowsky, and Gaynor (1982) compared the accident rates of U.S. Navy pilots who had experienced stressful life events to those who had not, events that included marital problems, major career decisions, relationship difficulties, job-related problems, as well as impending marriages and recent child birth in the immediate family. Pilots who had experienced stressful events had sustained higher accident rates than pilots who had not. Despite these findings, it is important to recognize that the mere presence of person-related stressors does not imply that an operator's performance was adversely affected by stress because of the noted individual variations in reaction to stressors.

System-induced stress Operators may find unexpected system events to be stressful, such as displays with information that cannot be interpreted, unexpected aural warnings, and controls that appear to be ineffective. Operator reaction to these stressors are influenced by their experiences and previous encounters with similar events.

Operator actions can also lead to stress, particularly if severe consequences might result. The more adverse the consequences, the greater the stress the operator can be expected to experience when encountering that event.

Summary

Two general categories of operator antecedents, behavioral and physiological, can lead to error. Physiological antecedents can impair performance either temporarily or permanently, through disease, medications, or alcohol or over the counter or illicit drugs. These can temporarily impair operators by altering perception, slowing reaction time, and causing fatigue, among other adverse effects.

Behavioral antecedents to error include fatigue and stress, originating from the operator's personal experiences or from company actions. Long work schedules, changing shift work schedules, abrupt change in time zones, or a combination of these, are company actions that can cause fatigue, a well-documented antecedent to error. Stress can be caused by factors related to the job, or events in an operator's personal life that are independent of the job.

Documenting operator antecedents

Medical condition

- Review operator medical records, both company-maintained and those maintained by a personal health care provider, with a health care professional.
- Note recent diagnoses of and treatment for medical conditions, and determine the possible effects of the conditions and associated medication on operator performance.
- Consult an occupational health expert if system features may have created particular physiological demands on operators.
- Interview colleagues, associates, relatives of the operator, and the operator if possible, to determine if he or she was experiencing even a mild illness or temporary discomfort at the time of the event.
- Interview operator family and colleagues to determine if they noted changes in the operator's daily routines, behaviors, or attitudes, and when these changes were first observed.
- Review company personnel records to detect changes in work habits, job performance, and attendance.

Drugs or alcohol

- Request, as soon as possible after the occurrence, a blood sample from the operator, or from the pathologist if the operator was killed, for a toxicological analysis.
- Ask local law enforcement authorities to recommend a reputable and qualified laboratory that can conduct toxicological analyses if local government laboratories are unable to do so.
- Review positive toxicological findings with the company's occupational health specialist, another toxicologist, or health care provider with the necessary expertise. Ask him or her to obtain and review the results of controlled studies on the medications in question.

- Give the toxicologist information about the care of the body or the specimen if the operator has been killed, the state of the operator's health before the event, and possible medication that the operator may have been taking.
- Consult a physician, pharmacist, toxicologist, or a pharmacologist to learn about the effects of single or multiple drugs on operator performance when evidence confirms that an operator took medications before an occurrence.

Autopsies

- Arrange for an autopsy by a forensic pathologist if possible, or one with additional training and experience in accident investigations beyond that of most pathologists.
- Give the pathologist information on the nature of the accident, the state of the body, the role of the operator at the time, the nature of the machinery with which the operator was interacting, and data obtained from medical records, peer interviews and other sources.
- Provide the pathologist with photos of the operator's body and of the accident site.
- Ask the pathologist for information on preexisting physiological conditions, the effects of impact forces, (if in a vehicle or other dynamic environment) thermal injuries, or toxic fumes, and the presence of corrective lenses, hearing aids, or other supplemental device on the body of the operator.

Fatigue

- Document the times that an operator went to sleep and awoke for each of three 24-hour periods before the event, and the times that he or she usually slept and awoke.
- Characterize those who receive four or more hours less sleep than typical in a 24-hour as acutely fatigued and those who receive two hours less sleep than usual over four 24-hour periods to be chronically fatigued.

- Reconstruct the times the operator went to sleep and the times the person awoke for each of the days since the travel commenced, using the home time zone as the standard for those who have traveled across time zones.
- Note the number of days that the traveler was away from the base schedule, and the number of days since the traveler returned to the base schedule.
- Document the time of the accident to determine whether it occurred between 3:00 am to 5:00 am local time.
- Identify characteristics of fatigue in the critical errors, including preoccupation with a single task, slowed reaction time, and difficulty performing tasks that had been performed effectively before.

Stress

- Interview family and colleagues to determine whether the operator experienced stressors before the event, and how he or she reacted to them.

5 The Company and the Regulator

> The Japanese nuclear accident three weeks ago occurred largely because managers counted on workers to follow rules but never explained why the rules were important. (Wald, 1999a)
>
> *The New York Times*

Introduction

The company's role in creating antecedents to error has been increasingly recognized. The *New York Times* account of the 1999 accident at a Japanese uranium processing plant suggests that the operator errors that led to the accident resulted from management actions. A subsequent *New York Times* article revealed that plant managers compounded the effects of their initial actions by not developing an emergency plan in the event of an incident (French, 2000). Apparently, the managers believed that an accident could not possibly occur and therefore, none was needed. This chapter will address how companies and regulators involved in complex system operations can create antecedents to error.

Organizations

Companies that operate complex systems influence the safety of those systems in many ways. They hire and train operators, establish operating and maintenance procedures, oversee compliance with these procedures, and establish cultures than influence attitudes and performance. Each of these has the potential to create error antecedents, and companies are ultimately responsible for ensuring that their actions help to minimize the role of potential antecedents, so that the systems they operate do so safely.

Hiring

Companies implement selection standards to improve the likelihood that those whom they hire will successfully perform their requisite duties and responsibilities. Ineffective selection will not only be expensive in training and selection costs, it can lead to error as well. Companies generally consider several factors when selecting candidates for operator positions. These include requisite skills and knowledge, predicted performance as operators, and the number of operators needed to oversee system operations.

Skills, knowledge, and predicted performance Companies need to identify the knowledge and skills operators need to operate the systems effectively, so that they can predict the applicants that can perform their required tasks safely and those who cannot, and those expected to commit a disproportionate share of errors. For example, maintenance technicians generally perform any of the following tasks–

- Read and understand instructions
- Understand the structural and mechanical relationships among components and subsystems
- Apply instructions to tasks
- Identify and locate appropriate components and tools
- Diagnose and correct mechanical malfunctions
- Recognize when the tasks have been completed
- Complete written documentation
- Communicate, either orally or in writing, the maintenance actions taken
- Verify that the intent of the maintenance instructions had been carried out.

Deficiencies in any of these tasks could lead to errors. The more of the critical skills that an applicant can carry out, the more effective the applicant will likely perform as an operator, and the fewer the errors he or she will be expected to commit. Of course, companies also are responsible for training operators to compensate for identified deficiencies, and for determining the point at which they will be considered sufficiently skilled to perform error free. Selecting a person and assigning that person to a position of responsibility without the requisite training will serve as a company antecedent to error.

Companies have also created error antecedents by selecting operators based on certain skills or experiences, but assigning them to perform tasks that did not match those skills and experiences. In some fields regulators establish operator-licensing criteria, which companies adopt as minimum selection standards. Should investigators identify deficiencies in the skills of licensed operators, they would need to focus on both the regulator's licensing standards and the company's hiring criteria to identify antecedents to error.

Because interpersonal skills are critical to the effectiveness of multi-operator teams, companies need to consider these among their selection criteria when appropriate. Those members of multi-operator teams with deficient interpersonal skills may commit errors, or contribute to the errors of others.

The number of operators   The number of operators interacting with a system, whether too many, too few, or optimum, affects the quality of individual and team performance and system safety. Paris, Salas, and Cannon-Bowers (2000) believe that an insufficient number of operators can create excessive operator stress because of the resultant increased individual workload. However, hiring too many operators is wasteful and can create low individual workload, which can lead to operator boredom and inattention, both potential antecedents to error (e.g., O'Hanlon, 1981).

Designers, regulators, companies, or operators themselves may determine the number of operators needed to operate the systems. In aviation regulators require at least two pilots to operate air transport aircraft, even if only one can effectively control the airplane. Companies in other systems may have more discretion to determine the number of operators they need. They may base the decision on the nature of the tasks, the degree of difficulty in performing the tasks, and the amount of time available to complete them. For example, when scheduling maintenance tasks, companies may want to return the equipment to service quickly and may assign more operators than usual to the task. The greater the need, the more personnel they will likely assign.

In some systems, the operating cycle or phase of operation may influence the number of operators needed. Some companies determine the number of operators they need based on an "average" workload level. In other systems, where individual workload varies according to the operational phase, companies can match the number of operators to the workload level. During periods of high workload that require additional operators, they may add operators to match the workload and likewise, they may reduce the number needed during low workload periods. For example, air traffic control sectors or airspace segments are often combined at night, during low activity periods.

Researchers have studies methods of determining the number of operators needed to operate safely. Lee, Forsythe, and Rothblum (2000) developed a mechanism to determine the appropriate number of operators needed in one complex system, commercial shipping. They incorporated factors such as phase of voyage (open waters, restricted waters, and in port), port call frequency, level of shore-based maintenance support, and applicable work/rest standards into their analysis. The number of crewmembers needed varied considerably with changes in these factors, factors that would have different weights according to the particular system and its operating environment.

Training

In general, operator performance deficiencies are more likely to result from deficiencies in company training than from deficiencies in hiring. Training decisions are among the most significant actions companies can take to reduce error opportunities.

Unlike academic or professional training, training in operating complex systems generally involves two components. One, initial training, designed to convey the overall knowledge and skills necessary to effectively operate the systems, is administered to newly hired operators. The other, ongoing training, is designed to maintain the skills and knowledge of existing operators and introduce them to changes in the system or to other safety-related topics. Most companies that operate complex systems employ some type of initial training to introduce newly hired operators to system operations, however, not all conduct ongoing training.

Training content After companies have hired system operators, they need to give them an overview of the system, information on the company and system operating procedures, and the skills to operate the equipment. Some companies employ on-the-job training to accomplish these objectives. New employees first observe experienced operators and then slowly learn to operate the system under their supervision. Other companies use formal training curricula to train new operators.

Initial training should describe the system, its components and subsystems, their functions, normal and non-normal system states, and general company policies and operating procedures. Initial training can also introduce employees to potential system shortcomings. New systems, no matter how thoroughly they had been tested before their introduction to the operating environment, can be expected to have difficulties or "bugs" that designers had not recognized. Although training should not be expected to compensate for design deficiencies, the training environment is often used to introduce operators to potentially unsafe elements of system operation so that operators will be familiar with them and, if necessary, respond appropriately should they encounter them.

Ongoing training is designed to ensure that system operators learn about design changes, new operating procedures and regulations, and changes to other pertinent system features, so they can continue to perform effectively. Some industries require ongoing training at regular intervals, others schedule it only as needed, and some do not conduct additional training. Similar differences can be found among the standards accrediting organizations apply to the certification of professionals (Menges, 1975). Some establish criteria for ongoing training, including the curricula, instructional media, and intervals between training sessions while others specify a minimum number of continuing education credits or courses to be completed within a certain period.

Instructional media Technological advances have improved the quality of training systems, and enhanced operator training in many respects. For example, equipment simulators have improved system safety, despite acquisition costs that can exceed several million dollars (e.g., Moroney and Moroney, 1998). Simulators can duplicate operating stations and their associated displays and controls, and they can replicate many of the sounds and kinesthetic cues associated with the operating environment. They can present operators with almost the full range of both expected and unexpected conditions, enabling them to learn and practice their skills in a safe environment, free of error consequences.

Initial and ongoing training may employ various instructional media, including computer-based instruction, CD-ROM and Internet-based presentations, videotapes, 35mm and electronic slide programs, as well as text and written material. Each has particular advantages and disadvantages for students, instructors, and course developers. Some allow more flexibility, others are more responsive to individual students, and some may offer reduced development and delivery costs. Some training programs combine instructional media, for example with instructors providing a systems overview and electronic media addressing specific topics at the students' own pace, without disrupting the class or distracting other class members.

However, despite their particular benefits, instructional media only deliver instructional material; they cannot compensate for deficiencies in the material they present. Although the particular medium can influence the quality or pace of learning, the quality of the training program is predicated upon the content of the material presented and not the instructional medium delivering it.

Costs versus content Companies strive to maintain effective training programs within budgetary limitations, and they can be expected to make compromises to balance the competing objectives of high quality with low cost. They exercise considerable control over the content of their training programs, notwithstanding regulatory standards, and try to keep costs down, recognizing that effective training in complex systems can be so expensive that they may have to make compromises in other areas as a consequence. Reason (1997) suggests that the need to maintain the operations that produce the resources necessary to fund training influences companies to weigh production needs more than non-production needs, such as training.

Because of the often substantial costs of operator training, managers may devote considerable effort into operator selection to ensure that those hired will be likely to successfully complete the training. These high costs may also produce an additional unintended result–inducing companies to retain operators whose skills may have deteriorated over time to avoid the expense of training new operators. Such decisions could create company antecedents to error.

The caliber of a company's training serves as a measure of its commitment to reduce opportunities for error. Those that provide training beyond the minimum that the regulator requires, and that spend additional resources to ensure that their operators are skilled and proficient, make positive efforts to reduce opportunities for error. By contrast, companies with training programs that meet only minimum standards may create opportunities for error. Issues such as these, reflecting on corporate culture, will be more fully discussed in Chapter 8.

Procedures

Complex systems require extensive rules and procedures to guide operators when interacting with the equipment, and to serve as the final authority on how they conduct operations. Procedures also guide operators when they respond to new or unfamiliar situations, and can help to standardize operations across companies and even across international borders. The International Civil Aviation Organization, for example, has established operating rules governing air traffic control procedures and aircraft operations that govern operations across international borders, while its marine counterpart, the International Maritime Organization, has developed rules and procedures for use in international maritime operations.

To be effective, operators must perceive the procedures as logical and necessary to ensure safe and efficient operations. Otherwise, over time they may disregard them, as seen at the beginning of this chapter–unless their fear of adverse managerial action will be sufficient to ensure that they comply.

Designers generally develop operating procedures for the systems they design, but companies are ultimately responsible for the procedures they implement. For many reasons companies often modify procedures after they have begun operating the equipment. They may wish to standardize procedures across different equipment, or they may intend to improve their operations as they gain familiarity and experience with the equipment.

General versus specific Companies and regulators face a fundamental dilemma in developing and implementing procedures. Procedures should be sufficiently specific and unambiguous to guide operators, yet operators may encounter unexpected situations with no applicable procedures. As Flach and Rasmussen (2000) note, "it is impossible to have conventions for unconventional events" (p. 170).

Operators must follow procedures to assure system safety, yet they need to retain sufficient authority to bypass the procedures if they believe that the circumstances warrant. Explicit procedures provide the guidance operators need to operate systems as intended and ensure that different operators control the system similarly. However, overly restrictive procedures can work against safety. Reason (1997) argues that these may actually encourage operators to develop their own shortcuts, circumventing the intent of the procedures. Overly restrictive or comprehensive procedures also need extensive management oversight to ensure that operators comply with them.

Most companies recognize that it is impossible to develop procedures that present the steps necessary to operators to respond to all possible circumstances. Ideally, procedures they develop and implement will be both comprehensive and specific, applying to as many potential circumstances as possible.

Oversight

Oversight helps ensure that operators adhere to their companies' operating procedures, and informs companies of critical aspects of system operations. Effective oversight requires pertinent employee performance data, and frequent and thorough acts of managerial data gathering and inspection.

Employee data should reveal the quality of employee performance in a variety of operating conditions. Many large companies, with thousands of operators, have too large a span of supervision to allow effective oversight of all operators, and they depend on operator performance data for effective oversight.

Effective oversight informs companies about all critical aspects of their operations. Well-informed companies can quickly respond to operational difficulties as they emerge, and thus help to reduce the likelihood that they will become opportunities for error.

The quality of oversight varies according to the system, the operating conditions, the operators, and the severity of the consequences of operator error. Since constant oversight is economically unfeasible in most companies, they must maximize the frequency and thoroughness of their oversight, through as many of the operating cycles, as possible. Yet, effective oversight does not require constant surveillance. For example, to determine the extent of taxpayer compliance with the tax code in the United States, the federal government inspects or audits the tax returns of fewer than 5% of taxpayers in a given year. Yet, sampling of taxpayers reveals that the overwhelming majority of taxpayers comply with the tax laws, despite the low probability that an individual's returns will be audited. Most taxpayers know the stiff penalties that they can receive if they are convicted of evading tax laws, and are unwilling to face the penalties, irrespective of the actual risk of being caught.

New operators

Many companies place newly selected operators in probationary periods that give them full discretion to evaluate employees, and decide whether to retain them beyond these periods. Effective oversight requires companies to identify and address difficulties that their operators may demonstrate. Organizations that fail to act can create antecedents to error.

Experienced operators

System safety requires companies to respond to operator performance deficiencies, and most support this need. Consequently, operators with manifestly deficient performance are rarely encountered, but investigators may occasionally encounter marginally performing operators. The operators may, for example, perform satisfactorily most of the time but on occasion perform unacceptably, or they may perform well during routine or expected situations, but poorly otherwise.

Some operators may knowingly violate company procedures, and oversight of these operators calls for a response. Ultimately, companies may have to remove operators who have disregarded operating procedures from safety-sensitive positions, or re-evaluate their oversight of the operators. Companies that do not address reported instances of noncompliance are, in effect, communicating to their operators that they need not comply with the procedures.

Investigators of a 1993 aircraft accident, involving a pilot alleged to have ignored critical procedures, encountered this type of deficient oversight (NTSB, 1994b). The airplane, owned and operated by the FAA, struck the side of a mountain before air traffic controllers could permit the plane to climb through clouds and depart the area. The pilot chose not to delay takeoff to wait for air traffic controllers' authorization, most likely in the belief that he could obtain it sooner once airborne.

Fellow pilots made numerous allegations to investigators regarding his unsafe practices, allegations that corresponded to the nature of his performance on the accident flight. According to the investigation report, his fellow operators reported that he–

Continued on a VFR [visual flight rules] positioning flight into IMC [instrument meteorological conditions],

Conducted VFR flight below clouds at less than 1,000 feet above the ground in marginal weather conditions [violating safe operating practices],

Replied to an ATC [air traffic control] query that the flight was in VMC [visual meteorological conditions] when it was in IMC,

Conducted departures without other flightcrew knowing essential flight planning information, such as IFR [instrument flight rules]/VFR/en route filing/weather briefing/ultimate destination or routing,

Departed on positioning flights without informing other crewmembers whether he had obtained weather information or filed an appropriate flight plan,

Disregarded checklist discipline on numerous occasions,

Refused to accept responsibility that his failure to adhere to a checklist had caused an engine damage incident in January 1993, [an event that precipitated a letter of reprimand],

Performed a "below glide path check" in IMC when VMC conditions were required by FIAO [the FAA organization operating the flight] requirements, and refused to answer a SIC [co-pilot] query regarding the reason for his alleged violation of VFR requirements in an incident 2 weeks before the accident. (p. 8)

Despite repeated complaints to their management about his performance, the pilot's supervisors failed to address his reported performance deficiencies. Their failure allowed an unsafe practice–his continued operation in their system–to continue uncorrected. Consequently, investigators considered the supervisors' role in this accident equivalent to the captain's. As Reason (1997) notes, opportunities for "rogue" operators to ignore procedures increase in organizations that have deficient oversight, or managers who are unwilling or unable to enforce compliance with the organization's operating rules and procedures.

"Good" procedures

By establishing the circumstances under which operators interact with the systems, and by setting the tone for their "corporate culture," companies and organizations can positively or negatively affect operator performance. They can encourage operators to keep management informed of perceived safety hazards, including instances of operator non-compliance with operating procedures.

Some companies have established self-reporting systems that assure the anonymity of those who submit these reports, even when they describe their own instances of non-compliance, to increase company awareness of their operations. Companies can also develop and implement salary and incentive programs that reward suggestions for improving safety. Where technical capabilities are in place, companies can read data from system recorders to monitor system state and operator performance. All have increased supervisor knowledge of potential safety issues in their operations.

The regulator

In one form or another, regulators are fixtures of complex systems. Whether independent overseers of systems or elements of them, regulators provide a degree of oversight of most complex systems.

Throughout the world some level of independent supervision and inspection of complex systems has become expected. In the United States, with some exceptions, government agencies carry out the oversight, although the level of oversight activity varies across systems. The nuclear power industry is heavily regulated, while the medical community is less so. Some regulators establish rigorous operating standards that companies will have to maintain for continued approval of their operations, while others play a less active role in the systems they oversee.

The two regulator functions

Regulators primarily perform two critical functions. They establish rules governing system operation and equipment design, and they enforce compliance with the rules that they establish. The rules are designed to provide a minimal level of safety of the systems they oversee. Organizations that chose to operate at that level and no higher should still operate safely.

System operators and equipment designers are expected to establish their own rules, methods, and standards, at a level sufficiently rigorous to provide a minimally acceptable standard of safety. At the same time, overly constrictive regulations may inhibit operations and companies' abilities to operate profitably.

However, regulators face a critical difficulty meeting their responsibility, what Reason (1997) refers to as "the regulators' unhappy lot." As the pace of technological change has increased, regulators have found it increasingly difficult to maintain the necessary expertise to properly evaluate the system and the procedures needed to operate them. In addition, regulators themselves adhere to procedures that are, of necessity, slow and methodical, not allowing for the type of rapid evaluation needed to keep pace with technological change. Yet, as advanced equipment is introduced into service, regulators are expected to anticipate potential operating errors in the use of the new systems, even if they lack the technical expertise to evaluate them. As Reason (1997) explains,

> Regulators are in an impossible position. They are being asked to prevent organizational accidents in high-technology domains when the aetiology of these rare and complex events is still little understood. (page 171)

Further, because regulators are usually supported by public funds, they are often under-funded. Yet, as systems become increasingly complex and the consequences of error more severe, they are expected to increase the quality and quantity of their oversight. As Reason (1997) notes, this leads to less than satisfactory consequences,

> In an effort to work around these obstacles, regulators tend to become dependent upon the regulated companies to help them acquire and interpret information. Such interdependence can undermine the regulatory process in various ways. The regulator's knowledge of the nature and severity of a safety problem can be manipulated by what the regulated organization chooses to communicate and how this material is presented. (p. 174)

Regulator activities

Regulators govern licensing and training, maintenance and inspection, and in some cases even organizational structure, activities that parallel many of those that organizations and companies perform in their own establishments. Investigators can assess the adequacy and effectiveness of regulator performance similarly to that of companies, by examining the role of many of the antecedents previously outlined. For example, the effectiveness of rules governing equipment design features can be gauged by the standards of conspicuity, interpretability, and other characteristics discussed in Chapter 4.

Summary

Students of human error have recognized the role of companies that operate complex systems in creating antecedents to operator error. The selection processes used to hire system operators can identify recognizable or predictable operator skills and deficiencies, and thus influence safety by the quality of operators they hire. Companies determine the optimum number of operators needed to run the system during both routine and non-routine system states, and they train operators to safely operate the system, and to remain current with changes in system design or operating procedures.

Companies also establish operating procedures and, within reason, enforce adherence to those procedures. Procedures should guide operators to interact with systems throughout the range of expected system states, yet provide sufficient flexibility to operators in the event that the procedures do not apply to an unexpected event.

Regulators establish the rules of the systems they oversee and ensure compliance with those rules. Regulators may establish and enforce rules governing system design, system operation, maintenance, and personnel qualifications. Many of the antecedents relating to equipment design and organizational antecedents apply to regulator antecedents as well.

Documenting Company and Regulator Antecedents

The company

- Refer to company manuals and related written documentation, interview managerial and operations personnel, human resource specialists, experienced operators, and both newly hired operators and if possible, applicants who were not hired, to obtain their accounts of the selection process, training, procedures, and oversight.

Selection

- Determine the extent to which both the company's selection criteria and selection process changed over a period of several years.
- Match company-employed selection criteria to the skills that operators are expected to perform routinely. Note inconsistencies between the two, and determine the extent to which the process can adequately predict effective operator performance among applicants.
- Assess the extent to which the company recognizes operator deficiencies during their probationary period and after they have fully qualified as operators.
- Determine the number and proportion of operators in each of several years from the time of the accident, who were not retained beyond the conclusion of their probationary periods, or whose employment was terminated thereafter, because of performance deficiencies.
- Describe performance deficiencies that led to the company actions.

Training

- Compare the content of company training to the knowledge and skills operators need to effectively and safely control the systems.
- Document the training material presented, the methods of instruction, and instructional media, such as control station simulators, that the organization uses in training.
- Determine the extent to which the content of company training pertained to the event under investigation.
- Assess the extent to which company training surpasses, meets, or falls below the minimum level of instruction mandated.

Procedures and oversight

- Determine the extent to which the operating procedures that the company established prepared operators to respond to the event being investigated.
- Document the type and frequency of company oversight over a finite period from the time of the accident.
- Determine the extent to which the oversight informed the company of operator application of company procedures.

The regulator

- Examine regulator inspector selection criteria and inspector training.
- Apply the presentation and control design standards outlined in Chapter 4 to assess the quality of the regulator's oversight of equipment design.
- Determine the extent to which the regulator effectively assessed the technology incorporated in the equipment.
- Evaluate the extent to which the regulator's operator-licensing requirements provided an acceptable level of safe system operation.
- Examine the effectiveness of regulator approval of operating rules and procedures as applied to the circumstances of the event.
- Determine the extent to which the regulator met the oversight standards it established.
- Assess the extent to which the regulator inspection standards provided effective surveillance over the full range of operations that the organization conducted.

6   Maintenance and Inspection

Maintenance can seriously damage your system. (Reason, 1997)

Managing the Risks of Organizational Accidents

Introduction

Complex systems need maintenance to remain in working order. In time components wear out, fluids become depleted, and critical elements fail. Maintenance prevents these from adversely affecting system operation, and repairs systems when component failures or malfunctions occur. Systems generally undergo two types of maintenance, scheduled and unscheduled. Scheduled maintenance is preventive, intended to inspect and replace components, fluids, belts, etc., before they wear out or fail. Unscheduled maintenance repairs the system after an equipment anomaly.

Despite the importance of maintenance, until recently researchers have paid scant attention to maintenance errors. Exceptions include Boeing Corporation's study of commercial aircraft maintenance errors, and their development of a maintenance error decision aid (or MEDA) to help maintenance personnel identify the antecedents to maintenance errors and implement strategies to reduce the likelihood of their reoccurrence (Allen, Rankin, and Sargent, 1998). The FAA has also devoted substantial effort to understand maintenance and inspection errors, work that has greatly enhanced our understanding of the maintenance system. This chapter will examine the maintenance environment and maintenance tasks to explain how antecedents to error in maintenance tasks can occur.

Maintenance tasks

Maintenance in complex systems is marked by the work of multiple operators who perform numerous, often unrelated tasks, with limited immediate feedback on the quality of their activities. "It is this frequency of contact," Reason (1997) writes, "and hence greater error opportunity, rather than any lack of competence on the part of maintenance personnel, that lies at the heart of the problem" (p. 86).

The frequency of contact, or numerous operator interactions with the equipment that Reason refers to, results from just a few maintenance activities. Drury (1998) contends that maintenance and inspection tasks consist fundamentally of a handful of discrete steps, in which technicians primarily interpret and diagnose, act (i.e., repair, replace, or inspect), and evaluate or inspect the maintenance action.

Interpret and diagnose

Before beginning a task, maintenance technicians usually receive either verbal or written instructions that describe an anomaly, or present a task and list the actions that need to be performed. In response to an anomaly, they will diagnose the nature of the anomaly and select an appropriate action based on their diagnosis.

Task descriptions often take the form of computer-generated steps that are obtained from a central source, such as a general maintenance manual. Drury (1998) found that printed instructions given to maintenance technicians occasionally contain flaws that can lead to maintenance errors. These include insufficiently sized font, and incomplete or poorly written instructions.

Because of the length of time needed to perform some maintenance tasks, technicians may not complete them within their duty periods. In that event they will be expected to brief technicians in the subsequent shift on the tasks they had completed and the tasks that remain. Those receiving the information will then apply the instructions they received to the task to be performed. Deficiencies in either communicating or comprehending the instructions, or in applying them to the task, may lead to errors. Ambiguity in the verbal description of the system condition, or the receiver's misunderstanding of the information, can also lead to error. Yet verbal instructions are common, particularly if tasks were partially completed.

Act

After interpreting and diagnosing, technicians generally perform one or more of the following actions, each of which calls for different skills–

- Removing a component and replacing it with a repaired, reassembled, or new component
- Repairing a component
- Disassembling and reassembling a component
- Disconnecting and reconnecting a component
- Emptying and replacing fluids.

Because there are numerous opportunities for error in reinstalling and reconnecting components and in replacing fluids, these steps are most prone to error.

Reason (1997) suggests that because of the numerous ways that components can be incorrectly reassembled and reconnected, or the ways that incorrect types or quantities of fluids can be used, in contrast to the single way that they can be removed or disassembled, technicians are more likely to commit errors when completing these tasks than when performing other maintenance tasks. Reassembling components not only calls for using the correct component, but the correct attachment parts, e.g., screws and bolts, in the correct amount, placed in the correct location, with the correct torque or tension. Errors can occur in any one of the steps.

Evaluate

After receiving instructions, technicians inspect components and may observe the operation of the system to diagnose the anomaly or evaluate the type of maintenance actions needed. Evaluation and inspection are subject to distinctive antecedents and, depending on the procedures, the setting, and the type of task performed, the rate of detecting flaws may vary. For example, Leach and Morris (1998), who studied maintenance actions in an unusual environment, welds performed underwater, found that inspectors failed to detect defects at a rate well above the accepted tolerance level, with no correlation between experience of the inspector and error rate.

Often, inspectors are asked to identify barely perceptible defects. Because many of the components that they inspect are flawless, inspectors often have little or no history of detecting flaws and, as important, may have little or no expectation of finding them. Their expectancies may then play a role in their performance since previous experience helps to guide technicians and inspectors. Previous experience can help inspectors locate and identify flaws, but it could also lead to potential error-inducing expectancies when flaws had not been encountered previously.

On some components there is little to help inspectors ensure that they have inspected all critical areas. Specialized tools have been designed to highlight defects in some types of inspections; however, the effectiveness of these tools is largely dependent on the user's expertise. Here again, previous experience in detecting flaws can increase an inspector's ability to detect subsequent flaws. However, these tools often place considerable demands on inspectors' vigilance and over extended periods, their visual searching and monitoring skills degrade.

Failure to detect flaws has occasionally led to accidents. An inspector did not detect a flaw in a jet engine component that led to its disintegration during a flight, and the death of two passengers (NTSB, 1998a). Nine months before the accident the inspector had examined the component using an instrument designed to enhance the conspicuity of flaws. However, he failed to detect the flaw, a small crack that was believed to have originated shortly after the component's manufacture. Investigators concluded that the defect was sufficiently large that he should have been able to detect it. As they note,

> To detect the crack on the aft-face of the hub, the inspector would have had to first detect a bright fluorescent green indication (if there was such an indication) against a dark purple background. To detect the indication, the inspector would have had to systematically direct his gaze across all surfaces of the hub. However, systematic visual search is difficult and vulnerable to human error. Research on visual inspection of airframe components, for example, has demonstrated that inspectors miss cracks above the threshold for detection at times because they fail to scan an area of a component. It is also possible that the inspector detected an indication at the location of the crack but forgot to diagnose, or reinspect, the location. [Moreover,] a low expectation of finding a crack might also have decreased the inspector's vigilance. Further, research on vigilance suggests that performance decreases with increasing inspection time. (pp. 63 and 64)

The maintenance environment

Unlike control stations in complex systems, which are generally climate controlled, well lit, and quiet, maintenance environments are susceptible to noise, temperature variations, and poor illumination, among other adverse effects. Maintenance personnel work directly on system equipment, and equipment location and design features dictate many of the parameters of their work environment.

Lighting

Lighting deficiencies arise because the external light that technicians rely on is often designed to illuminate the general work environment, and not the areas on which they focus. Illumination shortcomings can be present in confined or enclosed spaces, or in open spaces where general overhead lighting is the primary source of illumination. Technicians could employ portable lighting fixtures to compensate for these deficiencies; however, using hand held fixtures require technicians to dedicate one hand to holding the fixture, leaving only the other hand for the maintenance task itself. If hands-free operation is not possible, the technician's ability to work effectively will be impeded, either because of constraints from the use of only one hand, or because of the poor illumination, leading to a maintenance or inspection error.

Noise

Maintenance environments can be quite noisy, many are not sound-controlled and ambient noise from ongoing activities may interfere with technicians' work. As discussed in Chapter 3, sounds can distract operators and interfere with their job performance. If sufficiently loud, sounds can also limit technicians' ability to converse or to hear verbal instructions. Although maintenance personnel can wear protective devices to limit the adverse effects of noise, these devices can interfere with their duties if they are uncomfortable, hinder conversation, or restrict movement.

Environment

Technicians may be exposed to wide variations in temperature and humidity because maintenance tasks are often performed outdoors or in environments that are not climate controlled. People perform effectively at a fairly narrow temperature and humidity range. Although cultural and geographical factors affect sensitivity, research has demonstrated that as temperatures extend beyond a fairly narrow range, from about 60°F or 15°C to about 90°F or 35°C (e.g., Ellis, 1982; Van Orden, Benoit, and Osga, 1996; and Wyon, Wyon, and Norin, 1996), temperature increasingly becomes a stressor that adversely affects operator performance. Humidity increases sensitivity to temperature and exacerbates its effects. The higher the relative humidity, the narrower the temperature range in which people can work without being affected by the temperature-related stress.

Other potentially adverse environmental factors can also degrade performance in the maintenance environment. These include pollution, such as from smoke, dust or allergens. Strong odors and vibrations from the equipment or its operating environment are also distracting and can degrade performance.

Accessibility

Tight quarters, exposed wires, chemicals, moving objects, protruding sharp objects, the lack of protective barriers high above the ground, and other hazards may be present in the maintenance environment. These hazards, and technicians' concern for and efforts directed at self-protection, can degrade performance. Although they can wear protective equipment or work in protected surroundings when working in hazardous conditions, often the protection itself interferes with technicians' mobility and thus, limit performance. To illustrate, heavy gloves that protect operators from sharp objects also restrict operator dexterity.

Features of the maintenance environment played a role in technicians' errors in an incident in which one of the four engines on a Boeing 747 became partially detached from its pylon–the component that attaches the engine to the wing–upon landing (NTSB, 1994c). No one was hurt, but had the engine fallen off while the airplane was in flight, the safety of flight could have become compromised. Investigators found that the pin that connected the engine to the pylon was missing.

About a week before the incident a mechanic who had performed maintenance on the pylon failed to reinstall the pin. Following the mechanic's actions an inspector examined the pylon, but he failed to notice the missing pin. These maintenance and inspection errors led to the incident.

Investigators found that the relative inaccessibility and poor illumination of the critical component played a part in the errors. The inspector had to lean about 30° to the side, from scaffolding without barriers, to inspect the component. The scaffolding itself was located about 30 feet or 10 meters above a concrete floor. As investigators report,

> The combination of location of the scaffolding (at a level just below the underside of the wing that forced him [the inspector] into unusual and uncomfortable physical positions) and inadequate lighting from the base of the scaffolding up toward the pylon, hampered his inspection efforts. Moreover, portable fluorescent lights that had been placed along the floor of the scaffolding illuminated the underside of the pylon. These lights had

previously been covered with the residue of numerous paint applications that diminished their brightness. (p. 30)

Tools and parts

Poorly designed tools, parts, and equipment can degrade maintenance quality and lead to error. They can be awkward to hold, difficult to use, block the technician's view of the maintenance action, or present technicians with any of a number of difficulties.

Poorly labeled or poorly designed parts may be used incorrectly, or applied to the incorrect component. Many parts are relatively indistinguishable, differing in seemingly imperceptible ways, yet the use of even "slightly" different parts can lead to an accident. In addition, since those who store tools and parts do not generally perform the maintenance, they may not appreciate the needs of those who do. They may insufficiently differentiate among tools and parts when storing them, or fail to label them clearly, actions that can lead technicians to select incorrect parts for the critical tasks.

Case study

In 1991 a BAC 1-11 lost its windscreen after takeoff from London, almost killing the captain (Air Accidents Investigation Branch, 1992). As the aircraft climbed the cabin pressure increased, to compensate for the decrease in the outside pressure. When the airplane reached an altitude of 17,300 feet, or about 5,300 meters, the pressure differential between the two created a force that blew the captain's windscreen out of its moorings and pulled the captain halfway out. Only the first officer's quick actions of grabbing and holding onto his legs, and a flight attendant's subsequent continued forceful restraint of the captain, prevented his death.

The night before the accident, a weekend night when the maintenance facility had a partial complement of technicians on duty, a maintenance supervisor had worked on the airplane. He reinstalled a cockpit windscreen of the aircraft, securing it with bolts that resembled, but were slightly narrower than the correctly sized bolts. Investigators, examining the circumstances of the windscreen replacement and the airline's system for storing windscreen bolts, concluded that the supervisor–

- Used incorrectly sized bolts to secure the windscreen
- Performed the windscreen maintenance between 0300 and 0500 local time, on his first night of a new shift, after being off duty for several days and then working the day shift for several days thereafter
- Visually compared the previously used bolts to the replacement bolts, in a dimly lit area, without using the corrective lenses that he needed, and without referring to an illustrated parts catalog, as the airline had required
- Retrieved the bolts from a bin that was not controlled by the airline's computerized parts storage and retrieval system because the bin that was under the system's control contained fewer bolts than needed
- Obtained bolts that had no labels or identifiers, from a bag in the storage bin that was labeled
- Used an uncalibrated wrench to apply and tighten the bolts because he was unable to locate a calibrated one
- Tightened the bolts to a torque about 33% higher than called for by the maintenance manual
- Was unable to visually examine the torquing process because the wrench covered the bolt heads, and because he had to stretch outside the safety rail of the platform on which he stood, and use both hands to access and apply the bolts on the external side of the windscreen
- Performed work that was not inspected because no one inspected his work; he usually inspected and approved the work of others.

Colleagues considered the supervisor to be a dedicated employee who worked hard to facilitate the airline's maintenance activities. However, in examining his activities it became evident that, despite his good intentions, numerous antecedents, some of his own making, contributed to his errors. He performed the work at a time when he was most prone to the adverse effects of fatigue, between 0300 and 0500 and on his first night of a night shift, having been off for several days and then working on a day shift.

Because the shift in which he had replaced the windscreen was short staffed, the supervisor bypassed many of the procedures that the airline required, because adhering to them would have been time consuming. His shortcuts, such as his decision to replace the windscreen himself and inspect his own work afterwards, were well intentioned and designed to expedite the aircraft's return to service.

However, in doing so the supervisor violated a tenet of maintenance in complex systems. To ensure that inspectors have no expectancies regarding the focus of their examinations, and to increase the objectivity of their inspections, those who inspect maintenance actions are not the ones who perform the maintenance. Yet, the supervisor's reason for performing the maintenance and the subsequent inspection was consistent with objectives that most companies admire and reward–he sought to expedite the process and finish the job.

To further hasten the maintenance action, he visually examined and selected the bolts needed to secure the windscreen, rather than stopping to locate and use the corrective lenses he relied upon for close visual inspection. Then, instead of verifying that the bolts he selected met the maintenance manual specifications, or waiting until a parts specialist was available to retrieve the correct bolts, he selected bolts that he believed matched the bolts that had previously secured the windscreen. Unfortunately, the bolts he selected were slightly narrower than required.

He selected and used an uncalibrated wrench to tighten the bolts to the windscreen, because he had been unable to locate a properly calibrated one. He secured the windscreen from a scaffold that was near, but not adjacent to the cockpit exterior. He bent over, outstretched one hand to lean against the cockpit exterior, and tightened the bolts. Although providing stability, this position prevented him from adequately observing the bolts as he tightened them, bolts that were further obscured by the tool itself. He then tightened them with a higher torque that than was called for.

In brief, he applied bolts slightly narrower than required to retain the windscreen, secured them improperly, and did not inspect his work. The next morning, as the airplane climbed following takeoff, the bolts were unable to hold the windscreen in place against the increasing pressure differential.

Operator, company, and maintenance antecedents contributed to the supervisor's error. His uncorrected near vision was insufficient to allow him to effectively discriminate among the bolts. His probable fatigue, a result of the company's scheduling practice and time of day, likely degraded his decision making. Maintenance factors, such as poorly illuminated and relatively inaccessible components, poorly labeled parts, and inappropriate tools, then contributed to his using the wrong bolts, the error that led to the accident.

Summary

The research community has only recently focused on the maintenance environment and distinctive features of inspection and maintenance that can become antecedents to error. Maintenance largely involves three critical acts, recognizing and understanding the maintenance to be performed, carrying out the maintenance, and evaluating or inspecting the effectiveness of the action taken. Most errors take place in performing the maintenance task itself, largely because of difficulties in the maintenance environment, the task itself, or the tools and parts used.

The maintenance environment also differs substantially from those of most system control stations in complex systems. Unlike those, the maintenance environment may be subject to temperature extremes, poor illumination, distracting ambient noise, and difficult to access components.

Flaws or defects that inspectors examine may be relatively inconspicuous and difficult to detect. Inspectors may use devices to enhance flaw and defect conspicuity, but after extended visual inspection their effectiveness in detecting flaws will deteriorate. Previous experience detecting flaws will affect inspectors' expectations and the likelihood of finding flaws in subsequent inspections.

Documenting maintenance antecedents

Maintenance and inspection

- Document the illumination, sound, temperature, humidity, and component accessibility. Measure the temperature and humidity several times a day over a period of several days, as close as possible to the time of the accident, and use the average temperature and humidity if the information is not available.
- Document company deadlines to complete the required tasks.
- Evaluate the nature of written or verbal maintenance instructions, information on equipment, tools, and parts used, difficulties in their use, company training, and other relevant information by interviewing those who performed the critical maintenance, or were performing maintenance nearby at the time.
- Measure the illumination of the critical component and document the source of the light, its power, preferably in foot or meter candles, the area being illuminated, and the location of blind spots, dark areas or other deficiencies.
- Determine the presence of allergens or irritants by collecting residues from ventilation units and flooring, and air samples from the operator's work environment.
- Measure the ambient sound level at a time close to the time of the event if sound recordings at the time of the accident are not available.
- Obtain data concerning the work of the maintenance personnel at the time of the event from security cameras, audio recorders, and other devices.
- Determine accessibility to the component of interest from the location at which the maintenance technician performed the maintenance or inspection.
- Document material or components that blocked access to a component, and any exposed wiring, hazardous chemicals, or other potentially dangerous material in and around the work area.

Maintenance

- Measure differences among the dimensions of tools and parts used in the maintenance task and those of tools and parts approved for the task.
- Determine the availability of documentation on the correct tools or parts to be used and impediments to accessing the information.
- Examine the accessibility of the correct parts, and document the type and availability of information available to operators that described the parts to be used.
- Note the distance between the location of the parts and the location of the component that was maintained.

Inspection

- Document the amount of time the inspector devoted to inspection.
- Note the number of inspections of the particular component he or she had carried out previously, and the number of times the inspector found flaws, defects, or incomplete maintenance.
- Measure the length of the flaw if possible, and document features that distinguish a flawless component from a flawed one, or a completed maintenance task from an incomplete one.

The technician

- Obtain medical, financial, and personal information, as appropriate, to document potential operator antecedents that could pertain to the technicians.
- Document the technician's visual acuity. Obtain a visual examination, if possible, if a year or more has elapsed since the inspector's vision was last assessed.
- Determine whether the operator wore corrective lenses at the time of the event, and the extent to which the lenses corrected for any visual impairment.

7 Multi-Operator Systems

In [the University of] Miami's pass-oriented offense, they [the offensive linemen] do this by acting as one, a solid wall, so that their individual achievement is less visible than their group achievement. The Cane's offensive line is the best such group in the country, Gonzalez says, because they are selfless and because they adjust to one another's strengths and weaknesses. They act as a unit, both on and off the field. (Jordan, 2001)

The New York Times Magazine

Introduction

Many complex systems assign more than one operator to control the equipment. If one makes an error, the second could correct the error or minimize its consequences. The sheer complexity of these systems, the number of tasks that must be performed, and the amount of information that must be processed–also call for multiple operators. Using multiple operators also gives operators the flexibility to share system control duties as needed, which helps balance individual workload as operating cycles change.

Multiple operators working together to oversee system operations form multi-operator teams. Teams have certain characteristics, as Dyer (1984) describes,

A team consists of (a) at least two people, who (b) are working towards a common goal/objective/mission, where (c) each person has been assigned specific roles or functions to perform, and where (d) completion of the mission requires some form of dependency among the group members. (p. 286)

This definition, applying to all teams, helps explain the common objective of multi-operator teams in complex systems: safe and effective system operation.

Multi-operator teams offer several advantages over single operators and an extensive body of research supports the efficacy of operator teams in complex systems (e.g., Sundstrom, De Meuse, and Futrell, 1990; Ilgen, 1999; Paris, Salas, and Cannon-Bowers, 1999, 2000; Annett and Stanton, 2000). Moreover, several accidents in complex systems demonstrate that multi-operator teams can provide greater levels of safety than could single operators. For example, in a 1989 accident, a McDonnell Douglas DC-10 experienced a catastrophic engine failure that severed all hydraulic lines, leading to the loss of hydraulic systems and with that the loss of airplane control with traditional pilot techniques (NTSB, 1990a).

Fortunately, an instructor pilot who was seated in the cabin quickly recognized the severity of the problem and offered to assist the pilots. The instructor pilot had earlier practiced controlling and landing a DC-10 with a similar hydraulic failure in a flight simulator, using extraordinary and unconventional control techniques. He then guided them, helped manipulate the available controls, and assisted in bringing the airplane to an emergency landing. Their joint efforts saved the lives of over half the passengers and crew.

Team errors

Operators in any complex system can commit errors, but certain errors are can only be committed by two or more operators. For example, Janis (1982) identified errors that teams of highly qualified individuals committed in several prominent historical events, such as the decision to invade the Bay of Pigs in Cuba in 1961, and the failure of Admiral Husband Kimmell, the commander of U.S. forces in Pearl Harbor in 1941, to prepare for a Japanese assault.[3] Janis suggests that the cohesiveness of select groups and their subtle deference to respected leaders, lead to what he termed "groupthink." Groups that succumb to groupthink have difficulty considering ideas or assessing situations that are contrary to their often unspoken norms.

Teams need time to develop the necessary cohesiveness and deference to the leader that groupthink requires. However, these are not characteristic

---

[3] Since Janis completed his work, historians have reexamined Admiral Kimmel's role in the lack of effective preparations against the Pearl Harbor attack. A number believe that some in the U.S. government, while not knowing of the Pearl Harbor attack in advance, had critical intelligence of possible Japanese military strikes in the Pacific region, which they did not share with Admiral Kimmel.

of complex systems. Although severe consequences resulted from the groupthink errors Janis cited, the environments in which the errors were committed were relatively static and the team members had sufficient time to fully evaluate the costs and benefits of decision options.

Errors in multi-operator systems

Features of both team members and the environments in which they operate influence the likelihood of multi-operator team errors. The roles of the operators, companies, equipment designers, and regulators, among others, in influencing operator error have previously been discussed. In this chapter errors and antecedents characteristic of multi-operator teams operating complex systems will be examined.

In addition to the errors that any individual operator can commit, multi-operator teams can commit these types of errors in turn–

- Failing to notice or respond to another's errors
- Excessively relying on others
- Inappropriately influencing the actions or decisions of others
- Ineffectively delegating team duties and responsibilities.

Failing to notice or respond to another's errors

The most common type of error of multi-operator teams is committed when operators fail to notice or respond to the errors of other team members. This error may result from any number of antecedents, such as one operator not attending to or monitoring the actions of the other. However, in some circumstances operators notice the errors of others but fail to respond appropriately, a failure that may be due to cultural influences, to be discussed more fully in Chapter 8.

The NTSB (1994d) studied errors in 37 accidents that occurred in the multi-operator environment of a complex system–the cockpit of air transport aircraft. This error, which they referred to as failure to monitor/challenge the performance/errors of another, was one of the two error types they noted that were specific to multi-operator systems. The other, which the NTSB referred to as resource management, will be discussed shortly.

Excessively relying on others

This type of error can occur when operators possess different types or levels of expertise. It can lead to severe consequences when operators rely on other team members to such an extent that they fail to perform their own tasks effectively.

Junior operators, who typically work alongside those with more experience, seniority, authority, or status, occasionally commit this type of error. They may disregard their own knowledge and rely excessively on others to decide, act, or perform critical duties. A multi-operator error could result if the person being relied upon makes an error, or if his or her skills or knowledge is inadequate for the task requirements.

Inappropriately influencing the actions or decisions of others

Operators may not have sufficient time to effectively assess the situations they encounter, and in such circumstances one operator could exert extraordinary influence on the situation awareness and subsequent actions of the others. In highly dynamic conditions an operator that assesses the situation incorrectly could adversely affect another's situation awareness, even if that person had initially assessed the situation accurately. The operator with the inaccurate situation assessment could then create a multi-operator team error by interfering with the assessments of other team members.

Failing to delegate team duties and responsibilities

Operators cannot ignore ongoing system operations when responding to emergency situations, but must effectively control the system while responding to the emergency. Situations such as these call for multi-operator teams to respond to the differing situational requirements. Failing to delegate responsibility among team members to both operate the system and respond to the anomaly can lead to a multi-operator error as the response to either the anomaly or the system operation may be erroneous.

A team of three pilots committed this type of error in a 1972 accident involving a Lockheed L-1011 that crashed in the Florida Everglades (NTSB, 1973). The three had put the airplane into a hold or circle over the Everglades while they attempted to determine the cause of an indicator failure. The indicator, which had failed to illuminated, signified the status of the landing gear, whether extended or retracted. The three pilots attended to the indicator light but not to the airplane's flight path. No one noticed that the mechanism that controlled the airplane's altitude had disengaged, and that the airplane was slowly losing altitude. It continued to descend until it struck the ground.

Researchers at the National Aeronautics and Space Administration, later studied this type of error. Using a Boeing 747 flight simulator they examined the response of pilots to a system anomaly (Ruffell-Smith, 1979). They presented pilots with a scenario that included an anomaly, and then tried to distract them with non-essential questions during their response to the anomaly, using actors who were pretending to be cabin crewmembers. Several pilots responded to "flight attendants," became distracted, and committed errors that exacerbated the severity of the situation. As in the Everglades accident, the pilots allowed an anomaly in the simulator to become what would have been a serious event if in the aircraft, by failing to ensure that team members were monitoring the system, and by not responding to non-critical distracters.

In response to these findings, and to the findings of several accident investigations, airlines and the research community developed "cockpit resource management," (now referred to as crew resource management or CRM) to help crewmembers contribute fully to both routine and non-routine system operations. The programs stressed the need for clear, unambiguous delineation and assignment of operator duties and responsibilities in response to non-routine situations (e.g., Foushee and Helmreich, 1988; Helmreich and Foushee, 1993; Helmreich and Merritt, 1998). Today, CRM is widely accepted in aviation, marine, rail operations, and other systems where multi-operator teams are used to control the systems.

The research findings on CRM have not been consistent. Helmreich, Merritt, and Wilhelm (1999), in observing actual flights, found that CRM training improved the quality of crew performance. However, other studies on CRM effectiveness suggest that its effects on crew behavior may not be long lasting (Wiegmann and Shappell, 1999). CRM programs in aviation have not generally been subject to formal evaluation, because, as Helmreich et al. (1999) suggest, the overall accident rate in aviation is so low, and the variability among training programs so great, that meaningful formal evaluation is difficult.

Antecedents to errors: single- or multi-operator systems

The antecedents to individual operator errors lead to team errors as well. However, in some instances antecedents influence multi-operator teams in ways that do not affect individual operators. The influence of these antecedents on operators in both single and multi-operator systems will be reviewed more fully to understand their effects on multi-operator team errors.

Equipment

As discussed in Chapter 3, features of information presentation and control design affect operator performance. Those that apply to single-operator systems apply to multi-operator systems as well, with some additions. These pertain to an operator's ability to 1) interact with other team members, 2) access the information presented to other team members, and 3) control the system for other team members.

   Equipment designed for multiple operators enables team members to communicate with each other when needed, access critical information, and maintain system control. However, design features of some systems may interfere with team performance (e.g., Bowers, Oser, Salas, and Cannon-Bowers, 1996; Paris, Salas, and Cannon-Bowers, 2000). For example, some designs prevent operators from learning of other team members' control inputs and the system information they receive. This type of shortcoming can degrade both individual and team situation awareness.

Operator

Physiological and behavioral antecedents that lead to errors in single-operator systems can affect multi-operator teams as well. The influence of these antecedents on operator performance in single- or multi-operator systems is comparable.

Company

Companies have substantial influence on the quality of the teams they employ, as discussed in Chapter 4. Companies evaluate candidates' interpersonal skills, in addition to their technical expertise, when selecting candidates for multi-operator team positions. Those who are unable to interact effectively with other team members can adversely affect the quality of their team's performance and companies should screen applicants to ensure that those it hires do not manifest these characteristics.

To illustrate, Foushee (1984) described an incident on an air transport aircraft in which a captain demeaned a first officer and expressly discouraged him from providing input to the conduct of the flight. The captain's actions degraded the quality of team interactions, by deterring a team member from contributing to its performance. Because of the captain's behavior, the first officer was less likely to speak up in response to an error of the captain, or even unwilling to mitigate the effects of that error. Today, because social values have changed, there is little tolerance for individuals in positions of responsibility in safety-critical systems that openly demean others and discourage their input. Their behavior reflects on the company's selection criteria, training, and oversight as much as on them as individuals.

The quality of a company's procedures can also affect the quality of team member interaction and serve as an antecedent to multi-operator team errors. For example, companies can require operators to challenge and respond to each other, so that one verifies that another has performed a task, or one confirms that he or she received information from the other. Procedures can increase the level of operator contribution to team tasks, encourage operators to observe and participate in aspects of each other's performance, and reduce antecedents to error among team members.

Antecedents to errors–multi-operator systems

Certain antecedents to errors are specific to multi-operator teams. These include the number of operators, team structure, team stability, team leadership, and cultural factors.

Number of operators

The number of operators performing a given task can influence the quality of the task. An excessive number can degrade communications within a group and lower individual workload to the point that operators become bored, adversely affecting system monitoring and other aspects of performance (O'Hanlon, 1981). However, because of financial concerns, most organizations are more likely to have too few rather than too many operators, and as a result, this will not be considered further.

Circumstances with too few operators for the tasks to be performed may occasionally occur, especially during non-routine situations. The literature has indicated that an insufficient number of operators can increase operator workload, increase individual team member stress and reduce levels of operational safety (Paris, Salas, and Cannon-Bowers, 2000).

Yet, the dynamic nature of complex systems can make it difficult to plan for a constant workload. Operating cycles, with differing operator workload requirements, need different numbers of operators. A team that has sufficient operators for one operating phase may be insufficient for another, and a team that is insufficient for non-routine operations may be excessive for routine conditions. The adequacy of the number of operators assigned to a task will vary according to the operating phase, its complexity, and the level of operator workload.

Team structure

Team structure refers to the assignment of responsibilities and roles to individual team members, a factor that can influence the quality of intra-team interactions and team performance (Paris, Salas, and Cannon-Bowers, 1999). Operators in multi-operator systems work best when each team member understands his or her tasks, and contributes to the work of the other team members without interfering with them.

However, as with team size, a structure that is effective for routine operations may be ineffective for non-routine situations. As seen in the 1972 accident involving the Lockheed L-1011 that crashed in the Florida Everglades, a team structure effective for routine operations could break down in non-routine circumstances. Despite their response to what turned out to have been a relatively benign situation, a failed visual alert, the team members failed to monitor a critical element of system operations, the airplane's altitude.

Some have found that operators' roles within the teams can affect their situation awareness and other critical performance elements. For example, in commercial aviation one pilot typically performs the flying duties and the other monitors the subsystem performance and supports the "flying" pilot, although the captain remains in command throughout. On subsequent flights they generally alternate duties as pilot flying and pilot not flying. Jentsch, Barnett, Bowers, and Salas (1999) reviewed over 400 anonymous reports that pilots had filed describing their own errors to an anonymous self-reporting system. They found that captains were more likely to lose situation awareness when they were flying the airplane, that is, actively engaged in system control, and the subordinate pilots, the first officers, were monitoring the captains' performance. They were less likely to lose situation awareness when the first officers were performing the flying duties and they were monitoring the first officers' performance. The findings contradict a common belief that active engagement in system control enhances situation assessment. The researchers suggest that monitoring gave the captains the ability to observe system parameters and obtain situation awareness better than would have been true had they been flying the aircraft themselves. In addition, the superior-subordinate positions of captains and first officers, which made the latter somewhat reluctant to alert the captains to their errors when they were the flying pilots, may have also contributed to reduced situation awareness when the captains were flying.

Team stability

Team stability, the extent to which team members remain together as a working team, can also affect the quality of team performance. Working together allows team members to learn about each other's performance and work styles and develop reasonably accurate expectations of other's predicted performance, as often occurs with members of athletic teams who have played together over a period of time. The players and the team members learn subtle aspects of each other's performance that enable them to reliably predict each other's actions before they begin, facilitating communications and enhancing performance. In emergency operations, when operators may face intense workload and have little available time, stability can lead to enhanced communications as the operators can accurately anticipate each other's actions without articulating them.

However, in some systems long-term stability may not be possible. Contractual obligations and prevailing customs may dictate different work schedules among team members with different levels of seniority. Several airlines, for example, employ thousands of pilots, many of who fly with pilots they had neither flown with nor even met previously. In systems such as these, the consistent application of standard operating procedures can compensate for the lack of team stability. Well-defined and practiced procedures enable operators to anticipate their fellow operators' actions in each operating phase, during both routine and non-routine situations, regardless of the length of time they had been teamed with the other operators.

Companies can also use operator selection to counteract the potentially adverse effects of team instability. Paris, Salas, and Cannon-Bowers (2000) suggest that the most critical determinant of the effects of instability on team performance is the skill level of the operator leaving the team. "As a general rule," they note, "there is little disruption of team performance from turnover, as long as only one team member is replaced at a time and that replacement is as skilled as the person he replaced" (p. 1060).

Leadership quality

Team leaders in complex systems contribute to the climate in which the group operates, whether autocratic, democratic, or something in between. Leaders implement rewards and punishments, and assign tasks. In these and other daily interactions, leadership quality affects team performance quality. Military organizations, where unquestioned adherence to a superior's orders is expected, recognize that effective leaders elicit superior team member performance rather than compel it. Leaders are encouraged to obtain voluntary cooperation from their subordinates rather than demand what can become reluctant or grudging cooperation. Similarly, in complex systems multi-operator team leader quality can impact team performance quality, particularly during critical situations.

In commercial aviation early CRM programs addressed leadership quality as a critical element for successful interaction between superior and subordinate pilots. Good leaders attended to both operating tasks and subordinate concerns. Later CRM programs addressed additional elements of team performance and broadened the scope of team membership to include other operators as well as pilots.

Cultural factors

Different cultures respect and defer to leaders, rules, procedures and teams differently, and their values can affect the quality of operating team performance. The influence of cultural factors on team performance and related topics will be discussed more fully in Chapter 8.

Case study

The relationship of multi-operator team antecedents to errors can been seen in the collision of two commercial aircraft, a McDonnell Douglas DC-9 and a Boeing 727, in heavy fog at Detroit Metropolitan Airport in December 1990 (NTSB, 1991a). The DC-9 was destroyed and eight of the 44 people onboard were killed in the accident, although no one on the Boeing 727 was injured. During severely limited visual conditions, the DC-9 pilots mistakenly taxied their aircraft onto an active runway and into the path of the Boeing 727 as it was taking off. The Boeing 727 pilots were unable to see the DC-9 in time to prevent the collision.

Heavy fog places substantial burdens on both pilots and controllers at airports that lack ground radar, as was the case at the Detroit airport at the time of the accident. If visibility is sufficiently limited, pilots are unable to see beyond a short distance in front of their airplanes, and they would be prohibited from taking off or landing. Conditions at the time of this accident approached, but did not exceed the visibility limits, but Detroit air traffic controllers were unable to see taxiing aircraft from the control tower, and pilots had great difficulty establishing their positions on the airport. In these conditions—when planes could still operate but visibility is quite limited—both controllers and pilots rely on each other for information. Controllers depend on the pilots to inform them of their positions on the airport, and pilots depend on the controllers to keep them separate from other aircraft.

The limited visibility added to the workload of both pilots and controllers. Controllers were unable to verify airplane positions and pilots lacked many of the visual cues they needed to verify their positions on the airport surface. Even markings that had been painted on runways and taxiways were not visible because a thin layer of snow had obscured them.

The multi-operator team on the DC-9 consisted of two pilots, a captain, the superior, who was making his first unsupervised air transport flight after a six-year hiatus, following his recovery from a medical condition that was unrelated to aviation, and a subordinate, the first officer. In the six-year interval between medical disqualification and his return to flying, airline ownership had changed, and the airline that had employed him had been purchased by another airline. When he returned to flying the captain had to not only requalify to operate the DC-9 but learn his new employer's operating procedures as well.

The DC-9 first officer had retired from the U.S. Air Force, where he had been a pilot in command of large bomber aircraft. At the time of the accident he was within his probationary first year period with the airline. The airline's personnel rules allowed it to terminate the employment of pilots in their probationary periods without cause. In the six months since he joined the airline, he had flown into and out of Detroit 22 times, only one or two of them, according to his estimates, were in restricted visibility conditions.

Cockpit voice recorder data revealed that the first officer exaggerated an attribute of his background to the captain. Unsolicited, he told the captain that he had retired from the air force at a rank that was higher than the rank that he had actually attained. During the taxi from the gate he committed several errors, while ostensibly assisting the captain. Even when uncertain, he unhesitatingly gave their location to the captain, and he continued to do so after misdirecting the captain, necessitating a new taxi clearance to the active runway from air traffic controllers.

Although captains steer while taxiing this type of airplane, both pilots work together using airport charts and external visual information to verify that the taxi route they follow corresponds to the assigned route. Both also simultaneously monitor air traffic control communications for pertinent information, and they monitor the aircraft state.

Early in their taxi the first officer told the captain, "Guess we turn left here." The captain responded, "Left turn or right turn"? The first officer answered by describing what he believed to be their position. The captain then answered, "So a left turn," and the first officer agreed. Ten seconds later he directed the captain, "Go that way" and the captain complied. This type of exchange between the captain and first officer continued for about two minutes, until the first officer, in response to an air traffic controller's question about their location answered, "Okay, I think we might have missed oscar six," the name of the taxiway to which they had been assigned. By misdirecting the captain to a wrong turn on the airport he had endangered the safety of the flight, but neither had apparently recognized the significance of his error.

Yet, even after being misdirected, the captain continued to accept the first officer's guidance. For the next five minutes the captain continued to ask the first officer, "What's he want us to do here," "This a right turn here Jim," and "When I cross this [runway] which way do I go, right" and other similar questions. The first officer continued to direct the captain until they entered the path of the departing Boeing 727. By the time of the accident, the first officer had provided all taxi instructions to the captain, which the captain followed without hesitation.

The captain made a key multi-operator team error by over-relying on the first officer. His error is understandable given his return to active flying after the long hiatus, and his likely belief in the first officer's superior airport knowledge gained from more recent experience operating at Detroit. The first officer's seeming confidence in his knowledge of the airport routing exacerbated the captain's pre-existing tendency to rely on the first officer while navigating on the Detroit airport surface. The interaction of an overly assertive subordinate, with a tendency to exaggerate his accomplishments and knowledge, albeit a tendency the captain could not have been aware of, and a superior relatively inexperienced in the circumstances that existed at the time, combined to create unique multi-operator team errors. Had the captain relied less on the first officer, and been more attentive to information on their airport position, the accident may have been avoided.

Summary

Complex systems often require multi-operator teams, two or more operators working towards a common goal or objective. They can enhance team performance by helping to prevent errors and mitigating the effects of errors that have been committed. Multiple operators can reduce individual workload, and assure that necessary tasks are performed during non-routine or emergency situations.

Multi-operator teams in complex systems can also commit distinctive errors. These include failing to notice or to respond to another's error, relying excessively on others, incorrectly influencing the situation assessment of others, and failing to ensure that duties and responsibilities are delegated. Antecedents to these errors may lie within the culture or the company, or result from other factors specific to multi-operator systems.

Antecedents of error in both single- and multi-operator systems include those discussed in previous chapters, such as equipment design, operator factors, company and regulator factors, as well as several that are specific to multi-operator teams. These include the number of operators, team structure, team stability, leadership quality, and cultural factors.

Documenting antecedents to errors in multi-operator systems

General

- Determine the critical errors that are believed to have led to the event and identify the team members who likely committed those errors.
- Determine the number of tasks that operators attempted to perform, the amount of time available to perform those tasks, and the actions and decisions of each team member by interviewing operators, examining recorded data, and referring to operating manuals and other documents.
- Document pertinent antecedents to single-operator type errors (such as those resulting from performance or procedural deficiencies, discussed in previous chapters) and examine potentially relevant equipment, operator, and company factors if the error appears to be a multi-operator type error.

Multi-operator team antecedents

- Document the number of operators called for and the number of operators involved in system operation at the time of the event.
- Assess the adequacy of the number of operators available to perform the tasks in the allotted time.
- Identify the duties of each team member and determine the extent to which each team member understood his or her duties, and performed them.
- Determine how the length of time that the team members had worked together as a team.
- Describe communications among the team members, and supervisor/subordinate communications.
- Document company training, guidelines, and procedures that relate to team performance, and assess the extent to which these encourage team integration and team performance.
- Assess the proportion of training, guidelines, and procedures devoted to team performance and the extent to which they call for team, as opposed to individual operator tasks.
- Document interpersonal skills of operator applicants and leadership skills of supervisor applicants by examining company selection criteria and history, and interviewing supervisors, subordinates and colleagues.

- Assess the extent to which the training, guidelines, and procedures pertain to team structure, team member responsibilities, and leadership qualities.

8 Culture

At Korean Air, such teamwork has been nearly impossible," says Park Jae Hyun, a former captain and Ministry of Transportation flight inspector. Its cockpits have operated under an "obey or else" code, he says. Co-pilots "couldn't express themselves if they found something wrong with a captain's piloting skills. (Carley and Pasztor, 1999)

The Wall Street Journal

Introduction

On August 6, 1997, a Korean Air Boeing 747 crashed into a hill several miles short of the runway in Guam, killing 228 passengers and crewmembers (see Figure 8.1). This accident was the latest in a string of major accidents that investigators had attributed, at least in part, to errors that the airline's pilots had committed (NTSB, 1999b).

In the 16 years before this accident the airline had experienced one of the highest accident rates of any airline. These included the following–

- August 1983: A Boeing 747 inadvertently deviated more than 300 miles off course into Soviet territory before the Soviet Air Force shot it down
- December 1983: A DC-10 crashed in Anchorage after the pilots tried to take off from the wrong runway
- July 1989: A DC-10 crashed in Libya after the crew mishandled an instrument approach
- August 1994: An Airbus A300 crashed in Cheju, Korea, after the crew landed at an excessive airspeed.

Even after the Guam accident, its most serious event since the Soviet Air Force had shot down the Boeing 747, pilot error-related accidents continued to plague the airline. These included the following–

- August 1998: A Boeing 747 crashed after the captain misused the thrust reverser while landing at Seoul
- September 1998: An MD-80 ran off the end of the runway at Ulsan, Korea
- March 1999: An MD-80 ran off the end of the runway at Pohang, Korea
- April 1999: An MD-11 freighter crashed in Shanghai.

Courtesy National Transportation Safety Board

Figure 8.1 The site of the Boeing 747 accident in Guam

In 1999 the *Wall Street Journal* implied that factors rooted in Korean society and culture affected the airline and its safety record (Carley and Pasztor, 1999). The newspaper stated that,

> Korean Air's history has emphasized hierarchy. It is easy to discern the hierarchy: former [Korean] air force pilots, then fliers from other military services, and Cheju men [civilians that the airline trained] at the bottom. Red-stone rings worn by Korean Air Force Academy graduates command instant

respect. And ex-military men, while training co-pilots in simulators or during check rides, sometimes slap or hit the co-pilots for mistakes. In the cockpit, friction and intimidation can cause trouble. For a civilian co-pilot to challenge a military-trained captain "would mean loss of face for the captain," says Mr. Ludwin...[a] former Pan Am captain. For the co-pilot, he adds, "it's more honorable to die, and sometimes they do." (Carley and Pasztor, 1999, pp. A1 and 2)

The newspaper raised a critical issue by suggesting that specific Korean cultural factors adversely affected the airline's safety. Was it correct in its implication? Can cultural influences serve as antecedents to errors? This chapter will examine cultural factors in complex systems and discuss the relationship of cultural factors to operator performance.

Culture

Cultural influences have affected the behavior of people who work in the same companies, live in the same regions, and belong to the same groups. Recently, some have suggested that cultural factors affect operator performance (e.g., Orasanu, Fischer, and Davison, 1997) and hence, system safety. "Performance of a plant," Moray (2000) notes, "is as much affected ...by the expectations of society, as by the engineering characteristics of the design and the ergonomics of individual work and the design of communication within and between groups and teams" (p. 860).

Before exploring culture and its effects on system safety, culture needs to be understood. Schein (1990, 1996) defines a culture as,

a) a pattern of basic assumptions, b) invented, discovered, or developed by a given group, c) as it learns to cope with its problems of external adaptation and internal integration, d) that has worked well enough to be considered valid and, therefore e) is to be taught to new members as the f) correct way to perceive, think, and feel in relation to those problems. The strength and degree of internal consistency of a culture are, therefore, a function of the stability of the group, the length of time the group has existed, the intensity of the group's experiences of learning, the mechanisms by which the learning has taken place, and the strength and clarity of the assumptions held by the founders and leaders of the group. (1990, p. 111)

The assumptions that Schein refers to are commonly known as norms, ways that people act, perceive, and interpret the values that they share, that may be unspoken but are nevertheless perceived, felt, and practised by members of a group. Over time, new group members tend to incorporate these norms into their own behavior, beliefs, and perceptions.

Much of the recent work relating cultural factors to system safety began with Hofstede (1980, 1991), and his study of a multi-national corporation, IBM, then with offices in 66 countries. He found differences on several dimensions of behavior among IBM employees of the different cultures, three of which will be considered. One, termed "power distance," refers to the extent to which people perceive difference in status or power between themselves and their subordinates and superiors. In cultures with high power distance, subordinates and supervisors perceive the differences between them to be greater than do those in cultures that score low on power distance. In those cultures subordinates would be less willing to confront a superior, or call a superior's attention to an error that he or she may have committed, than would their counterparts in countries with low power distance.

A second dimension, "individualism-collectivism," characterizes the degree to which individuals accept and pursue the goals of the organization or group to which they belong, relative to their own individual goals. An individually-oriented person is more self-sufficient and derives more satisfaction from pursuing personal goals than organizational goals. Collectivist-oriented persons identify more with the companies that employ them than do individually oriented persons. They tend to view errors as reflections of the company or group as much as on themselves as individuals.

"Uncertainty avoidance," a third dimension, refers to the willingness or ability to contend with uncertain or ambiguous situations. People in cultures with high uncertainty avoidance generally find it difficult to deal with ambiguous or unclear situations that have few applicable procedures. They would be expected to respect and adhere to rules more readily than would their counterparts in cultures with low uncertainty avoidance. Those in cultures that are low in uncertainty avoidance feel comfortable responding to uncertain or novel situations that they had not experienced before, or situations to which few rules and procedures apply.

Researchers have corroborated Hofstede's findings in a variety of settings and identified additional differentiating cultural characteristics (e.g., Helmreich and Merritt, 1998). Maurino (1994) described five cultural dimensions among operators in aviation that are related to those Hofstede identified. These include adherence to authority compared to a participative and democratic approach, inquiry in education and learning as opposed to rote learning, identification with the group rather than identification with the individual, calm and reflective temperament as opposed to a volatile and reactive one, and free expression and individual assertiveness compared to deference to experience and age.

Some believe that the inability of early CRM programs to substantially impact the quality of operations was due to the influence of cultural factors. For example Helmreich, Merritt, and Wilhelm (1999), and Helmreich, Wilhelm, Klinect, and Merritt (2001) contend that these programs were developed in the United States, but when they were applied to other countries difficulties developed. Unlike the United States where CRM programs had originated, organizations found that when CRM programs were implemented in countries where employees scored high on power distance, the junior operators resisted efforts to be more assertive in dealing with their superiors, and senior operators did not accept their subordinates as fully contributing team members.

Researchers have applied Hofstede's work to a complex system, military aviation, to assess the relationship between cultural factors and safety. Soeters and Boer (2000) examined the safety records of members the North Atlantic Treaty Organization (NATO), and the air forces of 14 of its member countries. Many NATO pilots operate the same aircraft, and instructors from two of its member countries train almost all of its pilots. The air forces, although distinct, often practice together, follow the same procedures, and use similar criteria to select their pilots.

Soeters and Boer found a significant relationship between the accident rate of each country and the country's score on Hofstede's cultural dimensions, particularly individualism-collectivism. Countries with cultures that scored high on individualistic traits had lower accident rates than countries considered more group oriented.

Culture and operator error

The effects of cultural factors on system operations are evident; cultural factors influence a variety of operator-equipment interactions, and can make the difference between effective and erroneous performance. In applying cultural factors to operator performance, two cultural antecedents to error can be identified, one acceptance of authority, and the other identification with the group. Each can affect operator performance and lead to error, independently of the effects of other system elements.

Acceptance of authority

Operators across cultures differentially interpret and defer to the authority of their employers and superiors, and as important, to the products of their authority–including training material, guidance, rules, and procedures. Operators in some cultures, for example, learn material by rote memorization and apply it with little interpretation to system operations, while in others operators learn the principles underlying the material and are given more discretion to apply them.

Rules and procedures are necessary to guide operator performance in complex systems and operators are expected to adhere to them, as discussed in Chapter 5. In routine circumstances, learning by rote memorization and applying memorized material to system operations can be effective. However, when systems do not operate as intended operators may not be able to rely on memorized procedures. Their ability to recognize circumstances that call for them to depart from what they have been taught, and respond to circumstances in ways not specified in rules and procedures–"knowledge based performance" according to Rasmussen–may mean the difference between effective response and error.

Investigators of the Korean Air Boeing 747 accident at Guam (NTSB, 1999b) found that operators were expected to rely on rote memorization in training and not on a deeper understanding of principles. Investigators examined the airline's training in the type of landing maneuver, a nonprecision approach, which the pilots had attempted in this accident. The airline repeatedly presented the same landing maneuver, at the same airport, and at the same runway, to its pilots to practice during training. Investigators conclude that,

> The repeated presentation of a single nonprecision approach scenario throughout simulator training (to the exclusion of all other kinds of nonprecision approaches) provides insufficient training in nonprecision approaches. Specifically, the repetition limits pilots' opportunity to understand and practice the flying techniques necessary to perform the different kinds of nonprecision approaches and limits their ability to successfully apply these techniques to novel situations or unusual approach configurations encountered in line operations, such as the localizer approach at Guam. (p. 151)

In short, operators' unquestioning acceptance of a scenario with which they had repeatedly been presented works against their ability to apply the techniques underlying the scenario to similar, but different circumstances.

Although the B-747 pilots had mastered the necessary skills, they had practiced them only in one setting and when they encountered a situation somewhat different from that one, they were unable to apply the same skills to the new circumstances.

Identification with group

Operators often identify with and incorporate the norms of the group to which they belong. Although this is expected and often desired, taken to the extreme it could also limit an operator's contribution to system safety. Ideally, they should identify with a company, but not to the point that they unquestionably accept its goals, objectives, and procedures when they perceive that these conflict with safety. Operators should be sufficiently objective to recognize potential conflicts between company goals and safety, and sufficiently independent to perform in the best interests of safety.

Investigators of an accident involving a Douglas DC-8 cargo flight, which crashed in Anchorage, Alaska, in January 1977, shortly after takeoff, found operators that had been unable to retain such objectivity, and unable to bridge the authority distance between themselves and their superior (NTSB, 1979). The captain, an American, was intoxicated at the time; the two subordinate pilots were Japanese. His alcohol-induced impairment led him to mishandle the controls on takeoff and caused the accident, killing the three pilots and a cargo handler.

His intoxicated behavior was sufficiently apparent that the taxi driver, who had driven the pilots to the airport, telephoned his dispatcher and informed him of the captain's intoxication. The dispatcher then called the airline, but it took no action. Despite his obvious impairment, neither of the two subordinate pilots attempted to either prevent the captain from handling the controls or counter his control mishandling. Their failure to overcome the prohibition against overriding the captain's authority, even at the expense of their own safety, was a factor in the cause of the accident.

Organizational culture

Companies, as tribes, religious groups, and nations, can influence their employee's behavior through the norms that they develop–norms that can be as powerful an influence on employee behavior as can cultural norms (e.g., Schein 1990, 1996). Numerous illustrations of organizational practices, even among companies seemingly dedicated to enhancing operational safety, demonstrate potentially adverse effects of norms on safety practices. For example, the *New York Times* described poor organizational practices in the National Aeronautics and Space Administration after it had experienced several major project failures, years after the 1986 accident of its Space Shuttle Challenger. The article reported that,

> In candid reports assessing recent problems with the National Aeronautics and Space Administration's (NASA) programs to explore Mars, two panels concluded that pressures to conform to the agency's recent credo of "faster, cheaper, better" ended up compromising ambitious projects. To meet the new constraints, the reports said, project managers sacrificed needed testing and realistic assessments of the risks of failure. (Leary, 2000)

Interestingly, the newspaper indicated that NASA management had been criticized for many of the same management practices and norms demonstrated after the 1986 Space Shuttle Challenger accident.

As with national cultures, corporate cultural factors can affect safety, and become antecedents to error or mitigate opportunities for error. Moreover, employee groups within companies develop their own norms based on commonly held professional standards and beliefs. Vaughan (1996) examined the influence of the cultures at NASA, its primary space shuttle contractor, Morton Thiokol, and the shared engineer culture of both, on the Challenger accident. She suggested that engineers and their supervisors at both Morton Thiokol and at NASA had developed techniques of responding to the risky technology involved in space operations that minimized the perception of and appreciation for the risks inherent to the mission. Despite considerable evidence suggesting that the low outside temperatures that were present at the time of the launch could seriously degrade the integrity of a system component, officials at both organizations agreed to the launch, which proceeded with disastrous results.

Company practices

Aspects of a company's culture are revealed in its selection policies, operating procedures and operational oversight, all of which can affect performance. Companies that operate complex systems are required to perform these tasks, but companies that are especially safety-oriented will perform them more thoroughly, and at a higher level, than others. Practices that encourage operator responsibility, professionalism, and participation in safety matters can enhance operator attention to safety details; punitive practices do not. A company's culture can also be reflected in its definitions of and response to employee transgressions. Companies that require extensive documentation of occasional and infrequent medical absences, for example, encourage their employees to report to work when ill, increasing the likelihood of errors.

Managerial instability, frequent changes in supervisory personnel, supervisory practices, and operating procedures, may reflect instability, an indication of a corporate cultural factor that could affect safety. Instability can adversely affect operator performance by leading to frequent changes in interpretations and enforcement of policies and procedures. One supervisor may interpret procedures literally and expect the same interpretation and compliance from operators. Another may interpret the procedures differently, and permit operators to comply with those he or she considers most important, while ignoring those that are perceived to have little or no influence on system operations. Instability can also signal dissatisfaction with the company and its practices.

Previous company incidents and accidents can also reveal much about corporate commitment to safety. Numerous incidents and accidents relative to those of comparable companies suggest deficiencies in company practices, standards, and oversight. Common issues found in multiple events may indicate an unwillingness to identify and address potential system safety hazards. On the other hand, thorough company investigations of their events and sincere efforts to address identified safety deficiencies reveal aspects of a positive corporate culture.

Investigators noted the adverse effects on safety of some organizational norms in a January 1996 rail accident outside of Washington, D.C. (NTSB, 1996). A Washington Metropolitan Area Transit Authority subway train was unable to stop during a heavy snowstorm and struck a train stopped ahead on the same track, killing the moving train's operator.

The track had been exposed to heavy snow that had fallen throughout the day, reducing friction on the exposed tracks. Several times before the accident, the train operator had requested authorization to disengage automatic train control and operate the train manually to better control braking on the slippery track. However, the Authority's director of operations had prohibited manual train control under any circumstances, in an effort to reduce train wheel wear. Supervisors were reluctant to violate his order and grant the train operator's request, despite their awareness of the slippery track conditions. Not one of the supervisors believed that he had the authority to countermand the policy, even though all knew that adhering to it posed a threat to system safety.

The lessons of this accident apply to others in a variety of settings. Corporate norms that encourage unquestioning acceptance of rules risk jeopardizing safety when they no longer apply, and companies that manage through fear will, over time, increase the probability of unsafe operations.

High reliability companies

Companies that operate complex systems can establish practices that promote safe operations. After studying high-risk systems, Rochlin (1999) described what he calls "high reliability organizations." Expecting to focus on avoiding errors and risk management, he found that some organizations tended to anticipate and plan for, rather than react to, unexpected events. They attended to safety while efficiently operating complex systems, rewarded error reporting, and assumed responsibility for error rather than assigning fault. These companies actively sought to learn from previous errors by maintaining detailed records of past events and applying the lessons of those events to system operations. As Rochlin writes,

> Maintenance of a high degree of operational safety depends on more than a set of observable rules or procedures, externally imposed training or management skills, or easily recognized behavioural scripts. While much of what the operators do can be formally described one step at a time, a great deal of how they operate, and more important, how they operate safely, is "holistic," in the sense that it is a property of the interactions, rituals, and myths of the social structure and beliefs of the entire organization, or at least of a large segment of it. (p. 1557)

Rochlin argues that an organization's "interactions, rituals, and myths"– essentially its norms–can either help to create antecedents to error, or can anticipate and minimize their presence. An organization with a "good" culture encourages safety, even at the expense of production. It fosters communication among its employees and can proactively uncover problems in its operations. Westrum and Adamski (1998) offered techniques for companies to enhance safety through internal communications and error reporting.

Reason (1990) describes the benefits of programs that allow employees to report mistakes without retribution. Industries in several countries have implemented such self-reporting programs, which have provided considerable information about potential antecedents to error, before the antecedents could affect operator performance. The aviation industry has implemented a number of these programs, such as ASRS–Aviation Safety Reporting System in the United States, and CAIR–Confidential Aviation Incident Reporting, in Australia.

Summary

Cultures develop norms that influence the values, beliefs, expectations, behaviors, and perceptions of their group members. Recent studies have identified several cultural factors, including power distance, the perceived differences between superiors and subordinates, individualism-collectivism, the extent to which people accept their own goals relative to those of their group's, and uncertainty avoidance, the willingness to deal with uncertain situations, that can distinguish among members of different cultures and influence system safety.

Companies also develop norms through their actions, statements, practices, and policies. Hiring criteria, training programs, operating procedures, and oversight reflect these norms. Some companies actively encourage safety by recognizing and addressing potential operational hazards. Differences between "good" and "bad" organizational cultures are suggested.

Documenting cultural antecedents

National culture

- Refer to existing research to determine the effects of norms that are believed to influence safety (e.g., Hofstede 1980, 1991; Helmreich and Merritt, 1998; Soeters and Boer, 2000; Helmreich, Wilhelm, Klinect, and Merritt, 2001), when national cultural issues need to be examined.

Organizational culture

- Identify organizational cultural factors and assess their effects on system safety by interviewing employees at all pertinent company levels, and examining written documentation such as memos, organizational policies, and procedures.
- Document the extent to which company policies are enforced, and the extent to which operator expectations regarding company enforcement practices are met.
- Identify company recognized transgressions and the penalties it administers to operators who transgress.
- Evaluate the comprehensiveness of selection practices, training programs, maintenance practices, and operational oversight and, if possible, compare them to other companies in the same industry.
- Document managerial and operator turnover each year for a period of several years from the time of the event, and the reasons given for employees' willingness to leave the company.
- Determine the number of incidents and accidents the company has experienced over several years from the time of the event, assess the comprehensiveness of the organizational investigation of the events, identify common issues that may be present, and the remediation strategies the company has implemented to prevent future events.
- Document the resources that companies have devoted to programs that directly affect system safety, such as self-reporting error programs, rewards for suggestions to enhance safety, and efforts to remain current with industry and government safety programs.

Part III
Data and Data Analysis

9 System Recorders

The telltale recorder, known as a Sensing and Diagnostic Module or S.D.M., was one of six million quietly put into various models of General Motors [G.M.] cars since 1990. A newly developed model being installed in hundreds of thousands of G.M. cars this year records not only the force of collisions and the air bag's performance, but also captures five seconds of data before impact. It can determine, for example, whether the driver applied the brakes in the fifth second, third second or last second. It also records the last five seconds of vehicle speed, engine speed, gas pedal position and whether the driver was wearing a seat belt. (Wald, 1999b)

The New York Times

Devices that record parameters of system performance, found in many complex systems, provide valuable investigative data. Traditionally associated with commercial aircraft, these devices are increasingly found in other systems, including railroad locomotives, marine vessels, and, as noted, automobiles.

Types of recorders

In general, two types of devices capture data in complex systems, audio/video recorders and system state recorders, although on occasion devices intended for other purposes may provide helpful information. Each device collects information that could give investigators insight into the state of the operating system, its components and subsystems, the operating environment, as well as its operators' actions.

Audio/video recorders

Because of their prominence in aircraft accident investigations, cockpit voice recorders, often referred to as "black boxes," are among the most

121

well known recorders that investigators use. These record aircraft cockpit sounds in a flight's final 30 minutes to 2 hours.

Audio recorders are also found in other systems. Air traffic control facilities record communication between pilots and controllers, and electronically transmitted voice communications among controllers. Marine vessel traffic centers capture communications between vessel operators and ground station personnel, and railroad control facilities record voice communications between dispatchers and train crews.

Video recorders are not extensively used in complex systems at present, primarily because of both technical and legal reasons. Until recently, the costs of rewiring systems to employ video recorders and store the recorded data were prohibitive, and the size of recording equipment interfered with system operations. However, technical improvements have lessened the scope of these shortcomings.

The use of video recorders in accident investigations has also raised legal issues that have limited their use (Fenwick, 1999). Concerns such as operator privacy, post-event litigation, and unauthorized release of video data have yet to be resolved, and many potential users are reluctant to use them until they are resolved to their satisfaction. However, many investigators have called for the installation and use of video recorders to enhance safety (e.g., NTSB, 2000c). As these calls increase and as technical advances continue, video recorder use in complex systems will almost certainly increase. Nonetheless, because video recorders are not widely used at present, and because many of the principles governing the use of other recorders apply to video recorders as well, video recorders will not be addressed further in this text.

System-state recorders

System state recorders are found in many systems. They continuously record as many as 300 flight parameters over a 25-hour period in air transport aircraft. The International Maritime Organization recently required marine vessels to be equipped with voyage data recorders, devices that record the date, ship's position, speed, heading, echo sounder, main alarms, rudder order and response, hull stresses, and wind speed and direction, for 12 continuous hours (Brown, 1999). The U.S. Federal Railroad Administration requires trains that can exceed 30 miles per hour to be equipped with event recorders that record speed, direction, time, distance, throttle position, brake application, and, in some cases cab signals, for 48 continuous hours (Dobranetski and Case, 1999).

The value of the data that system recorders capture was evident in the investigation of a 1997 passenger train derailment. The accident occurred after a flash flood had weakened the underlying support of a bridge that the train was traversing (NTSB, 1998b). According to investigators,

> All four locomotive units were equipped with GE Integrated Function computer event recorders...The data from the lead locomotive indicate that the train was traveling approximately 89 to 90 mph, with the throttle in position 3 (with a change to 4 and then 1), when the brake pipe pressure decreased from approximately 110 to 0 psi, and the emergency parameter changed from NONE to TLEM [Train Line Induced Emergency]. Within the next 2 seconds, the pneumatic control switch (PCS) parameter changed from CLOSED to OPEN. Between 2 and 4 seconds after the PCS OPEN indication, the position of the air brake handle changed from RELEASED to EMERGENCY, and the EIE [Engineer Induced Emergency] parameter changed from OFF to ON. (p. 39)

These recorded data told investigators that the emergency brakes had been applied before the derailment, information that was critical to understanding the engineer's performance. The data allowed investigators to determine that the engineer had attempted to stop the train before the derailment, but was unable to do so in time.

Recorders need not necessarily be physically close to a system to capture potentially valuable data. For example, large airports are equipped with detectors that record weather data such as ceiling level, visibility, wind direction and velocity, barometric setting, and precipitation amount and duration. Some electrical generating facility smokestacks are equipped with detectors that measure and record wind direction and velocity, and some bridges can record the water levels underneath them.

Other recordings

Investigators obtain recorded data from a variety of sources, some of which may have been designed for purposes other than accident investigation. For example, companies place security cameras in and around buildings, equipment, yards, and other facilities, equipment which could provide information on the actions of critical people, as well as changes in lighting, weather, and equipment condition. Personal or laptop computers, or other data storage devices that operators, supervisors, and others use may also contain valuable data.

The value of data from these recorders was apparent in the investigation of a September 1989 accident involving a DHC-6, an airplane that was not equipped with recorders at the time (NTSB, 1991b). Investigators obtained a videocassette from a personal video camera that a passenger had used during the flight. Because there was no barrier between the airplane's cockpit and the cabin, passengers had an unobstructed view of the pilots. The video showed the pilots' arm and hand movements during the accident sequence, information that demonstrated that they had difficulty controlling the airplane during the landing, and attempted to stop the landing to try again. However, in attempting to reject the landing each pilot tried to operate the same controls at the same time. Their arm motions interfered with each other's actions, and they rapidly lost control of the airplane. The information was invaluable, without it investigators would have had substantial difficulty determining the accident's cause.

System recorder information

Audio recorders

Audio recorder data provides real-time information on both the operator and the equipment.

The operator Audio recordings reveal operators' verbal interactions in multi-operator systems. For example, in airline operations pilots perform procedures in strict order, established on checklists that are specific to the different operating phases. Generally, one pilot identifies the item, and the other performs and articulates the action taken in response, or describes the status of a particular component. Recordings of pilot statements or comments can help investigators determine whether they completed the required tasks, and the sequence in which they performed them.

This information was particularly helpful in the investigation of an August 1987 MD-80 accident in Detroit, Michigan (NTSB, 1988b). The pilots were following the appropriate checklist while they taxied the airplane from the terminal to the runway. The checklist included a step that called for one pilot to extend the flaps and slats for takeoff, and the other pilot to verify that this had been accomplished, a critical action because taking off with the flaps and slats retracted will jeopardize the safety of flight.

Audio recorder data revealed that the pilots' checklist review was interrupted when an air traffic controller requested information from them. The pilots responded to the controller and resumed reviewing the checklist but at the wrong place. They inadvertently omitted several required steps, including verifying the flap and slat extension. They attempted to takeoff but the airplane was unable to climb. It crashed shortly after the start of the takeoff, killing all but one of the more than 150 passengers and crew onboard. Cockpit voice recorder data enabled investigators to learn not only the nature of the operators' error, but the context in which they committed the error as well, giving investigators a fairly comprehensive view of the circumstances of the pilots' error.

Audio recorder information can also complement other operator-related data. For example, after an extensive inquiry, investigators of a September 1994 accident involving a Boeing 737 that crashed near Pittsburgh, Pennsylvania, determined that the rudder had abruptly moved to one side just before the accident (NTSB, 1999c). This caused the airplane to turn left and dive abruptly to the ground. Investigators had to determine whether the airplane's turn had been initiated by deliberate pilot action or by the rudder itself, because the flight recorder data showed the turn but not its source.

Investigators used different techniques to understand the cause of the turn. They analyzed sounds that the pilots made during the accident sequence and compared them to the sounds that they had made during routine portions of the flight. By examining elements of pilot sounds, including voice pitch, amplitude, speaking rate, and breathing patterns, investigators determined that,

> The first officer emitted straining and grunting sounds early in the upset period, which speech and communication experts stated were consistent with applying substantial physical loads; the CVR [cockpit voice recorder] did not record any such sounds on the captain's microphone channel until just before ground impact. After about 1903:18 (about 5 seconds before ground impact)...the captain's breathing and speed patterns recorded by the CVR indicated that he might have been exerting strong force on the controls. (pp. 247-248)

These sounds, with other information, convinced investigators that the pilots did not initiate the turn and subsequent dive. The straining and grunting sounds heard on the recording were characteristic of those made during utmost physical exertion. Pilots would make these sounds when forcefully attempting to counteract a maneuver, not when initiating one that would have taken little physical effort.

Audio recorder data can also reveal operators' perceptions of the events they are encountering, giving investigators critical information about their decision making. For example, in the January 1982 accident of a Boeing 737 that crashed in Washington, D.C., cockpit voice recorder information showed that neither pilot understood the meaning of engine performance display data (NTSB, 1982).

The flight had been delayed during a snowstorm. To speed their departure from the gate, the captain inappropriately applied reverse thrust, designed to redirect jet engine thrust forward to slow the airplane on landing. On other aircraft, reverse thrust is permitted for exiting the gate area. However, on airplanes with wing-mounted engines, such as the Boeing 737, engines are close to the ground and the use of reverse thrust in the terminal area could redirect debris into the front of the engines and damage them.

The pilot's use of reverse thrust at the gate caused snow and ice to block critical engine probes in the front of the engines, invalidating data that one of five engine displays presented. The other four gauges, which displayed data from internal engine functions, presented accurate information. With two engines on the Boeing 737, five engine-related displays were presented in each of two columns, one for each engine, a total of 10 gauges in all. The two inaccurate displays were located in the second of the five rows (Figure 9.1).

After he applied takeoff thrust, the first officer recognized that the engine instruments were providing unexpected information. Yet, neither pilot could understand the nature of the unfamiliar data, or the significance of the presented information. Neither appeared to have encountered the data previously, either in training or during an actual flight. The first officer asked the captain, "That don't seem right, does it?" Three seconds later he again said, "Ah that's not right." The captain responded, "Yes it is, there's eighty [knots]." Almost immediately, the first officer answered, "Nah, I don't think that's right." Nine seconds later he again expressed uncertainty, "Ah, maybe it is," he said. Four seconds later, after the captain declared that the airplane's speed had reached 120 knots, the first officer said simply, "I don't know." They continued with the takeoff, and the accident occurred 38 seconds later.

Figure 9.1   Engine data for 737-200, corresponding to displays on
accident aircraft. [Displays on 2nd row from the top
point to the 10:00 position, all others to the 8:00
position]

The pilots' comments, with other data, showed investigators that–

- They were unable to interpret the displayed engine data.
- The captain misinterpreted the displayed data.
- The first officer was uneasy with the captain's interpretation.
- He nevertheless acceded to it.

This information allowed investigators to understand the nature of the crew's decision making and suggest strategies to improve pilot performance.

Recorded audio data can also allow investigators to compare changes in operator vocalizations, potentially revealing much about operator performance. For example, investigators of the 1989 grounding of the oil tanker Exxon Valdez, in Alaska's Prince William Sound, compared changes in the tanker master's voice during communications with the U.S. Coast Guard's Port of Valdez vessel traffic center 33 hours before, one hour before, immediately after, one hour after, and nine hours after the grounding (NTSB, 1990b). His speech rate significantly slowed, and other vocal characteristics, such as articulation errors, were found that were consistent with the effects of alcohol consumption. With other evidence, the recorded audio information supported investigators' conclusions that the master was impaired at the time of the grounding, and that his alcohol-related impairment contributed to the accident.

The equipment Recorded data can disclose critical features of aurally-presented information such as alerts, their sound characteristics, time of onset and of cessation, and operator statements in response to these sounds. Investigators used this information in their investigation of a 1996 Houston, Texas, accident in which the pilots of a DC-9 failed to extend the landing gear before landing, causing substantial damaged to the airplane (NTSB, 1997d).

Airplanes are required to have alerts that sound if the pilots do not extend the landing gear before landing. Investigators sought to determine whether the warnings alerted, and if so, the nature of the pilots' response. Cockpit voice recorder data revealed that the pilots had omitted a critical step on the pre-landing checklist, which called for one pilot to engage the hydraulic system, the mechanism that powers the flaps and the landing gear, and the other to verify that the system had been engaged. However, because they had omitted this step and did not engage the hydraulic system, they were unable to extend the flaps and landing gear. Although they knew that they could not lower the flaps, the cockpit voice recorder indicated that they did not realize that they had not extended the landing gear.

Cockpit voice recorder information revealed that an audible alert, indicating a retracted landing gear, sounded before landing. Concurrently another more prominent alert, the ground proximity warning system alert, was also heard. The simultaneous sound of the two alerts (a result of a single phenomenon, the retracted gear), interfered with the pilots' ability to determine the cause of the alerts. Instead, they focused on maintaining a safe landing profile and did not recognize that the gear had not been extended.

Audio recorders may, on occasion, document information that they had not been designed to capture. For example, in the Washington, D.C., Boeing 737 accident discussed previously, the cockpit voice recorder recorded changes in the sounds of engine pitch, corresponding to increases in engine thrust for the takeoff. Investigators analyzed these sounds to measure the approximate amount of thrust that the engines generated; a parameter that flight data recorders capture today but not at that time.

The analysis showed that the amount of thrust actually generated was considerably less than the amount the pilots had attempted to establish, and less than what they believed the engines had been generating. As shown in Figure 9.1, the amount actually generated was consistent with data that eight of the 10 engine-related gauges displayed, but inconsistent with data that the other two gauges presented, the gauges on which the captain was primarily focusing. The discrepancy between the amount of engine thrust actually generated and the amount the pilots expected proved critical to understanding the accident. The thrust actually generated was insufficient to overcome other adverse weather-related characteristics of the flight. However, because the pilots focused primarily on displays of the amount of thrust that they had selected, in the second row of the five rows of displays, believing that it displayed the amount actually generated, they were unable to understand or resolve the discrepancy.

System-state recorders

System state recorders can provide data captured in the period leading up to and through the event that give extraordinary insights into operator actions and system responses. In railroad operations for example, event recorder data describe several aspects of system responses to engineer actions, data that alone would be quite valuable, but when combined with other data, such as obstructions to visibility, track curvature, grade, and bank angle, the information could enable investigators to identify antecedents to operator errors and understand their effects on operator performance.

The value of system state recorder information was evident in the investigation of the January 1997 crash of an Embraer Brasilia, in Michigan (NTSB, 1998c). The flight data recorder captured 99 parameters of airplane performance, information that, combined with other recorded data from the cockpit voice recorder, air traffic control radar and communications, and meteorological sources, gave investigators a comprehensive understanding of the state of the airplane and operator actions up to the time of the accident.

These data showed that the pilots had slowed the airplane to a speed that would ordinarily have been acceptable. However, analysis of the airplane's flight path suggested that it likely passed through an area of icing just before the accident, leading to ice accumulation that investigators determined was likely imperceptible. Its flight characteristics were consistent with those of an aircraft adversely affected by ice accumulation on its wings. Although the airspeed would otherwise have been adequate, it caused a control loss at the particular airspeed that the pilots had established in those meteorological conditions.

Integrating information from multiple recorders

When combining data recorded in different recorders, applying a common standard or metric to align and match the data, helps to clarify the often diverse information. Because many recorders capture elapsed time, the use of a measure of time as a standard allows investigators to compare data from multiple recorders. For example, using time as the standard allows one to compare operator statements obtained from audio recorders to parameters obtained from system recorders, to assess changes in operator statements that may relate to changes in other system features.

Investigators of the May 1996, DC-9 accident in the Florida Everglades, plotted the data from the flight data recorders, cockpit voice recorder, and air traffic control radar on one diagram to create a three-dimensional plot of the airplane's flight path. By comparing data from the three sources of recorded information, investigators found that,

> The flight was normal until 1410:03, when an unidentified sound was recorded on the cockpit voice recorder. At 1412:58, after about 30 seconds at 7,400 feet msl altitude with a gradual heading change to 192°, the radar indicates an increasing turn rate from the southerly direction to the east and a large increase in the rate of descent. Flight 592 descended 6,400 feet (from

7,400 feet to 1,000 feet) in 32 seconds. Computations of airspeed, based on radar data, indicate that the airspeed of flight 592 was more than 400 KIAS and increasing at the time of ground impact, which occurred about 1413:40. (pp. 55, 58)

Assessing the value of recorded data

Audio recorder data

The quality of the recording components and the level of ambient noise affect the quality of audio recorder data. Defects in microphones, recording media, and drive speed, can degrade the recorded sound quality and detract from the ability to identify and interpret the sounds. Although solid-state equipment can eliminate some of the shortcomings in the recording media, many recorders continue to use magnetic tape.

The distance of the microphone from the operators or system sounds also affects sound quality, unless microphones that are designed to detect sounds at great distances are used. In general, the greater the distance between the microphone and the sounds that are being recorded, the lower the quality of the recorded data.

System-state recorder data

The quality of system state recorders, though relatively immune to many of the features that could degrade audio recorder data, is primarily influenced by two factors, the frequency with which the data are sampled, and the number of system parameters that are recorded. Because at any one point complex systems measure a potentially unlimited number of parameters, the more parameters that are sampled and recorded, the more comprehensive the subsequent portrait of the system. Recorders that capture hundreds of system parameters provide a more comprehensive, and hence more valuable, description of the system and its operating environment than those that record only a few parameters.

Similarly, because of the dynamic nature of many complex systems, the more often system recorders obtain and record the data, the more accurate the view of the system that is obtained. A device that captures data every second gives a more complete, and hence more accurate, account of system operations than one that captures data every third second.

Summary

Many systems are equipped with recorders that record critical information about system equipment, components, operating environments, and operator actions. Audio recorders chronicle operator comments and other sounds heard in operating stations, and system state recorders record key system parameters. Investigators may also obtain valuable data from other devices, such as security cameras.

The level of background noise, and the quality of the recording media and related components, affect audio data quality. The number of recorded parameters and the rate with which the system samples the parameters affect system data quality. Using a common measure such as time, allows investigators to compare information from multiple sources and better interpret operators' actions and decisions, the context in which these occurred, and how they changed over time.

Interpreting recorded data

- Match pertinent data against a common metric, such as elapsed time, local time, or Universal Coordinated Time, also referred to as Greenwich Mean Time, when examining data derived from multiple recorders.
- Select the parameters that best reflect the overall system state, the components of greatest benefit to the issues of the investigation, and that offer the most information on operator decisions and actions, if considerable recorded data are available.
- Develop multiple data plots, or use multiple time intervals as the period of interest increases or decreases, when numerous system state parameters have been recorded.
- Determine an appropriate interval to be used when examining recorded data, taking into account the number of parameters, the proximity to the event, and the number of changes that the system is undergoing at the time.

---

10 Written Documentation

(a) Each certificate holder shall-
(1) Maintain current records of each crewmember…that show whether the crewmember…complies with…proficiency and route checks, airplane and route qualifications, training, any required physical examinations, flight, duty, and rest time records.
(2) Record each action taken concerning the release from employment or physical or professional disqualification of any flight crewmember…and keep the record for at least six months thereafter. (14 Code of [United States] Federal Regulations, Part 121.683)

Introduction

Investigators routinely examine information maintained in various types of written records during error investigations, records that contain information describing characteristics of the system, operators, and the companies that operate the system. Recognizing the value of written documentation and knowing when and how to apply the information they contain to an error investigation are critical investigative skills. In this chapter the types of written documentation available to investigators will be reviewed, preparation for examining written documentation discussed, qualitative aspects of the data considered, and the application of the data to various situations examined.

Written documentation

Regulators in some industries specify the data companies are to collect, the frequency and regularity of data collection, and the format of the data they are to maintain. For example, the FAA requires airlines to retain substantial information on pilots, airplanes, simulators, training programs, maintenance activities, and dispatch releases. Whether required or not, most companies maintain written information that investigators will want to examine. This information can take several forms.

135

Company maintained documentation

Personnel records These contain information pertaining to operators' educational and employment histories, and their current jobs, such as supervisor appraisals, letters of commendation or reprimand, and other relevant material.

Investigators of the grounding of the tanker Exxon Valdez, in Alaska's Prince William Sound (NTSB, 1990b), used this information to help understand the nature of the grounding. Investigators examined the personnel records of the third mate, the officer actually overseeing the tanker's path in the confined waters of Prince William Sound. Performance appraisals of the third mate, the senior officer on the bridge at the time, showed that just three years before the accident his performance had been rated low on several critical performance elements. As the report documents,

> In one performance appraisal as a third mate his "overall effectiveness" had been evaluated as "high," one rating below "outstanding." The two lowest ratings he received as a third mate were given to him while he was on the EXXON JAMESTOWN in 1987 and contained the following comments: "performs adequately" in the rating categories of "seeks advice or guidance at the appropriate time and informs supervisor when appropriate" and "demonstrates thorough knowledge of ship and its handling characteristics." In a summary of employee weaknesses, the evaluator wrote, "He [third mate] seems reluctant or uncomfortable in keeping his superior posted on his progress and/or problems in assigned tasks. (p. 33)

His supervisor's comments in his performance appraisal gave investigators background information to help understand and explain the errors he committed during the accident, where he failed to inform his superiors of his difficulties attempting to steer the vessel in the confined waters of Prince William Sound. Unfortunately, companies have tended to decrease the amount of these types of comments in written documentation, to the detriment of error investigations.

Training records Training records contain information on operator training that the company and others have conducted, and may include test scores and other performance measures. Instructor comments and other information, which go beyond test scores, may also be included.

Medical records Company maintained medical records contain data associated with regulator- or company-mandated medical requirements, such as physical examinations, vision, and hearing evaluations. The records may also include medical information outside of direct company control, such as descriptions of operators' medical evaluations, treatment, and prescriptions that were paid for by company-sponsored medical insurers.

As described in Chapter 9, investigators of the grounding of the Exxon Valdez concluded that the master had been impaired by alcohol at the time of the event. Information in the company's medical records of the master indicated that he had been treated for alcohol abuse about four years before the accident. As investigators noted,

> An Exxon Individual Disability Report, signed by the attending physician and dated April 16, 1985, showed that the master was admitted to a hospital on April 2, 1985, and "remains in residence at the present time." The report stated: "He is a 38 yo W/M [year old white male] who has been depressed and demoralized; he's been drinking excessively, episodically, which resulted in familiar and vocational dysfunction." A treatment program was suggested that included a recommendation that he be given a leave of absence to get involved in Alcoholics Anonymous, psychotherapy, and aftercare. (p. 32)

Because of the information in the company's own records, investigators believed that the company had been aware of his medical history, and should have monitored his alcohol use continually. That he had consumed alcohol while on duty on the vessel before the accident suggested that its oversight was deficient, and that the rehabilitation program that he had entered was flawed, or his commitment to rehabilitation was poor.

Some operators may attempt to conceal information from their employer about potentially adverse medical conditions, and one should not assume that a company's medical records contain all relevant medical information about an operator. The discussion in Chapter 4 of the 1996 New Jersey rail accident, in which the train operator was unable to recognize the stop signal because of his visual impairment, demonstrates that company-retained medical records may be incomplete. The train operator had successfully hidden his diabetes and the diabetes-related visual impairment from his employer, and the company's evaluation of the operator's vision failed to detect his impairment.

Documentation not maintained by the company

Sources unrelated to the operator's employer might also retain operator-related information. For example, documentation on financial, legal, and family matters, as well as driving history, may reveal aspects of an operator's behavior that, although not necessarily job-related, may nevertheless affect performance.

The information may reveal the presence of stressors that could degrade operator performance. The value of the information depends and the relationship of this information to antecedents to these errors. However, unlike company-maintained documentation, access to such information may be restricted to law enforcement personnel, and error investigators may need their assistance to examine it.

Financial information Bank transactions, mortgage applications, stock and bond purchases and sales, credit card transactions and credit reports, tax filings, and financial disclosure forms (required for some government and personal positions), may contain data indicating possible financial reverses. Increases in borrowing and debt, wage garnishment, and other legal action may indicate the presence of financial stressors that could degrade operator performance.

However, this information, though valuable, may be difficult to relate to operator performance because of differences in individual tolerance of financial reverses and debt. With the exception of such events as evictions or asset repossessions that affect quality of life, perception of financial distress is largely relative. Financial stressors that one person considers negative may not affect someone else.

Information from legal proceedings Pending civil actions or criminal charges are stressors. To take an extreme example, nearly all would consider criminal charges and a possible prison sentence to be stressful. By contrast, pending civil action may not necessarily be stressful. Although many find civil action stressful, others do not, particularly if they are not liable for financial penalties or legal expenses. For example, drivers involved in automobile accidents in the United States could be sued for damages that considerably exceed the direct costs of the accident itself. However, because most jurisdictions require drivers to be insured for protection against such losses, the accident-related expenses may be negligible and therefore, the experience may not necessarily be stressful.

Family-related information Family-related information may reveal likely stressors such as divorce, child custody disputes, or similar experiences.

Driving history A record of an operator's driving transgressions may suggest a pattern of behaviors, attitudes, and physiological dependencies that are pertinent to an investigation of error. Because many operators are exposed to law enforcement authorities when driving, those with records of infractions for driving while intoxicated may also manifest an alcohol or drug dependency because the infractions suggest an inability to avoid alcohol use outside of the work setting (McFadden, 1997).

However, although information contained in driving history and similar written documentation may relate to operator antecedents, that information pertains to events occurring outside of the system. Therefore, the information should not be applied directly to the examination of the errors, but should instead be used to complement other data about the operator. The data can also suggest avenues of inquiry that investigators may wish to pursue regarding an operator's error, such as possible chemical dependency or financial reverses.

Information value

As with other accident investigation data, whether from written documentation, recorded media, or interviews, investigators should evaluate written documentation data to assess their value. Quality may vary among, and even within, company written documentation. Poor quality information contributes little to an investigation, regardless of its relevance to the event.

In general, these factors influence the value of written documentation data–

- Quantity
- Collection frequency and regularity
- Length of time since collected
- Reliability
- Validity.

Quantity

All things being equal, the more data collected about a parameter, the more that is learned about the parameter, and the greater the value of the data. Similarly, the greater the number of parameters documented, the more that is revealed about potential antecedents. Because of the impossibility of infinitely documenting a system parameter, written documentation data are considered to be samples of the universe of data that can be potentially derived about the relevant parameters. Hence, the more data obtained, the closer the measure corresponds to dimensions of the actual attribute rather than to a sample of it.

For example, a single health measure, pulse rate, provides a limited portrait of an individual's cardiovascular state. Generally, health care providers measure pulse in 15- to 30-second increments to derive a baseline rate. However, to obtain more accurate measures they could document pulse over a one- to two-hour period. Although the obtained data would more closely correspond to a person's baseline pulse on that day, the cost of obtaining the data would not justify the benefits that would be derived from the increased accuracy. Therefore, the relatively brief measures of pulse provide data that effectively, but not perfectly, measure the parameter of interest.

Collection frequency and regularity

The more often a trait is measured, the better the data can reveal changes in measures of the trait. Frequent measures provide a more complete portrait of a parameter than would infrequent measures. For example, people who weigh themselves only once every five years would not notice small weight variations in that period. By contrast, if they weighed themselves 100 times in the 5-year period, they would obtain a more complete picture of their actual weights than possible from a single measure.

Frequent measures of attributes should also be reasonably spaced to reveal variations in the trait over time. Using the same example, weights measured 100 times, every three weeks, over the 5-year period more accurately describe weight than 100 weights measured in one month of that 5-year period. The greater the number of measures of a parameter, and the more equal the intervals between those measures, the greater the value of the obtained data.

Length of time since collected

The closer to the time of the event in which measures of a parameter are obtained, the closer the measures will correspond to the actual parameter value at the time of the event, which is the period of investigators' greatest interest. Investigators may find that data obtained after, but close to the time of an event, are more valuable than data obtained before the event, provided that the experience of the event did not affect the value of the parameter. In this way a measure of an operator's performance taken two days after an accident will likely be more valuable to investigators than a comparable performance measure obtained a year before, so long as the operator's performance did not change as a result of the accident experience.

Reliability

Reliability refers to the consistency of measures of a trait. Reliable measures vary little, while unreliable measures vary. Using the illustration of weight, if people were to weigh themselves on well-calibrated scales throughout the day, the weights would change little, except for minor weight fluctuations throughout the day. However, if they were to weigh themselves on several uncalibrated scales in the same period, and those weights varied by several pounds or kilograms, the differences would most likely result from differences in the scales' accuracy rather than changes in their weights, because variations of that magnitude are extremely rare.

Validity

The relationship between the measurement of a parameter and its actual value is known as validity. The closer a measure of a trait corresponds to the value of that trait, the greater its validity. For example, a test used to select candidates to operate a nuclear reactor should predict how well they would operate the reactor. A vocabulary test that applicants complete to be selected as reactor operators may be a valid measure of verbal achievement, but it would likely be of limited value predicting performance as a reactor operator. The knowledge needed to operate reactors extends well beyond vocabulary knowledge. A more valid measure would directly assess skills needed to operate reactors, developed from closely observing operator tasks.

Changes in written documentation

It is not unusual to find that, over time, the nature of information contained within written documentation changes. Measures of operator traits may change, as the operators gain experience; alternatively, measurement standards may change as the system evolves. Changes in two elements of written documentation, central tendency and organizational factors, are particularly noteworthy as they may reveal much about the operator and the operator's employer.

Central characteristic

Assessments of particular attributes, characteristics, or conditions should reveal what will be referred to as "central characteristics," general portrayals that should remain fairly stable from year to year. Performance appraisals, for example, generally include an assessment of overall job performance, a fairly stable measure over the short term. Someone who performs well one year would be expected to perform well the next. Because of its stability, marked inconsistencies in an operator's overall job performance over time would be cause for additional inquiry.

Investigators of the 1994 accident involving an FAA-operated aircraft used to inspect navigation aids, discussed in Chapter 5, found that a central characteristic of performance data in the pilot in command's personnel records was positive, with one inconsistency (NTSB, 1994b). His supervisor had consistently evaluated the pilot's performance positively, however, six months before the accident he reprimanded the pilot in writing for a performance-related event.

After interviewing the pilot's peers and supervisors, investigators resolved the inconsistency. Co-workers provided a different account of the pilot's performance than that described in the central characteristic of the performance appraisals. Interviewees described instances in which the pilot disregarded safe operating practices, information that corresponded to the gist of the letter of reprimand and his performance at the time of the accident, but not to the central characteristic of the performance appraisals. Therefore, the value of the central characteristic was diminished.

Organizational factors

Written documentation data may reveal characteristics of the company as well as the person. In the above-described accident for example, investigators resolved the discrepancy within the captain's personnel records by interviewing the pilot's peers and supervisors. Their comments raised critical issues regarding the role of the supervisor and the organization in overseeing the pilot and responding to safety-related concerns.

Comparing written documentation data of one operator to comparable data of others in an organization may also give insights into company actions. To illustrate, consider a locomotive engineer whose documentation shows numerous citations for rule violations in a five-year period, an individual who may well be a poor performer. However, if the records of other engineers in that railroad contained relatively equivalent infractions over similar intervals, then the engineer's performance would be "average" among other engineers.

Summary

Companies generally maintain data in three types of written documentation, personnel, training, and medical records. The data in these records may provide information about the operator and his or her employer. Driving history, and financial and legal records may also contain information that could help to identify operator-related antecedents to error.

The quantity of information about a trait, the frequency and regularity with which the information was collected, and the reliability and validity of the measures that provide the data, affect the quality of data in written documentation. Investigators should also examine general trends within the data, departures from consistency, relative rate and direction of change, similarity to information in the company records of others, and organizational factors, when reviewing data in written documentation.

Applying written documentation to investigations

Preparation

- Prepare to review written documentation by first identifying the information likely to be pertinent to the event, and the most likely sources of that information.
- Identify experts when reviewing unfamiliar information, such as financial and medical data, for assistance in interpreting the data.

Medical information

- Examine operator medical records of both company-sponsored medical care and sources independent of the company, if available.
- Document operator visits to health care providers that occurred within the three years before the event, results of diagnostic tests and health care provider's diagnoses, treatments, and prescribed and recommended over the counter medications.

Financial information

- Obtain and review financial information, if possible, if the evidence suggests that the operator may have encountered financial difficulties near the time of the event.
- Document evidence of recent financial losses, increases in debt, requests for payment, and legal documents requiring payment.
- Obtain law enforcement or prosecutorial assistance to obtain access to the information.

Family information

- Obtain family information if there is reason to believe that the operator experienced family-related difficulties near the time of the event. Obtain law enforcement or prosecutorial assistance to obtain access to the information.

Assessing the data

- Note the amount of data available on a given trait, the frequency and regularity of data collection, and the reliability and validity of the data.
- Determine the central characteristics of the data that pertain to each trait.
- Resolve inconsistencies in the data, generally by interviewing those who can comment on the discrepant information.
- Look for information on the company as well as on the operators within company maintained documentation.

After reviewing the data

- Summarize the major points of the information contained within the written documentation.
- Contact the person familiar with the information if there is still uncertainty about the meaning of some of the information.

11 Interviews

Did I see DiMaggio famously kick the dirt as he reached second, a moment replayed on countless television biographies of him because it was the rarest display of public emotion on his part? Again, I think I did. Who knows? Memory is often less about truth than about what we want it to be. (Halberstam, 2000)

The New York Times

Interviews can provide information unobtainable from other sources and give unique insights into critical operator errors. Their value to investigations is undeniable, and nearly all investigations rely heavily on interviews, yet many investigators conduct interviews poorly. Experienced interviewers understand how the conduct of an interview can affect its outcome. No information collected in an investigation is as susceptible to variations in investigative technique as are interview data. The interviewees selected, the questions asked, and the interviewing methods used, are just some of the elements that can affect interview quality. This chapter will examine interview quality and discuss methods to enhance the quality and quantity of interview information.

Memory errors

Research into memory errors has shown how inaccurate memory can be, primarily because people do not passively receive and record information but actively reconstruct memories (Buckhout, 1974; Haber and Haber, 2000). The reconstructions are influenced by their abilities, experiences, attitudes, motives, and beliefs. Because of these influences, people experiencing the same event may have different memories of it.

Dynamic events in particular can lead to memory errors. As Buckhout explains,

The length of the period of observation obviously limits the number of features a person can attend to. Yet, fleeting glimpses are common in eyewitness accounts, particularly in fast-moving situations. Less than ideal observation conditions usually apply; crimes [and incidents and accidents] seldom occur in a well-controlled laboratory. Often distance, poor lighting, fast movement or the presence of a crowd interferes with the efficient working of the attention process. (p. 25)

Errors in eyewitness recall of dynamic events were evident in the interviews that Federal Bureau of Investigation (FBI) representatives conducted with over 670 eyewitnesses to the 1996 in-flight explosion of a Boeing 747 off the coast of Long Island, New York (NTSB, 2000d). Over 250 eyewitnesses described aspects of the event that were directly contradicted by the physical evidence; they claimed to have seen a streak of light or flame ascend to the airplane. However, the physical evidence was unequivocal; flames fell from the airplane, not the other way around.

Hyman (1999) describes three categories of memory errors that people can make: incorrectly reconstructing event recollections, incorrectly attributing the source of information, and falsely believing that events that were not experienced had been experienced. To Hyman, memory errors occur because people "view the event as plausible, they construct a memory that is partially based on true experience and that is often very vivid, and they erroneously claim the false memory as a personal recollection" (p. 247).

Interviewers can also influence interviewee recollection and response. Loftus (1997) found that interviewers could lead people to believe false information as fact by subtly introducing the false information into their questions. Wells, Malpass, Lindsay, Fisher, Turtle, and Fulero (2000), summarizing the literature on eyewitness recollection errors, conclude that,

The scientific proof is compelling that eyewitnesses will make systematic errors in their reports as a function of misleading questions. From a system-variable perspective, it matters little whether this effect is a result of introducing new memories or altering old memories or whether this is a compliance phenomenon. The important point is that witnesses will extract and incorporate new information after they witnessed an event and then testify about that information as though they had actually witnessed it. (p. 582)

Despite the potential for memory errors, witnesses can provide valuable information; provided interviewers recognize the substantial influence they can exert on the quality of the interview itself. Interviewers can take steps to enhance interviewee recall, even before they begin the interview.

Interviewees and their concerns

Some interviewees have much at stake in the findings of an investigation while others have little or none. Differences in background, experience, and education can also affect their ability to understand and respond to questions, and their willingness to assist an investigation.

Interviewees generally fall into one of three groups in accident and incident investigations, according to their relationship with the operator or their role in the system. These include those who have observed the event, operators whose actions are the primary focus of the investigation, and those who are familiar with critical system elements. Each may have important information to contribute, according to his or her knowledge and insights.

Eyewitnesses

Eyewitnesses to an event may have observed features that system recorders did not capture, heard noises beyond the microphone range, or felt movement that no device recorded. Their observations and experiences may enable them to enhance or confirm already existing information and provide information that is unavailable from other sources.

Eyewitness willingness to cooperate with investigators will likely be influenced by their confidence in the value of the information they can provide the investigation, and possible concern with the interviewer's approval of their responses. They will offer information more readily if they believe that it will help the investigation and that interviewers will appreciate their cooperation.

System operators

Operators may be able to describe their actions and decisions during the event and provide helpful background information about the system. At a minimum, they can discuss their experiences in system operations and thus provide information and insights regarding system design and company policies and practices.

However, if the event that occurred was dynamic, they may be unable to recall details, and if they feel responsible for the event, they may have difficulty responding. They may also be concerned about the effects of the event on their careers, perhaps the most challenging and difficult event they have encountered in their professional experience. If operators' feelings of personal responsibility or career concerns adversely affect their ability to recall events, interviewers can do little other than delay the interview, until the operators are sufficiently composed to effectively answer questions.

Those familiar with critical system elements

Those at the system's "blunt end" in Reason's terms, are familiar with critical elements of the system. They serve as the equipment designers, training managers, procedures specialists, financial managers, or direct supervisors. Their decisions and actions may have set in motion the circumstances that led to the errors of the operators at the "sharp end."

Those close to the operators, such as family and coworkers, may share many of their concerns. They should be asked to provide details about recent operator experiences such as sleep and work habits, and recently encountered stressful events, with the understanding that the information may give investigators better insight into the event than they might otherwise obtain.

Those who are familiar with aspects of the system may feel responsible for the cause of the event. For example, a maintenance supervisor may believe that he or she was responsible for the errors of the technicians whom he supervised, or for the quality of the procedures that he followed. Unfortunately, little can be said to address these concerns. These interviewees could describe their decisions and the actions they took that may have influenced the nature of the event.

Information sought

The information sought in an error investigation varies according to the role of the interviewee, whether eyewitness, operator, or someone familiar with critical system elements.

Eyewitness

Eyewitnesses should be asked to describe–

- What they saw, heard, felt, and smelled
- Details of the event that first caught their attention
- Time of day they witnessed the event
- Their own location and activities during the event
- Operator actions
- The names and locations of other eyewitnesses if known
- Additional information they believe relevant.

Operators

Operator should be asked to provide information about the event, and additional personal and company-related information, including–

Event-related actions and decisions
- Decisions they made before the event
- Approximate time when they made those decisions
- Actions they took before the event
- Approximate time when they took those actions
- Outcome and consequences of each.

Job/task information
- Their job/task duties and responsibilities in general
- Knowledge requirements of the job/task
- System operating phases and their approximate time intervals
- Their responsibilities, activities, and workload during each operating phase
- Abnormal situations and the frequency with which they have been encountered
- Their responses to abnormal situations.

Company practices and procedures
- General system operating practices and procedures
- Task specific practices and procedures
- Differences between company intent and actual practice in system procedures.

Personal information
- Overall health and recent illnesses, physician visits, and hospitalizations

- Emotional health, including major changes in family and/or job status
- Medications taken within previous 30 days, including prescribed and over the counter medications, and herbal supplements
- Sleep schedule previous 72 hours
- Activities previous 72 hours.

Those familiar with critical system elements

Those who are acquainted with the system operators should be asked for information that is unavailable from other sources, or that adds to existing information about the event. In general, the operator's close relatives or colleagues should be asked about his or her–

- Sleep and rest schedule previous 72 hours
- Activities previous 72 hours
- Opinions expressed toward the job, coworkers, and the company.

Those who are familiar with the system should be asked about the following, according to their expertise and role in system operation–

- Operator training and work history
- Training program history and description
- Operating policies and practices
- General company policies and practices.

Finding, scheduling, and placing the interviews

Rapport

Interviewer-interviewee rapport will considerably influence the quality of the interview. Because of the importance of personal contact in establishing rapport, particularly when interviewing operators and others knowledgeable about the system, interviewers should conduct face-to-face interviews when possible. Nevertheless, rapport is less critical to eliciting information from eyewitnesses and others who are not a central focus of the investigation. If numerous eyewitnesses are to be interviewed, and insufficient interviewers are available to conduct the interviews in person, face-to-face interviews may not be practical. In that case, it would be acceptable to conduct interviews by telephone.

When only limited information needs to be obtained from interviewees, and their information may not be critical, but will likely be helpful to the investigation, electronic/computer media and even post or mail service can be used. However, telephone interviews will be superior to these methods because they allow interviewers to readily follow up on points that interviewees may raise.

Eyewitnesses

Local media, law enforcement and rescue personnel, and those working near the event, often establish contact with eyewitnesses. Law enforcement and rescue officials are usually the first to arrive at the scene, are experienced in locating witnesses, and can encourage them to cooperate with investigators.

Media representatives, who generally arrive on scene quickly and are usually adept at locating and interviewing eyewitnesses, may be able to help locate eyewitness as well. Media representatives can also be asked to inform the public of a need for eyewitnesses.

Scheduling the interview There is usually extensive media attention and general discussion after a major accident, and eyewitnesses have difficulty avoiding exposure to accounts of the event. Therefore, eyewitnesses should be interviewed as soon after the event as possible to reduce their exposure to potentially contaminating information and other adverse influences on their recall.

Placing the interview Eyewitnesses may recall more of an event at the locations at which they witnessed it. Reencountering the cues associated with the event, such as buildings, objects, hills, or trees may help them remember additional information (Fisher and Geiselman, 1992). However, if traveling to the site where eyewitnesses came upon the event will delay interviewing them, they could become exposed to memory contaminants that outweigh the advantages of site-related memory enhancements. Consequently, if eyewitnesses can be interviewed quickly at the locations at which they observed the event one should do so, but interviews should not be delayed to interview them there.

Operators

The company managing the system should be able to coordinate interviews with operators who were on duty during the event.

Scheduling the interview Operators are also subject to recall contamination and this would ordinarily call for interviewing them quickly after an event. However, two factors argue for delaying their interviews for 24- to 48-hours. First, it often takes several days to obtain even routine system-related information after an event. Delaying operator interviews allows investigators to examine records, talk to eyewitnesses, and learn about the event, enabling them to ask more sophisticated questions about the event, and increasing the value of information they would likely obtain immediately after an event.

Second, operators involved in a major event are often distraught and may have difficulty concentrating. Delaying the interview allows them to compose themselves. A one- to two-day delay after the event is usually sufficient to serve both operator and interviewer needs.

If the operator was injured in the event, it is important to obtain the attending physician's approval before the interview. The physician should agree that the operator would not be harmed by the interview, and is capable of comprehending and responding to questions.

Placing the interview The location of an operator interview is critical. The wrong setting could increase the operator's anxiety and discomfort, and thus hamper his or her recall. Ideally, operators should be interviewed in a professional setting, free of distractions such as busy hallways, elevators, and noisy streets, and equipped with comfortable chairs and a table or desk. A hotel conference or meeting room is often a good choice. Telephones, pagers, cell phones, and other potential distractions should be disengaged or turned off, window shades or curtains drawn to minimize outside distractions, and thermostats set to a comfortable temperature. Operating and training manuals and other pertinent material should be accessible. Finally, water or other refreshments for the operator should be available throughout the interview .

When an operator is having difficulty recalling events, conducting the interview in a system mock up or simulator may enhance recall. If this is not possible, diagrams or photographs of system components, and equipment used at the time of the event, should be provided for reference.

Those familiar with critical system elements

Company management should assist in finding and scheduling interviews with company personnel. They can also usually help to find friends and close family members of the operators if needed.

Scheduling the interview It is not critical to minimize the exposure to memory contaminants of those who are familiar with critical system elements, and these interviews can safely be delayed for several weeks. On the other hand, family and acquaintances of the operators should be interviewed quickly because their memories of the operator's activities could be contaminated by exposure to subsequent accounts.

Placing the interview Whether the interviewee is a family member or a company supervisor, the interview should be professional and business-like, free of distractions, and large enough to comfortably accommodate those participating in the interview. Interviewees should have access to reference material, and other helpful items as needed.

Administrative concerns

Interviewers must attend to many logistical and administrative details to ensure a successful interview. These include–

- The written record
- Multi-operator team members
- Multiple interviewers
- Information to provide interviewees.

The written record

The interview's written record is the medium through which interview data are conveyed to others. Deficiencies in the record lessen its value, regardless of the overall interview quality. Several interview documentation methods are available, each with particular advantages and disadvantages.

Video or audio recordings provide the most accurate interview record and usually require the least interviewer effort during the interview. Interviewees generally adapt quickly to the presence of the recording equipment. However, the cost of transcribing interviews from recordings can be substantial, and obtaining accurate transcriptions may be difficult and time consuming. Interviewers must also follow appropriate rules governing interview recordings because some jurisdictions prohibit recording interviews without interviewee approval.

Professional transcribers or court reporters can generate interview transcripts, however the cost may be substantial and transcribers are often unfamiliar with technical terms that may arise. In addition, they are more obtrusive than recording devices, although interviewees will usually adapt to their presence as well.

Interviewers who are adept keyboarders can also enter interviewee responses directly into a laptop computer during an interview, an inexpensive alternative to transcribing the interview. Spell checkers facilitate this method by allowing keyboarders to input the data quickly without the need for much accuracy. However, interviewers may find it difficult to conduct an interview and keyboard the responses simultaneously. Many computers also allow an audio interview record to be entered directly onto audio files, giving an audio interview record to support transcribed notes.

The common method of preparing a written record calls for the interviews to write their own notes taken during the interview and add more details from memory afterwards. This method is inexpensive and requires little writing skill, but it is the least accurate of the interview documentation techniques.

Multi-operator team members

Multi-operator team members should be interviewed individually, outside the presence of other team members, to reduce the likelihood that one operator would influence another's responses. Operators should also be asked not to discuss the interviews with their colleagues, although enforcing this prohibition may be difficult.

Multiple interviewers

The number of interviewers should be kept to the minimum possible to maximize interviewer-interviewee rapport. The lower the number of interviewers who are present, the less intimidating the process will be to the interviewee. However, multiple interviewers can also enhance the interview. They can interview many eyewitnesses simultaneously, increasing the efficiency of the interview, and they can bring multiple perspectives to the interview, thus increasing the interview scope and depth.

To avoid potential administrative difficulties among multiple interviewers, it is important to establish and maintain rules governing the conduct of the interviews. These should including identifying the lead questioner, establishing the order in which interviewers question the interviewee, and determining how to deal with interruptions.

Order of interviewers The lead interviewer is generally the group's head or chairperson and therefore, the person who generally questions the interviewee first and sets the tone of the interview. Thereafter, each interviewer should be given the opportunity to ask an initial set of questions and at least one set of follow up questions, in the order appropriate to the group.

Interruptions Interruptions to either interviewees or interviewers should be prohibited, except when an interviewee does not understand the question or his or her response has deviated from the thrust of the question. In that event, only the lead interviewer should be permitted to bring the discussion back on track. Otherwise, interviewers should note additional questions they may have, and then ask those questions during follow up questioning.

Information to provide interviewees

Before the interview, interviewers should identify the information that they will be willing to provide interviewees. In general, information that cannot be shared with those outside the investigation, is speculative or analytical, or can influence the recollections of subsequent interviewees, should not be discussed.

Concluding the interview

The interview should be concluded when all issues pertinent to information sought from the interviewee have been addressed, and when it is clear that the interviewee has no additional information to offer. Interviewers should not have difficulty determining when they have reached this point. Interviews should not be concluded for other reasons, such as the need to attend to other investigative activities.

After responding to all questions, interviewees should be asked whether they have additional information to offer, and if there are important questions about the event that they had not been asked. Interviewers should then ask the interviewees whether they have questions, and give them previously agreed upon information, as needed. The lead interviewer should then give the interviewees his or her business card or contact information. Finally, interviewers should thank the interviewees for their cooperation and assistance to the investigation.

Applying interview data

Because of the many factors that could influence interviewee responses, interview data should not be considered in isolation, but only with other investigative data.

Eyewitnesses

Information from eyewitnesses should be used to supplement, but not supplant, other data because of the potential contamination of their recollections. Nonetheless, eyewitnesses can add details that may not be available from other sources. However, if data from more accurate and reliable sources contradict eyewitness data, credence should be given to the more reliable data.

Operators

Operators' first hand experiences in the complex system in which the event occurred can considerably enhance ones's understanding of the nature of critical errors. Operators with good recall of the event, who sincerely wish to help the investigation, can provide data that simply cannot be obtained elsewhere. Nevertheless, interviewers find that many operators have difficulty recalling specific details in the very dynamic or stressful environment in which events in complex systems often unfold.

Those familiar with critical system elements

System managers, designers, and others who are knowledgeable about a system can provide information that complements information from other sources. For example, instructors can describe the meaning of comments found in training records, managers can explain the intent that lay behind statements they wrote in performance appraisals, and equipment designers can describe their design philosophy and its manifestation in the operating system. Those operating in the system's blunt end can help explain the development of operating procedures, training programs, and other potentially critical investigative issues.

The value of the information that family and acquaintances of the operators provide depends on the availability of other supporting information, as well as on the relevance of the data to the event. Family and acquaintances of the operators can provide especially valuable information when there is little information available from other sources. Family members or friends of operators injured or otherwise unavailable may be able to give investigators accounts of the operators' activities in the 72 hours before the accident, while their colleagues can describe their work habits and attitudes to investigators.

Case study

The investigation of the collision between two marine vessels gives a good illustration of interviewing techniques. In February 2001 a U.S. Navy nuclear submarine, the USS Greenville, struck a Japanese fishing vessel, the Ehime Maru, off the coast of Hawaii, killing nine on board the fishing vessel. A month later the Navy conducted a Court of Inquiry to look into the cause of the accident, focusing particularly on the actions of the Greenville's officers, the Officer of the Deck, the Executive Officer, and the Commanding Officer. The Court of Inquiry also addressed the actions of a fourth officer, the Chief of Staff of the Navy's Submarine Force Pacific Fleet (SUBPAC), who was on the Greenville during the collision but was not part of its crew, and of an enlisted person onboard the submarine. The Court of Inquiry was open to the public and televised internationally.

Except for the counsels for the three officers of the Greenville, the members of the Court of Inquiry had not been trained to conduct interviews in accident investigations and it is likely that they had little opportunity before this accident to apply interviewing skills to formal investigations of error. Selections from the Court of Inquiry transcripts illustrate both effective and ineffective interviewing techniques.

Poor techniques

> *Question*: But as a submarine qualified officer would your expectations be that the Chief of Staff, in his position in the port aft side of [the] Control [Room], would have been able to detect poor reporting to the Commanding Officer and the Officer of the Deck in terms of support from the watchstanders? Would he–wouldn't he understand the climate of the Control Room? And wouldn't he have high expectations in terms of the quality of the reports and the timeliness of the reports? Would he have to be physically engaged in the control of the ship not to be able to sense whether or not those reports were of a quality enough to support the Officer of the Deck and the Commanding Officer?

This questions is quite lengthy and difficult to follow. Further, it contained multiple questions that pertained to the Chief of Staff. These were–

- Could he have communicated with the Commanding Officer?
- Did he understand the Control Room climate?
- Would he have had high expectations of the crew's actions?
- Could he have been able to evaluate the crew's actions without being actively engaged in controlling the vessel?

By asking four questions within one, the interviewer forced the interviewee to either respond to one of the four questions or interpret the questions and attempt to respond to the gist of all four, i.e., the quality of the Chief of Staff's actions. Had he asked the four questions individually, or had he asked, "what did you think of the Chief of Staff's performance during this portion of the accident," the interviewer would have better focused the questions and helped the interviewee respond directly to the issues he was raising.

After the response, another member of the Court of Inquiry asked the witness:

> *Question:* Along the same lines, the issue of time. With the Chief of Staff's experience, would he be able to be in the Control Room during this time frame that we're talking about here, and know that the transition of the submarine to go through the various target motion analysis legs; to go through the proper periscope procedures that everyone's been trained to and that we saw today in the simulator that there's a certain element of time for the ship to be able to safely conduct those events. And therefore, based on his operational experience, he knows the minimum time requirement basically to

do that safely. And therefore his position as the Chief of Staff at SUBPAC, he would know that something was amiss. Do you have an opinion as to whether, based on the timeline for these events, that the Chief of Staff was in a position to know that you can't do those events in that reduced timeline properly?

Unlike the first, this question addressed only one issue. The interviewer prefaced his query with a narrative that did little to enhance the question, and likely degraded the quality of the response. Further, he phrased the question in the form of a yes-no answer. The interviewee had to first understand what the interviewer was asking before responding, increasing the likelihood that the interviewee would provide incomplete information.

An additional question illustrates another ineffective technique.

Question: Was there any change that the quality of reports that came out of sonar? Was there any noticeable change as a result of the Executive Officer? That could be for a couple of reasons. Maybe there was nothing significant to report. But could you detect in any of your statements that you took that there was a change in the quality of the way those reports were made to Control?

Answer: No, sir, I can't make a statement one way or the other on that. I don't know. (p. 267)

The interviewer asked two very different questions within the one question–did the quality of the reports change and did the Executive Officer influence the quality of the reports–questions that were not answered. The interviewer then offered a possible opinion as to whether the target of the reports themselves had changed.

Another example of a poorly phrased question follows.

Question: Because in reality, if you are looking to do this event, and you plan on coming back up within 5 to 6 minutes–say 6 minutes–and you have all of the speed of your own ship in the line of sight of another contact–even a high-speed contact, maybe at 20 knots, and give yourself–maybe you're going 10 knots, that's, that's 30 knots in the line of site, that in 3 minutes, that's what 6,000 yards. So you need 3 to 4 miles assurance that's clear, is that a correct analysis?

Answer: Yes, sir. (p. 259)

In this question the interviewer gave a statement and asked the interviewee to agree with the statement, without elaboration or interpretation. The question was also wordy and hard to follow. Because it contained extensive analysis and much information, and sought only a single answer, it did not give the interviewee the opportunity to disagree with the nature of the analysis, only with the result of the analysis.

Later, the same interviewer asked:

> *Question:* In the case of the GREENVILLE would you discuss, as you did in your report, the material condition of her sensor suite to be able for her to execute safely the maneuver?
>
> *Question [from a different member of the Court of Inquiry]:* Can I interrupt Paul?
>
> *Answer [from the Member of the Court of Inquiry that had asked the initial question]:* Sure. (p. 261)

The second interviewer interrupted the first before the interviewee could answer the initial question. The initial question, which was well phrased and illustrates effective interviewing, gave the interviewee latitude to respond with the information he wished to provide. However, by interrupting the interviewer the second interviewer forced the interviewee to alter his initial train of thought, increasing the risk that the interviewee would forget information that he had recalled in preparing to answer the initial question. In the next selection, the interviewer leads the interviewee to provide particularly desired answers.

Good interviewing techniques

The same interviewers also asked questions that illustrate effective interviewing. They initially asked open-ended questions, then asked follow up ones that pursued issues in more detail.

> *Question:* Rear Admiral Griffiths, as part of your Preliminary Inquiry, did you have an opportunity to evaluate GREENEVILLE's performance with respect to search and rescue efforts after the collision?
>
> *Answer:* I did.
>
> *Question:* Sir, would you describe for the court how GREENEVILLE did? (p. 499)

Although the first question called for a yes-no answer, it was asked as a prelude to the second one, a question that was open-ended and succinct. The first question established a train of thought that the interviewer pursued with the second question, which related to issues raised in the initial question.

Question: Alright, sir. Let me ask you a question [that addresses a different issue]. Who orchestrated the search and rescue on GREENEVILLE?

Answer: The Captain [or CO-Commanding Officer] was in charge of the GREENVILLE still and was making the major decisions about how to operate the ship.

Question: Admiral, would you please tell the court–give your assessment of Commander Waddle's performance during the search and rescue phase?

Answer: Well I think remarkable. I mean they had just suffered a trauma–unimaginable trauma and you know I'm–I think it was a remarkably professional effort. (p. 505)

The questions were open-ended, and allowed the interviewee to respond in his or her words. The questions were also brief, which elicits more expansive answers from interviewees. In general, the ratio of the length of questions to the length of answers is a rough guide to the quality of the questions that the interviewer asks.

Summary

People are subject to memory errors, but interviewers can exercise some control over potential influences on these errors and increase the amount and value of the information interviewees provide. Investigators of error in complex systems generally question three types of interviewees, eyewitnesses, operators, and those familiar with critical system elements. Each interviewee has specific concerns and information to provide. Interviewers seek different information from each interviewee, and should recognize their different needs when eliciting the information.

Interviewers should identify the type of information that the interviewees can provide, and identify the issues to elicit the desired information before the interview. Interviewers should ask questions that correspond to the sequence of issues, by beginning with open-ended questions and following up with more specific questions that address points that the interviewee has made. Suggestions are provided for asking questions and chronicling the information from interviewees, with illustrations of effective and ineffective interviewing techniques.

Conducting interviews--The interview process

- Identify the information sought, then identify and locate interviewees that can provide that information.

Structuring the interview-beginning

- Thank the interviewees for their cooperation.
- Introduce each interviewer to the interviewees, giving titles and affiliations, if multiple interviewers are participating.
- Describe the purpose of the interview and mention the value of the information sought.
- Review the interview guidelines with interviewees and ask them if they have questions before beginning.

The question sequence

- Determine beforehand the order of issues to be addressed in questioning each interviewee.
- Introduce new issues after each issue has been addressed in turn.
- Use one of two types of sequences of issues with interviewees, chronological order or order of importance.
- Address issues that the interviewee may have raised while discussing another issue, even if it means going out of sequence.

Follow up questions

- Use follow up questions when one of several interviewers has not pursued an issue that an interviewee has raised, or when an interviewee has raised multiple issues in a response.
- Ensure that other interviewers wait until their turns to follow up on an issue rather than disrupt other interviewers.
- Allow each interviewer at least two opportunities to ask questions, one to ask the initial questions and a second to ask follow up questions.

Attending to the interviewee

- Show attention to the interviewee at all times.
- Be aware of and avoid nonverbal cues that may unwittingly be sent to the interviewee.

- Ensure that the interviewee is comfortable and that the interview location is free of distractions.
- Stop the interview if interviewees appear uncomfortable or begin to lose their composure.
- Do not offer the interviewee career or personal assistance, but demonstrate concern for the interviewee.

False responses

- Rephrase or refocus the questions if there is reason to believe that an interviewee has answered questions falsely.
- Do not express disapproval or attempt to coerce a truthful response from the interviewee.
- Do not use a prosecutorial tone in asking questions.

Asking questions

- Begin questions with verbs.
- Keep questions as brief as possible.
- Phrase questions to encourage interviewees to be as expansive as possible.
- Progress to more focused questions that follow up on the points interviewees make in response to initial questions.
- Attend to the interviewee answers and, to the extent possible, base questions on those answers.
- Avoid questions that permit one or two word answers, e.g., yes or no, unless following up on a response to a particular interviewee answer.
- Avoid asking questions from a predetermined list, in the predetermined order.
- Identify issues to be addressed and ask questions that relate to those issues.

- Practice asking questions that follow directly from interviewee's responses.
- Maintain an even and neutral tone of voice.

Ineffective techniques

- Avoid asking questions that call for yes or no answers, are long or wordy, or go beyond the interviewee's level of expertise.
- Do not agree or disagree with the interviewee.
- Avoid using technical jargon with those who are unfamiliar with the jargon.
- Do not ask interviewees whether they remember having taken an action.
- Do not interrupt the interviewee or allow other interviewers to interrupt each other or the interviewee.

Concluding the interview

- Conclude the interview when it is apparent that the interviewee has no additional information to offer investigators.
- Do not conclude the interview for other reasons, such as a need to perform other investigative activities.
- Ask interviewees if they have additional information to offer or additional issues to discuss before concluding the interview.
- Give interviewees business cards and ask them to contact you later if they have additional information to provide.
- Thank interviewees again for their cooperation.

12 Analysis

As is so often the case when we begin to learn the complexities of a situation, some of the issues that had seemed very clear at the outset had become more confused. Only much later would we fully understand the extent to which oversimplification obfuscates and complexity brings understanding. (Vaughan, 1996)

The Challenger Launch Decision: Risking Technology, Culture, and Deviance at NASA

Introduction

Many people routinely review and make inferences about data, perhaps without recognizing that they have done so. They examine the behavior of their friends, acquaintances, and political leaders and infer motives from the observed behavior to explain the actions that they have observed. This process–examining an action and developing an explanation of that action–is the foundation of the human error investigator's work.

Differences between this type of informal analysis and the more formal one used in error investigations result less from differences in the processes than in their application. Unlike the informal process applied to everyday situations, the investigative analysis is applied systematically and methodically to past events. This chapter examines the principles of human performance data analysis, the process in which investigators of error identify relationships between operator errors and their antecedents.

Investigative methodology

Accident investigation methodology and the scientific method have similar objectives, to explain observed phenomena or events using formal methods of data collection and analysis. Kerlinger's (1973) description of the objectives of science corresponds to those of accident investigations, "[the] systematic, controlled, empirical, and critical investigation of hypothetical propositions about the presumed relations among natural phenomena" (p. 11). Although the methods in accident investigations are not controlled and the process is not empirical, accident investigators apply a systematic and critical methodology to study the relationships between antecedents and errors, and between those errors and the incidents and accidents that the errors may have caused.

Ex post facto designs

Investigators collect and analyze data after the fact, a method similar to "ex post facto" research designs. Investigators and researchers using this method work backwards, after an event has occurred and the data collected, to understand the variables that led to the event. However, researchers have recognized that this method, although providing critical insights into event causation, can lead to analytical inaccuracy. Because data are gathered after the fact, researchers and investigators can select from and apply a favored explanation to account for the obtained results, rather than be compelled to accept the explanation that the data offer from experimental design techniques developed before the fact (e.g., Kerlinger, 1973).

Nevertheless, error investigators partially compensate for this limitation. Investigation findings can be applied broadly, unlike many laboratory studies. The influence of uncontrolled variables is always possible outside of the laboratory, especially in complex systems where antecedents that designers neither recognized nor anticipated may be present. Accident investigators obtain data on many measures, data that had been continuously collected throughout the event, unlike researchers who generally collect data on only a few performance measures, and often only at selected intervals. Further, operators in accident scenarios may be exposed to stressful conditions that no researcher could ethically present in a laboratory, allowing investigators to examine real world behavior under conditions that could not be examined in controlled settings.

Ex post facto analytical techniques allow investigators to effectively explain the nature of the relationships underlying the data, and apply them well beyond the immediate circumstances of the event under investigation. Well-conducted investigation analyses fall within Vicente's (1997) observation that, "science...encompass(es) naturalistic observation, qualitative description and categorization, inductive leaps of faith, and axioms that can never be empirically tested" (p. 325).

An illustration

A hypothetical accident illustrates the process. Assume that a train failed to stop at a stop signal and struck another train that had been standing just beyond the signal on the same track. The locomotive engineer had an unobstructed view of the signal.

The locomotive engineer claimed that he applied the brakes, but the brakes failed. If he is correct, investigators will have to look elsewhere for the cause. An incorrect determination could unfairly target an operator who performed well, and worse from a safety consideration, threaten future safety by failing to address the hazards that led to the accident in the first place. However, before they could accept the engineer's explanation as the most likely cause of the accident, investigators would have to test and accept the viability of several possible conclusions that are necessary to accept a failed brakes explanation. These are–

1) The brakes were defective at the time the engineer claims to have applied them.
2) Brakes with this defect would be unable to stop a similarly configured train in the same distance.
3) Other possible malfunctions that could also have failed to stop a similarly configured train in the same distance were not found.

To determine whether these conclusions could be supported, investigators would need to collect a variety of system data. If the data supported these conclusions, they could be reasonably confident that defective brakes caused the accident. If not, other explanations would need to be proposed, and the data reexamined and reanalyzed. The data would either support or refute the proposed explanations.

Analysis objectives

As discussed in Chapter 2, investigators bring their own perspectives to the analysis, depending upon their employer, their values, and the like. The investigation objective that is endorsed in this text is, *to identify the errors and their antecedents that led to the occurrence being investigated, so that future opportunities for error can be reduced or eliminated.* Investigators should examine the collected data to meet this objective until they are confident that the identified relationships conform to criteria that will be discussed shortly.

During an investigation, it is likely that investigators will collect different types of data of varying quality. Before analyzing the collected data, investigators evaluate the data to assess their value to the investigation. This will affect the weight they give to the conclusions that are derived from the data.

Assessing the quality of the data

Some of the data that investigators collect will pertain to the investigation objective while other data may not. Including incomplete data and data that do not address the antecedents of error in the analysis will lead to an analysis that contributes little to understanding the origin of the particular errors.

Determining the quality of data is critical because the quality of an investigation largely depends on the quality of the data that investigators collect. "Garbage in-garbage out" applies to the analysis of error in incidents and accidents as it does to analyses. Two standards of quality are used to assess data value, internal consistency and sequential consistency.

Internal consistency

Anderson and Twining (1991), describing legal analysis, believe that internally consistent data should converge into one conclusion. Converging data, they argue, even if derived from different sources and collected at different times, support the same conclusion. For example, if an operator's history reveals previous deficiencies and those deficiencies are similar to characteristics of the operator's performance at the time of the occurrence, the data would converge. One could reasonably conclude, in that instance, that the operator's performance during the event was not an aberration but was consistent with that of an operator whose quality of work would likely have led to an event in circumstances similar to those in which the operator had previously performed deficiently. In complex systems, internally consistent data converge by depicting aspects of the same event similarly, at the same points in time. If they do not, the data will not be internally consistent.

In any investigation, investigators collect a large amount of data. In the hypothetical railroad accident in which defective brakes are believed to have caused the collision, one can assume that at a minimum, investigators will collect data regarding–

- The operator's train orders and his or her interpretation of them
- The operator's commanded speed, power, and brake applications
- The actual locomotive speed, power, and brake settings
- Pertinent operating rules, procedures, and operating limitations
- The operator's performance history
- Toxicological analysis of specimens of the operator
- Medical evaluations of the operator
- The commanded and displayed signals
- Lights, flags, or markings at the aft end of the standing train
- Company oversight of its operations
- Regulator oversight of the railroad.

If the brakes had been defective and investigators determined that the defect caused the accident, internally consistent data should reveal the effects of the defect on much of the data. All data, except those pertaining to the brakes and those independent of the sequence of antecedents and errors/flaws leading to the event, should be consistent. However, if the data showed defects in other components that could have altered the sequence of occurrences, or if the brakes were found to have been defect free, the data would be inconsistent and the discrepancy would need to be resolved.

Inconsistencies could be caused by deficiencies either in the data or in the proposed theory or explanation of the cause of the event. Deficiencies in the equipment-related data could result from flaws in the recording devices, measuring instruments, or, with eyewitnesses, their perceptions and recall. Inconsistencies in operator-related data could be caused by any of several factors that will be discussed shortly. Otherwise, inconsistent data indicate the need to revise the theory or explanation of the cause of the accident, to reexamine the data or collect additional data.

Likely sources of inconsistent data Inconsistencies among the data, though rare, are most often found among eyewitness accounts and operator-related information. Substantial differences among eyewitness accounts are infrequent, but, as investigators found in the explosion of the Boeing 747 off the coast of Long Island, occur occasionally (NTSB, 2000d). Inconsistencies in eyewitness data largely result from perceptual and memory factors, and differences in interviewer techniques, discussed in Chapter 9.

Several factors may explain differences in operator-related information. For one, people interact differently with operators, based on their relationships with them. Colleagues, acquaintances, and supervisors have different perceptions of the operator, and these perceptions will affect the information they give to interviewers. In addition, as discussed in Chapter 8, changes that occur over time in such parameters as measures of operator performance and health may also lead to inconsistent data.

Investigators can safely discard inconsistent data, if the inconsistency is not a result of deficiencies in the way the data were collected. Investigators of the 1999 collapse of logs, intended for a bonfire at Texas A & M University, discarded numerous eyewitness reports that were not supported by the physical evidence, or were otherwise irrelevant (Special Commission, 2000). As investigators, who use the term Bonfire to refer to the stack of logs, describe,

> A large number of interview summaries prepared by Kroll [the investigative organization that conducted the interviews] contained information which was either not in agreement with the physical evidence, or not directly related to the Bonfire collapse. These summaries were not included with Packer's [the investigative organization conducting the physical examination of the logs] analysis. Of the remaining summaries, those containing information from witnesses who were physically on Bonfire at the time of the collapse were considered most accurate, while those of witnesses at Bonfire but not on the actual stacks were also considered highly accurate. (Packer Engineering, p. 25)

Because the physical evidence contradicted many of the eyewitness accounts, investigators could confidently discard the inconsistent eyewitness data without affecting the subsequent analysis.

Sequential consistency

Investigative data should consistently match the sequence of occurrences and the period of time in which they occurred during the event. Certainly, the sequential relationships between antecedents and errors are invariant; antecedents will always precede errors and errors will always precede the event.

In the railroad accident example used earlier, if a signal directing train movement commands a stop, locomotive event recorders would be expected to show, in order, power reduction first and then brake application, corresponding to the expected operator actions. The data should also match the passage of time corresponding to the occurrence, in the actual period in which the train approached the signal and struck the standing train. Regardless of the rate at which actions occur and system state changes, the two should correspond. Certain operator actions must still occur after certain events have taken place, and certain equipment events should follow particular operator actions. Sequentially inconsistent data may be the result of inaccurate data recorders, defective measuring devices, or deficiencies within the data. If the inconsistencies cannot be resolved satisfactorily, investigators may need to collect additional data, or reexamine the data selection and collection methods to resolve the inconsistencies.

Data value

Data vary in their value and contribution to the analysis. Depending on the event and the data, investigators rely on some data to understand what happened and why, and ignore other data. The greater the reliability, accuracy, and objectivity of the data, the greater their value to, and influence upon, the analysis. Reliable and objective data should describe the same phenomenon the same way, regardless of how or when investigators obtained the data.

In general, "hard" data, data directly measured by the system, contribute substantially to the investigation because of their high reliability, objectivity, and accuracy. By contrast, the value of "soft data," such as eyewitness accounts and interview data, is less because the data can change as a function of the person collecting the data, the time of day the data are obtained, and the skill of the interviewer, among other factors.

Relevance

Anderson and Twining (1991), referring to legal analyses, consider a statement relevant if it tends to make the hypothesis to be proved more likely to be supported than would otherwise be the case. Data that can help explain conclusions regarding the cause of the event, the critical errors, and the antecedents to the errors, are analogous to data that can support the hypothesis and are considered relevant to the investigation.

Most investigators routinely gather data that may not necessarily relate to their investigations, but are needed to rule out potential issues. If it is determined that an operator performed well, one can exclude data pertaining to the operator's performance history from the analysis without degrading the quality of the analysis or the investigation, unless the data relate to other critical issues. On the other hand, if operator error is believed to have led to the incident, almost all data concerning the operator would be considered relevant and included in the analysis.

Data relevance can change as more is learned about an event. For example, an initial focus on potential training deficiencies makes information pertinent to the development, implementation, and conduct of the training relevant to the investigation. If the data suggest that equipment design factors rather than training affected operator performance, operator training-related data would be less relevant.

Quantity

The more data obtained about a particular aspect of the system, the more confidence one can have in the value of the data and their contribution to the analysis. For example, in some systems multiple recorders capture a variety of operator performance parameters, documenting the operator's spoken words and any related sounds. These would provide considerable data that describe, both directly and indirectly, what the operator did before and during the event. These data may comprehensively describe operator actions and presumably, errors.

If there is little data available, other measures that can approximate the parameters of interest should be sought. If no data directly describe aspects of operator performance, investigators may need to infer operator actions from other sources, such as system recorder data. If there are insufficient data available to allow inferences about the parameters of interest, conclusions regarding the data of interest will have little factual support.

Identifying the errors

After the data have been examined and evaluated, one can begin to propose relationships among antecedents, errors, and the causes of the event.

The sequence of occurrences

To begin developing the critical relationships, investigators should first establish the correct sequence of actions and occurrences in the event. The sequence will determine the order of actions and decisions, and facilitate the investigator's job of establishing the critical relationships.

Investigators establish the sequence of occurrences in the event by working backwards from the event itself until the errors that led to the event, and the antecedents to those errors, are reached—what Rasmussen, Pejtersen, and Goodstein (1994) refer to as the "stopping point." Regardless of the event, whether airplane accident, chemical refinery explosion, or vessel grounding, the incident or accident is the point at which one begins the sequence of occurrences.

Using the railroad accident discussed earlier, the sequence of occurrences begins with the collision. Occurrences earlier in the sequence would likely include the engineer's brake application and power reduction, and progress to company brake maintenance practices, as far back as brake manufacture and locomotive assembly.

The sequence of occurrences includes major system elements. In this illustration, these would include the operator, the railroad, the regulator, and the brake manufacturer. However, few issues should be ruled out early in the investigation. Data pertinent to those issues would need to be collected to determine the role of each element in the event.

For example, if it is learned that the locomotive engineer did not attempt to stop the locomotive, then operator actions would be a focus of the investigation and investigators would need to identify potential antecedents to those actions. Other issues to be investigated would likely include the railroad's training and oversight of its operators, and the regulator's oversight of the railroad. Table 14.1 illustrates how an initial sequence of occurrences may appear.

Although investigators may include different occurrences, or use a different order of occurrences in the sequence of key occurrences, the general structure of the sequence should not change. The critical facts, including the collision, the record of inspections of the brakes and their manufacture, would not be in dispute.

Assume that in this example, after interviewing critical personnel and collecting and examining the data, investigators determine that the operator performed satisfactorily. In that case, occurrences relating to operator performance can be safely excluded from the sequence of occurrences and from subsequent data analysis. Table 14.2 illustrates the results of a second iteration of a sequence of occurrences, after first discarding occurrences irrelevant to the issues of interest.

The error or errors

After examining the data, assessing their relative value, and establishing the sequential order of occurrences, investigators can exclude from the analysis several additional factors that are no longer considered relevant to the accident. For example, if tested and found to have been in acceptable condition at the time of the event, factors related to the signal system may be considered irrelevant.

Table 14.1 Sequence of occurrences–railroad accident illustration–first iteration

Sequence of occurrences-beginning with the collision
1. The collision
2. Locomotive operator brake application
3. Locomotive operator power reduction
4. Railroad signal system maintenance and inspection
5. Locomotive operator initial and refresher training
6. Railroad brake system maintenance and inspection
7. Railroad brake system maintenance personnel selection
8. Brake system manufacture and installation
9. Railroad signal system selection and acquisition
10. Signal system manufacture
11. Railroad signal system selection and installation
12. Railroad signal installer, maintenance, and inspection personnel training
13. Locomotive operator selection
14. Railroad brake system maintenance personnel selection
15. Railroad signal system installer, maintenance and inspection personnel selection
16. Regulator oversight of railroad signal system
17. Regulator oversight of brake system.

The next step in the data analysis can now be conducted, identifying the errors that led to the event, perhaps the most critical step in the analysis. This step is distinct and separate from the formal or legal determination of the accident cause. The focus should be on the errors suspected of leading to the event.

Table 14.2 Sequence of occurrences–second iteration with non-essential events excluded

Events excluded
1. Locomotive operator brake application
2. Locomotive operator power reduction
3. Locomotive operator initial and refresher training
4. Locomotive operator selection.

Events retained
1. The collision
2. Railroad signal system maintenance and inspection
3. Railroad brake system maintenance and inspection
4. Railroad brake system maintenance personnel selection
5. Brake system manufacture and installation
6. Railroad signal system selection and acquisition
7. Signal system manufacture
8. Railroad signal system selection and installation
9. Railroad signal installer, maintenance, and inspection personnel training
10. Railroad brake system maintenance personnel selection
11. Railroad signal system installer, maintenance and inspection personnel selection
12. Regulator oversight of railroad signal system
13. Regulator oversight of brake system.

Central question If there is uncertainty determining whether a proposed error has contributed to the cause of the event, investigators should ask a central question; would the accident have occurred if this error had not been committed? If the answer is no, the accident would not have occurred, they can be confident that the error caused or contributed to the cause of the accident.

Using the train collision illustration, assume that: 1) the brake defect resulted from a manufacturing error and, 2) the defect was sufficiently conspicuous that inspectors should have noticed it during routine inspections, but they did not. In addition to the errors of those involved in the brake manufacture, the investigation would also examine the inspectors' errors and consider them contributory to the accident. In this accident, if neither error had been committed, the accident would not have occurred. Both errors are needed for the accident to occur, and each can be considered to have led to the accident.

If these errors have been identified, the list of relevant occurrences to be retained can be further narrowed, with concomitant expansion of the list of those excluded, as Table 14.3 illustrates. This list includes the accident itself, the errors that directly led to it, as well as the antecedents that may have allowed the errors to occur.

Assessing the relationship of antecedents to errors

After identifying the errors, the antecedents of those errors must be determined. The process is largely inferential, based on the preponderance of evidence pointing to a relationship between the two. The evidence consists of the nature of the error, and information from written documentation, interviews, system recorders, equipment, and other sources.

Inferring a relationship

Central question A relationship between antecedent and error must be logical and unambiguous. Investigators must establish that the antecedent, either by itself or with others, influenced the operator's performance so that he or she committed an error. To identify the antecedent, one should ask, would the operator have committed the error if this (and other) antecedent(s) had not preceded it? If the answer is no, one could be confident that the antecedent led to the error.

Assume that insufficient operator experience is one of several antecedents that affected the performance of an operator, and he misinterpreted system-related data as a result. A relationship between experience in operating a system and the error of misinterpreting data is logical; a more experienced operator is less likely to commit the same error than a less experienced one. This conclusion is supported by both research and the findings of previous accident investigations. This relationship between antecedent and error is clear and unambiguous, reached only after the necessary facts have been obtained and analyzed.

Table 14.3 Sequence of occurrences–third iteration with non-essential events excluded

Events excluded
1. Locomotive operator brake application
2. Locomotive operator power reduction
3. Railroad signal system maintenance and inspection
4. Locomotive operator initial and refresher training
5. Railroad signal system selection and acquisition
6. Signal system manufacture
7. Railroad signal system selection and installation
8. Railroad signal installer, maintenance, and inspection personnel training
9. Locomotive operator selection
10. Railroad signal system installer, maintenance and inspection personnel selection
11. Regulator oversight of railroad signal system.

Events retained
1. The collision
2. Brake system manufacture and installation
3. Railroad brake system maintenance and inspection
4. Railroad brake system maintenance personnel training
5. Railroad brake system maintenance personnel selection
6. Regulator oversight of brake system.

Statistical relationship

The logic used to establish a relationship between antecedents and errors is analogous to multiple regression analysis, a statistical technique used to determine the relationship between one or more predictor variables and a single variable (e.g., Harris, 1975). Economists, for example, employ multiple regression analyses to predict the effects of changes in variables such as the prime interest rate, unemployment, and government spending, on changes in an outcome variable such as inflation rate.

The stronger the relationship between the predictor or influencing variables and the outcome variable, the higher the *correlation* between the two sets of variables. In relationships that have high positive correlations, changes in the predictor variables are associated with corresponding changes in the outcome variables. As the value of predictor variables increases or decreases, the value of the outcome variable similarly increases or decreases. If the correlations were negative, predictor variable changes in one direction would be associated with outcome variable changes in the opposite direction. As the predictor variables increase or decrease in value, the outcome variable loses or gains value in the opposite direction.

Multiple regression analyses also describe another facet of these relationships that can be stated statistically; when the correlation between the two sets of variables is high the predictor variables account for much of the total variance in changes in the outcome variable. That is, the higher the correlation between the two, the more that changes in the predictor variables–and not some other variable or the effects of chance–account for changes in the outcome variable. The lower the correlation, the less that changes in the outcome variable can be attributed to changes in the predictor variables. In that case, changes in the outcome variable will more likely be associated with variables that had not been considered in the analysis.

In investigations of error, the predictor variables correspond to the antecedents and the outcome variable to the critical error. Investigators assess the relationship between one or more antecedents and the operator's error in the circumstances that prevailed at the time of the accident. The stronger the relationship between the antecedents and errors, the more the antecedents would account for "variance" about the errors, and the more the error can be attributed to those antecedents, and not to other variables or antecedents not yet recognized.

Relating antecedents to errors

Relationships between antecedents and errors should be simple, logical, and superior to other potential relationships among the variables. These criteria are related; if a relationship meets one criterion it will likely meet the others as well.

The influence of one variable on the other should be as simple as possible. One should be directly related to the other, with as few assumptions as possible needed to support it. A simple relationship should also be logical, one that makes sense to all concerned. It should require little analytical effort to understand the relationship between one and the other. In addition, it should be simpler and more logical than other, alternative proposed relationships.

Multiple antecedents

In a complex system multiple antecedents often influence operator performance. Multiple antecedents can affect performance cumulatively, by increasing the influence of each to bring a greater total influence on operator performance than would otherwise be the case. Multiple antecedents can also interact with each other to differentially affect operator performance. Investigators should search for multiple antecedents, even if one antecedent appears to adequately explain the error.

Cumulative influence

Multiple antecedents can increase each other's influence on operator performance so that their cumulative total influence is greater than would be true if the antecedents had individually influenced performance. For example, individual antecedents of fatigue can cumulatively influence performance beyond that of individual antecedents, as investigators found in a 1998 accident involving a commercial bus, discussed in Chapter 4. Investigators determined that the bus driver fell asleep while at the controls, and the bus then ran off the road and struck a parked truck (NTSB, 2000b).

Investigators identified three antecedents of the driver's fatigue. Individually each was probably insufficient to have caused him to fall asleep, but combined their effects were substantial. Toxicological analysis of a specimen from the driver's body revealed the presence an over-the-counter sedating antihistamine that he had consumed earlier. He had also maintained a nighttime work schedule for several consecutive days before the accident, a schedule that had disrupted his sleep patterns and caused a cumulative sleep deficit. Further, the accident occurred at 4:05 am, a time when he would ordinarily have been in his deepest phase of sleep. Those who stay awake at that time are especially prone to the effects of fatigue. Combined, the effects of the sedating antihistamine, disruptive schedule, and time of day were so powerful that the driver was unable to stay awake.

Interacting antecedents

Interacting antecedents differentially affect operator performance. To illustrate, assume that the control rooms of two electrical power generating stations, designed five years apart, are identical in all respects except that one employs "older" analog gauges and the other "newer" digital displays to present system information. The same information is shown in both, and in both generating station operators have received identical training and use identical procedures.

The operators of the two generating stations also have different levels of experience; one group has an average of 10 years of experience and the other, two. Thus, four different operator/equipment groups are possible–

1. Experienced operators with "old" analog displays
2. Inexperienced operators with "old" analog displays
3. Experienced operators with "new" digital displays
4. Inexperienced operators with "new" digital displays.

Further, in a certain non-routine condition, the displays present information that requires the operators to respond. The operators can only respond correctly or erroneously. With no interaction, differences in operator response would be affected either by their experience or by the display format, or there would be little or no difference in their responses. Inexperienced operators might respond erroneously while experienced ones would not, or operators working with the "newer" displays could respond correctly though the others not. Alternatively, with no interaction all four groups could perform correctly or all could commit errors, in which case the effects of either operator experience or display type would lead to performance that is independent of the other. Figures 14.1 – 14.5 below illustrate five of the possible outcomes.

An interaction would occur when experience and display type interact to differentially affect operator performance. Operators committing the greatest number of errors could be the inexperienced ones who worked with the "older" displays. Alternatively, experienced operators working with the "newer" technology could commit the greatest number of errors, and the inexperienced operators working with analog displays, the fewest.

Many interactions are possible in complex systems. The variety of human behavior, the diversity among procedures, training, and equipment, and the numerous component interactions within complex systems are such that the potential number of interacting antecedents that could affect performance is practically infinite. For example, training can interact with procedures or operating cycles so that certain types of training, say on-the-job training and classroom lectures, lead to different levels of performance, according to the particular procedure and operating cycle. Oversight may interact with managerial experience so that certain types and levels of oversight lead to superior operator performance. Less experienced operators may perform best with extensive oversight, and experienced operators may perform best with little oversight. Some operators may perform effectively with certain types of controls, but erroneously with others, according to the type of training they receive.

	Experienced	Inexperienced
Analog	Correct	Erroneous
Digital	Correct	Erroneous

Figure 14.1   Non-interacting antecedents: Operator experience

	Experienced	Inexperienced
Analog	Correct	Correct
Digital	Erroneous	Erroneous

Figure 14.2   Non-interacting antecedents: Display format favoring analog displays

	Experienced	Inexperienced
Analog	Erroneous	Erroneous
Digital	Correct	Correct

Figure 14.3   Non-interacting antecedents: Display format favoring digital displays

	Experienced	Inexperienced
Analog	Erroneous	Correct
Digital	Correct	Erroneous

Figure 14.4 Interacting antecedents: Interaction of performance quality with experience and format type

	Experienced	Inexperienced
Analog	Correct	Erroneous
Digital	Erroneous	Correct

Figure 14.5 Interacting antecedents: A different interaction of performance quality with experience and format type

Common elements

Antecedents may share a common underlying influence, referred to as a "common element," an antecedent that accounts for or influences numerous others. Often, common elements are related to equipment, organization, or regulator antecedents because of their substantial influence on operator performance. For example, operator errors could be influenced by deficiencies in company training, operating procedures, and equipment design, among others. If the regulator oversaw, and was required to approve, each of these elements, regulator oversight would be a common element among the antecedents because the regulator would have permitted poorly designed equipment, deficient training, and inadequate operating procedures to enter the system. Common elements generally include what Reason refers to as "latent conditions" (Reason, 1997) that are present in a system and can adversely influence performance in certain circumstances.

In the railroad accident illustration, assume that, in order to reduce expenses, railroad managers considered, but because of financial concerns delayed, implementing additional procedures to its brake system maintenance and inspection program, and hiring additional inspectors to perform more thorough inspections. If the evidence supports these findings, and it could be shown that those actions would have prevented the accident, a corporate objective of reducing expenses would be considered a common element that adversely influenced performance.

Unidentified antecedents-concluding the search for antecedents

Despite thorough evidence gathering and sound analysis, some uncertainty regarding the antecedents that were identified as influencing the errors is common. Statistical and experimental design techniques aid empirical researchers to reduce the role of unidentified variables, but even these techniques cannot exclude the possibility that variables that the researchers had not identified influenced the obtained results. Researchers control the variables they could identify, but because of unidentified variables may always be present, absolute certainty is not possible. Rather, researchers rely on statistical probability measurement, in which the possible presence of unidentified variables is measured and, if sufficiently low, acknowledged but considered so unlikely as to be absent.

Accident investigators must also acknowledge the possibility that unidentified antecedents contributed to the critical errors. Unidentified antecedents are always potential factors in investigations. Nevertheless, investigators can be confident that with thorough data gathering and sound analysis, they can minimize their possible effects, much as researchers can with sound experimental design and analytical techniques. By systematically and methodically examining the effects of antecedents that are believed most likely to have influenced the probable errors, antecedents that are supported by logic, research and previous investigation findings, the potential presence of unidentified variables will be addressed and minimized.

Sound analytical techniques will also enable investigators to recognize when they have reach the point at which the search for antecedents should be stopped. In Chapter 2 and earlier in this chapter, the "stopping point," the point at which the search for antecedents should be ended, was discussed. For the purposes of this text, *the stopping point is reached when investigators can no longer identify antecedents that can serve as the target of remedial action*. Theoretically, the search for antecedents is infinite and investigators can never be certain that they have identified all possible antecedents. Investigators should pursue all issues and seek to identify all potential antecedents and errors. However, at some point the increase in precision needed to understand the origin of the errors or mechanical failures is not worth additional investigative resources. When reaching the point at which logic dictates that little further activity will be worthwhile, further investigative activity becomes unproductive.

For example, suppose investigators identify deficient regulator oversight as a factor in the defective brakes, used in the previously discussed example. They determine that with effective regulator surveillance, deficiencies in the railroad's oversight would have been identified, the deficiencies corrected, and the defective brakes likely identified and repaired. However, the regulator could argue that it performed the best oversight it could with its limited resources. It could contend that it does not determine the number of its inspectors, rather, that Congress makes that determination in the budget that it approves. Further, the legislature acts on the budget that the President submits. Therefore, presumably, one could identify the President's budget as an antecedent to the error.

Of course, that is taking the search for antecedents to its ultimate conclusion. Pursuing the argument to that point is untenable because, if for not other reason, no agent could be identified that could implement effective remediation strategies. Well before that point, the investigation will have passed the point of diminishing returns, with little additional benefit gained from further activity.

Absolute versus probable cause

As noted in Chapter 2, "there is no absolute cause" of an accident and investigators must accept the imprecision that is an inherent part of error investigations. Precision is not possible in complex systems, and for that reason, absolute certainty in establishing the errors leading to an event is an impossibility.

As a result, some investigative agencies use the term "probable cause" of an accident rather than the more succinct and absolute term, "cause," acknowledging that, despite their best investigative and analytical efforts, the influence of an unidentified variable remains possible. Others do not use the term "cause" at all in their investigations, but list findings instead.[4]

---

[4] The Australian Transportation Safety Bureau is an example.

Some have criticized the use of any type of cause in an investigation for that reason. Miller (2000), for example, suggests that this,

> Relates back to a subject pursued for the past quarter century or so–that detestable preoccupation most people seem to have with "cause." If investigative processes and classifications of accident findings continue to be hung up on "cause" instead of pursuing the implementation phase [of remediation strategies and techniques] further, we are going to be static at best in prevention efforts. (p. 16)

Yet, examining the results of incident and accident investigations between organizations that determine a cause and those that do not suggests that neither approach is superior. Whether an organization determines a probable cause or not appears to make little difference in the quality of the investigation or proposed recommendations. Irrespective of a requirement to develop a cause to an event, investigators should focus on conducting a thorough and systematic investigation in order to reduce future opportunities for error. Doing so will contribute positively to effective investigations, regardless of the nature of the "cause" or "findings" that are determined.

Recommendations

After determining the relationships between errors and antecedents, investigators should identify the recommendations, the final step in the investigative process. Many investigative agencies propose recommendations as the vehicle for strategies and techniques to correct the system deficiencies they have identified. Others use other means, but for the purpose of this text, the term "recommendations" will be used to describe proposed remediation strategies.

Recommendations accomplish a major objective of error investigations, to address and mitigate the system deficiencies, the antecedents, which led to the operator errors identified in the investigation, so that future opportunities for error will be reduced. Recommendations describe at least three separate, but related entities, 1) the deficiency and its adverse effects on safety, 2) the proposed remediation strategy or technique, and 3) the mechanism by which the suggested remediation techniques will correct the identified deficiency and improve safety.

Recommendations begin with an explanation of the deficiency and its adverse effects on safety. When referring to error, deficiencies are the antecedents to errors, but deficiencies can also be mechanical malfunctions, design failures, or other system defect. In general, three types of system deficiencies are the subject of recommendations; those that 1) led to the accident, 2) contributed to the cause of the accident, or 3), were identified as system safety deficiencies, but were not involved in the cause of the accident.

The example of the rail accident cited earlier, in which inspectors failed to detect a flaw in the system, will be used again to show how to develop recommendations. Suppose that investigators identified these deficiencies regarding inspector performance in failing to recognize the defects in the brakes–

1. Inspector fatigue from abrupt scheduled shift changes
2. False inspector expectancy from having inspected flawless components exclusively
3. Inadequate inspection station illumination
4. Inadequate inspection procedures
5. Deficient equipment.

Recommendations can be proposed to address each of the safety deficiencies. Because the regulator and the company can correct each deficiency, the recommendations can be directed at either one. However, addressing recommendations to the regulator in effect, would direct them to all organizations that the regulator oversees. If similar deficiencies were present at other companies, the regulator would implement or require corrective actions with those organizations as well in response to the recommendation. For the sake of simplicity, the recommendations used in the illustration will be aimed at the regulator.

Investigators can take many directions in proposing recommendations. They can suggest specific solutions or leave it to the recipient of the recommendation to develop its own strategies to address the deficiency. The latter method is often preferred since it gives the recipient the latitude to develop corrective actions that meet its own needs, so long as investigators are satisfied that the corrective actions will be effective and meet the intent of the recommendation.

To develop a recommendation to address the first deficiency or antecedent–fatigue from an irregular work schedule–investigators can ask the regulator to revise its rules governing scheduling practices to prevent abrupt changes in shift schedules. Other recommendations can also be made, such as requiring companies to provide adequate rest periods before scheduling operators for night work, informing operators of the nature of fatigue and its effects, and providing information to both supervisors and operators to help them recognize operator fatigue.

Deficiency number two–expectancies from dealing with flawless components–can be corrected by requiring companies to randomly give inspectors brake systems with recognizable defects, to increase the likelihood of their encountering defects, and thus reduce their expectations of flawless parts. This action would have the additional benefit of creating a mechanism for both companies and operators to identify potential inspection problems.

To address deficiency number three–inadequate illumination–the regulator could be asked to require companies to install adequate lighting in inspection stations. A recommendation to address deficiency number four–inadequate company inspection procedures–could be corrected by requiring companies to review existing procedures, identify the inadequacies, and develop procedures that address them. Deficiency number five–deficient equipment–could be rectified by requiring companies to inspect their equipment, and replace or repair components found to be defective. The proposed recommendations address specific antecedents to acknowledged errors, by identifying the deficiencies and proposing either general or specific corrective actions to the proper recipient.

Summary

Analyzing human performance data in accident investigations is similar to empirical research; both apply formal methods of inquiry to explain relationships within data. In a human error investigation, the relationships under study are those between errors that led to an occurrence, and the antecedents that led to the errors.

Human error investigators usually collect a substantial amount of data. However, only internally and sequentially consistent data should be included in an analysis. Data that do not meet these standards may have to be discarded, additional data obtained, and hypotheses revised to account for the inconsistencies.

The sequence of occurrences of the event is determined by working backward from the event to identify critical errors, and the antecedents that influenced the errors. Relationships between antecedents and errors should establish that without one the other would not have occurred, and meet standards of simplicity, logic, and superiority to alternative relationships. The potential presence of multiple antecedents should also be considered. These can cumulatively increase each other's combined influence on operator performance, or interact to differentially affect performance.

After identifying the antecedents, investigators should develop recommendations to address safety-related deficiencies identified in the investigation. These will include the identified antecedents, as well as safety deficiencies that were identified but which may not have been antecedents to the errors involved in the cause of the event. The recommendations should identify the deficiencies and suggest ways to mitigate them.

Helpful techniques
• Discard data that do not meet standards of internal consistency, sequential consistency, reliability, objectivity, and accuracy, and if necessary, collect new data or revise the prevailing hypotheses.
• Determine the relevance of the data to the circumstances of the event, the critical errors, and the antecedents to the errors.
• Establish a sequence of occurrences by working backwards, beginning with the final phase of the accident sequence and progressing to the errors that led to the event and their antecedents.
• Identify errors by asking, "Would the accident have occurred if this error had not been committed"?
• Identify antecedents by asking, "Would the operator have committed these errors if these antecedents had not preceded them?"
• Establish relationships between antecedents and errors that are simple, logical, and superior to other potential relationships.
• Propose recommendations, after identifying errors and antecedents, that identify system deficiencies and suggest remediation techniques.

Part IV
Issues

13 Situation Awareness and Decision Making

The impetus of existing plans is always stronger than the impulse to change.
(Tuchman, 1962)

The Guns of August

Introduction

Throughout history poor decision making has led to undesired outcomes. In the first days of World War I, for example, the military commanders of several countries made decisions that led to disastrous consequences (Tuchman, 1962). In the face of overwhelming evidence that their initial plans needed to be revised in the light of battlefield conditions, they refused, decisions that ultimately led to their countries' defeat.

In complex systems deficiencies in operators' decision making have contributed to errors and accidents. Many of these errors resulted from deficiencies in situation awareness. Because of the importance of situation awareness to decision making, and the importance of decision making to system safety, investigators need to understand both. In particular, factors affecting situation awareness, the relationship of situation awareness to operator decision making, and the effects of deficient decision making on operator errors need to be examined to properly understand decision making. This chapter will review situation awareness and decision making, and discuss the types of data needed to assess decision making when conducting error investigations.

Situation assessment and situation awareness

Situation assessment is the process of acquiring data to understand or obtain a mental picture of the immediate environment; situation awareness refers to a person's understanding or mental picture of that environment. Situation assessment and situation awareness are closely related; at any point in time, the two are identical. Endsley (1995) lists three elements that form situation awareness, 1) perceiving the status, attributes, and dynamics of relevant elements in the environment, 2) comprehending the significance of these elements, and 3) projecting current assessment to future status. Thus, an operator would obtain situation awareness after receiving critical system-related information, understanding it, and using the information to predict the near-term system state. Endsley (1995, 2000) argues that situation awareness is based upon elements of both operators and equipment, suggestive of operator and equipment antecedents discussed previously.

Temporal factors can also directly influence situation awareness. Grosjean and Terrier (1999) propose a modified view of situation awareness, referred to as "temporal awareness." In their view, an operator has obtained temporal awareness when he or she can accurately recall previous events and reliably predict near term events. Temporal awareness can also refer to operators' awareness of the amount of time needed and the amount of time available to perform a task. The two are independent, critical features of operator performance. The more time an operator has available to assess a situation, the greater the likelihood that he or she will obtain situation awareness. Conversely, as the amount of time decreases, the less likely the operator will be to obtain situation awareness.

Situation awareness-operator elements

Characteristics that affect situation awareness include operator–

- Experience, expertise, training, and memory
- Expectancies
- Workload, attention, and automaticity
- Goals.

Each can affect situation awareness and influence operator performance.

Experience, expertise, training, and memory As operators gain system experience they become increasingly expert at interpreting system cues and as a result, they need less time and fewer cues to obtain situation awareness. The greater their memory capacity, the more experiences they can call upon to compare to current situations, and hence, the greater their expertise. Because experts can refer to previous system-related experiences to develop accurate situation assessments, as Orasanu (1993) notes, they can "see" the underlying structures of problems more quickly than can novices.

Experts and novices also differ in response to dynamic situations. Federico (1995) compared expert and novice military personnel who examined identical simulated battlefield scenarios, and found that experts were considerably more context-dependent in evaluating situations than are novices, allowing them to evaluate situations more completely than novices. Experts can also multi-task better than novices. Cara and LaGrange (1999) found that experienced nuclear power plant controllers anticipate events while they exercise system control, enabling them to quickly discern subtle system interactions. Endsley notes that in high workload conditions, experienced operators attend to cues that are likely to be most informative about the system and its environment. Given these differences, in comparable circumstances experts can be expected to gain situation awareness more quickly and with fewer cues than can novices.

Training can compensate, in part, for inexperience by providing novice operators with system-related knowledge that experts have acquired from their experience. Training can also introduce operators to challenging system states, enabling them to respond appropriately should they encounter similar circumstances in actual operations.

Expectancies Operators' mental models of system state guide them to the relevant situation cues, increasing the efficiency of their situation assessment. However, their mental models can also lead them to expect cues that may be unavailable in the actual environment. Jones (1997), and Jones and Endsley (2000), found that if operators' expectancies did not match the cues they encountered, whether because of their own incorrect mental models or because circumstances had changed after they had formed their mental models, they often failed to perceive cues critical to situation awareness, and hence they retained inaccurate situation awareness.

Unmet expectancies can also lead operators to misinterpret the cues they perceive, what Jones (1997) has termed "representational errors."

Unfortunately, as Endsley (2000) notes, initial situation assessments are particularly resistant to change after operators have received conflicting information. An operator with deficient initial situation awareness may have difficulty obtaining more accurate situation awareness subsequently. Should the situation change subtly, the operator may not recognize situational changes.

Workload, attention, and automaticity Workload affects an operator's ability to attend to and interpret necessary cues, and thus it can directly affect situation awareness. In high workload conditions operators might work so intensely that they have limited spare cognitive capacity to attend to multiple cues. In these circumstances they will attend to the most salient cues available, cues that may not necessarily be the most informative. On the other hand in low workload conditions operators may reduce their vigilance to the point that they attend to cues ineffectively, or fail to seek out the cues necessary for situation awareness.

Operators can compensate for the effects of high workload by using "automaticity" when completing tasks they had performed often. With repetition a task can become so familiar that it can be performed with little conscious effort. As automobile operators who repeatedly drive the same route, people can eventually become so adept at a task that they devote little attention to it, and attend to only limited situational cues (Logan, 1988). However, in the event that they encounter new or unexpected cues, operators may pay a price for automaticity because of the minimal attention they would pay to the cues. They may fail to notice changed cues and have difficulty modifying their situation awareness in response (Adams, Tenney, and Pew, 1995).

Goals Goals help to guide operators to the information needed for situation awareness. A familiar aural alert, for example, guides operators to the information needed to comprehend the circumstances that led the alert. The alert acts as a goal, orienting operators to the information they need to obtain and maintain situation awareness.

Situation awareness-equipment elements

Chapter 3 addressed many aspects of the presentation of system-related information and their effects on operator performance. The effects of two equipment features on operator situation awareness will be addressed presently, 1) cue salience and interpretability, and 2) automation level.

Cue salience and interpretability Displays that present information in a confusing manner require operators to expend more effort interpreting the data than do well-designed displays. Equipment designers have generally taken this into account when designing new systems. They have replaced displays with one-to-one relationships to system components, in which displays and aural alerts can closely match operators' informational needs. These displays present information corresponding in salience to the urgency of the needed response, and, if necessary, guide operators to the desired responses.

In the discussion in Chapter 9 of the Boeing 737 that crashed in Washington, D.C. (NTSB, 1982), the approximately 30 seconds available to the pilots proved to be insufficient to enable them to interpret the data from the 10 engine-related gauges. The pilots primarily attended to two gauges that presented the most salient information, those that they had typically relied upon. Unfortunately, those gauges presented inaccurate information. The other eight gauges presented the less salient, but accurate information.

The importance of cue salience is especially evident with respect to aural information. When multiple aural alerts are sounded, operators attend to the loudest or most prominent, especially when they are under stress or experiencing high workload. For this reason designers generally make alerts that are associated with the most critical system states the most prominent.

Automation level High levels of automation remove operators from direct involvement in system operations and alter the system-related information they receive. This could reduce operator situation awareness, often during critical operating phases when situation awareness is most needed. Because of the importance of automation to understanding operator error, this topic will be discussed more fully in Chapter 13.

Obtaining or losing situation awareness

Obtaining situation awareness

Research has increased our knowledge of how operators obtain situation awareness. Mumaw, Roth, Vicente, and Burns (2000) monitored nuclear power plant controllers and observed that they obtained situation awareness from a variety of sources, not exclusively from system displays and alerts, as many had previously thought. In addition to receiving information from the displays, they actively sought out information from the operating environment. For example, as their shifts changed, departing operators briefed incoming ones about system-related events, and incoming operators probed the outgoing ones to obtain information. They also used control room logs and interacted with other operators, both their own team members and those outside the immediate control environment. Finally, because of the size of the operating environment, they walked through the facility to observe operations, performing their own observations to obtain situation awareness.

Operators use a variety of techniques and strategies to obtain situation awareness. They rely extensively on displays for their information, and also actively solicit and obtain information from additional sources. As Mumaw et al. write,

> We emphasize the contribution of the various informal strategies and competencies that operators have developed to carry out monitoring effectively. Although these strategies are not part of the formal training programs or the official operating procedures, they are extremely important because they facilitate the complex demands of monitoring and compensate for poor interface design decisions. Thus one could effectively argue that the system works well, not despite but because of operators' deviations from formal practices. (p. 52)

Losing situation awareness

Limited operator exposure to a situation, inadequate training, poorly displayed system information, and high workload, with other factors, can individually or in combination adversely affect situation awareness. Other factors, such as automaticity, can also affect operator ability to deal with high workload situations, and limit their ability to perceive novel or unexpected cues.

Operators develop mental models of system state based on their training and experience with the system, and on the available information that they obtain. Adams, Tenney, and Pew (1995) studied the activities of airline pilots and found that pilots may fail to perceive cues that are subtly different from, but seemingly similar to, those associated with their mental models of the system state, especially if they are engaged in cognitively demanding tasks. Jones (1997) found, as did Adams et al., that operators can lose or fail to obtain situation awareness when exposed to situations in which cues are seemingly similar to, but actually different from, those associated with their mental image of the situations. Jones and Endsley (1996) found that operators were more likely to notice and alter their situation awareness when exposed to cues that were considerably different from those associated with their mental images. The less cognitive effort operators expend in monitoring the system, the more likely they will fail to attend to critical situational cues.

Nevertheless, excessive cognitive effort may also lead to deficient situation awareness. Adams et al. suggest that when presented with ambiguous or incomplete information, operators may expend considerable cognitive effort to interpret the information. Their efforts can be so extensive as to distort, diminish, or even block their ability to perceive and comprehend arriving information.

Operators can also lose situation awareness when they are interrupted while performing a task, as discussed in Chapter 9 with regard to the 1987 MD-80 accident in Detroit, Michigan. After the pilots had been interrupted during a critical checklist review they neglected to extend the flaps and slats before takeoff after (NTSB 1988b). Yet, during periods of high workload operators will almost certainly face competing demands on their attention, and can often be interrupted during their activities. When returning to their tasks their ability to maintain the situation awareness that they had acquired before the disruption will be reduced. As Adams et al. write,

> To the extent that incoming information is unrelated to the task in which the pilot is concurrently engaged, its interpretation must involve considerable mental workload and risk. The more time and effort the pilot invests in its interpretation, the greater the potential for blocking reinstatement of the interrupted task as well as proper interpretation of other available data. The less time and effort invested in its interpretation, the greater the likelihood of misconstruing its implications. In a nutshell, choosing to focus attention on one set of events can be achieved only at the cost of diverting attention from all others. (p. 96)

In summary, high workload, competing task demands, and ambiguous cues can all contribute to an operator's loss of situation awareness, even with experienced and well-trained operators.

Decision making

Accurate situation awareness is especially critical to decision making. Operators with deficient or inaccurate situation awareness have difficulty interpreting system-related information and are likely to commit errors. Because of the influence of decision making on operator performance, investigators should be familiar with the process and its role in error.

Heuristics and biases

Biases affect decision making in complex systems in ways that are counter to what would be predicted exclusively by decision making models. Researchers suggest that biases influence decision making for very practical reasons. As Tversky and Kahneman (1974) suggest, in ambiguous situations "...people rely on a limited number of heuristic principles which reduce the complex tasks of assessing probabilities and predicting values to simpler judgmental operations" (p. 1124).

Wickens and Hollands (2000) describe a bias that many decision makers demonstrate after they have made a decision. As noted at the beginning of this chapter, decision makers are often reluctant to alter decisions they have made, even in the face of evidence suggesting that their decisions and situation assessments were faulty. As in other domains, reluctance to alter a decision in a complex system in the face of contrary evidence can lead to error. Orasanu, Martin, and Davison (1998), following up on an NTSB study on pilot error accidents (NTSB, 1994), attribute many of the decision making errors that they examined to "...errors in which the crew decided to continue with the original plan of action in the face of cues that suggested changing the course of action" (p. 5).

Wickens and Hollands (2000) suggest that decision makers tend to seek information that supports their initial hypothesis or decision, and avoid or discount information that supports a different decision or hypothesis (what they refer to as *discomfirmatory evidence*). As they write,

> Three possible reasons for this failure to seek discomfirmatory evidence may be proposed: (1) People have greater cognitive difficulty dealing with negative information than with positive information. (2) To change hypotheses–abandon an old one and reformulate a new one–requires a higher degree of cognitive effort than does the repeated acquisition of information consistent with an old hypothesis. Given a certain "cost of thinking" and the tendency of operators, particularly when under stress, to avoid troubleshooting strategies that impose a heavy workload on limited cognitive

resources, operators tend to retain an old hypothesis rather than go to the trouble of formulating a new one. (3) In some instances, it may be possible for operators to influence the outcome of actions taken on the basis of the diagnosis, which will increase their belief that the diagnosis was correct. This is the idea of the "self-fulfilling prophecy." (p. 313)

An operator's reluctance or bias against altering decisions extends to a reluctance to accurately reassess the situation that led to the initial decision in the first place, and to an inability to accurately reevaluate the effects of that decision on the situation itself. Consequently, if an initial decision led to adverse consequences, the operator will likely be reluctant to revisit the decision.

Operators generally apply one of two types of decision making processes to the circumstances they encounter. One is appropriate to fairly static environments and one to the dynamic environments of complex systems.

Classical decision making

In relatively static environments operators usually employ "classical" decision making processes, in which they–

1. Assess the situation
2. Identify the available options
3. Determine the costs and benefits (relative value) of each
4. Select the option with the lowest costs and highest benefit.

Classical decision making scenarios generally allow decision makers sufficient time to effectively assess the situation, identify and evaluate the various options, and select the option with the greatest benefit and least perceived cost. Decision makers may value the benefits of a particular course of action to be greater than the value of an alternative one, the costs of an alternative path as greater than the costs of the selected path, or both.

Decision makers generally complete these steps in circumstances in which there is sufficient time to perform each, such as when making a major purchase, considering a job offer, selecting a candidate for a position, or even choosing the movie they will watch.

Errors involving classical decision making

Operators can make poor decisions even when they have sufficient time to carefully evaluate existing options. Operators may evaluate the options improperly, fail to consider possible alternatives, or inaccurately estimate their costs. The pilot of a small plane committed a classical decision making error in a 1986 accident in which airplane he was piloting collided with a much larger Boeing 727 (NTSB, 1987).

The pilot had been employed as a pilot with a major airline. He had flown his own airplane from his home to Tampa, Florida–a flight in his airplane of less than an hour–where he was scheduled to command an airline flight. Because of heavy fog in the Tampa area, he had been unable to see the runway as he was about to land. On a second attempt to land, he touched down on what he thought was the runway, but was actually a taxiway, where the larger airplane was stopped. He struck the large airplane after failing to distinguish the taxiway from the runway, or to even see the Boeing 727 in the fog.

Five years earlier, the pilot had received a written reprimand after reporting late to a flight that he had been scheduled to command. The airline was forced to delay the flight and it warned him not to repeat the offense. Although the airline exempted offenses over three years old from being considered in future disciplinary actions, investigators believed that he had been unaware of the policy. In addition, the airline was experiencing labor-management difficulties at the time. The pilot's supervisor told investigators that he believed that "since the merger [of the airline with another airline], there had been more emphasis on eliminating crew delays, and...morale...[was] the lowest he had seen" (p. 18).

Investigators believed that the pilot was trying to avoid reporting to work late and face a possibly severe disciplinary action, such as the loss of his job. The evidence suggests that he had likely made the decision to fly, rather than drive and depart at a considerably earlier hour, in the static environment of his home, when he had sufficient time to evaluate the options. However, at the time of his departure the Tampa visibility had changed substantially from what it had been when he had made his departure decision. At that point, he could no longer have driven to Tampa within the time available, and still have sufficient time to command the airline flight.

Because he had made his decision before he entered his airplane, and not in the dynamic environment of a scheduled airline flight, the classical decision making model is appropriate to his decision making processes.

Using this model, he had committed his decision making error before he had departed for Tampa, in selecting a departure time that did not allow him to modify that decision should circumstances later change. Thus, although visibility may have been acceptable at the time he made his decision, at the time of the accident it was below that necessary for safe flight. However, at that point he was no longer able to drive and he could only either continue to try to land at Tampa or divert to an airport with better weather. However, had he diverted to another airport, he believed that he would have risked possible job loss. In effect, because of the decision that he had made, the pilot no longer had a viable alternative available.

Naturalistic decision making

In the often dynamic environments of complex systems, operators may not have the luxury of sufficient time to fully assess a situation and the various options that are available. Cues may be ambiguous, conflicting, and changing, options may not be fully identifiable, and the operator may need to make a decision before he or she could complete each of the steps in the classical model. As Klein (1993b) explains,

> Most systems must be operated under time pressure. Many systems must be operated with ill-defined goals…[and] shifting goals [that] refer to the fact that dynamic conditions may change what is important. Data problems are often inescapable. Decisions are made within the context of larger companies [that have their own priorities]. Tasks generally involve some amount of teamwork and coordination among different operators. Contextual factors such as acute stressors can come into play [such as] time pressure and uncertainty about data…Operators can't follow carefully defined procedures [and] finally, the decisions…involve high stakes, often [with] risk to lives and property. (pp. 16-19)

Rather than identify and then compare and select among alternatives, Klein (1993b) suggests that decision makers in dynamic situations employ what is referred to as naturalistic decision making. They recognize a situation based on their experiences and select the course of action appropriate to their perception of the situation.

Orasanu (1993) argues that naturalistic decision making in complex systems is quantitatively and qualitatively different from the processes in classical situations. In dynamic situations naturalistic decision making is faster than classical decision making because decision makers bypass steps critical to effective decision making–identifying and evaluating alternatives. The process can be effective when applied to dynamic, rapidly changing circumstances.

The naturalistic decision making process may not necessarily lead to the "best" decision for the circumstances, but it will likely be good enough for the particular situation, a process also know as "satisficing" (e.g., Federico, 1995). As Orasanu (1993) notes, "A decision strategy that is 'good' enough, though not optimal, and is low in [the cognitive] cost [required to obtain the 'best' decision] may be more desirable than a very costly, and perhaps only marginally better, decision" (p. 151).

When the situation is highly dynamic, the decision maker experienced, and the available time brief, a naturalistic decision should lead to a more effective decision than one reached through the classical decision process. Because the decision will be reached quickly, it can be made with a reasonable likelihood of success, provided that the decision maker's initial assessment was accurate.

However, should decision makers inaccurately assess the situation, naturalistic decision making can lead to poor decisions. In highly dynamic conditions, operators facing time pressure or stress likely attend to the most salient cues and not necessarily the most informative ones. In the absence of thorough situation assessment they can misperceive a situation and make ineffective decisions because the foundations of their decisions will have been flawed. As with the 1982 Boeing 737 accident in Washington, D.C. (NTSB, 1982), the captain responded to cues–airspeed and engine thrust displays–that were inaccurate. His situation awareness was faulty and therefore his decision to takeoff was deficient, ultimately leading to the accident.

Errors involving naturalistic decision making

Klein (1999) argues that the concept of decision errors in real world settings may itself have little validity because of the often-untidy nature of those settings. Orasanu, Martin, and Davision (2001), cite additional difficulties with the concept of errors in naturalistic decision making. As they note,

> Defining errors in naturalistic contexts is fraught with difficulties. Three stand out. First, errors typically are defined as deviations from a criterion of accuracy. However, the "best" decision in a natural work environment such as aviation may not be well defined, as it often is in highly structured laboratory tasks. Second, a loose coupling of decision processes and event

outcomes works against using outcomes as reliable indicators of decision quality. Redundancies in the system can "save" a poor decision from serious consequences. Conversely, even the best decision may be overwhelmed by events over which the decision maker has no control, resulting in an undesirable outcome. A third problem is the danger of hindsight bias...a tendency to define errors by their consequences. These difficulties suggest that a viable definition of decision error must take into account both the nature of the decision process and the event outcome. (p. 210)

Yet, it is clear in reviewing accidents in complex systems that operators have made decisions that, even if appearing adequate at the time, are considered faulty after the fact.

This can be illustrated in a 1992 accident involving a Lockheed L-1011 that crashed after takeoff from John F. Kennedy International Airport in New York (NTSB, 1993). The pilots received a false aerodynamic stall warning just after the airplane lifted off from the runway. They unsuccessfully attempted to return the airplane to the remaining runway. By contrast, when they also encountered the same false alert on that aircraft at that point in the flight, other pilots had continued their flights without incident. However, on this flight the first officer, who was the pilot handling the controls and flying the airplane, immediately told the captain, "getting a stall" and then gave airplane control to the captain.

As noted previously, an aerodynamic stall is perhaps the most critical situation that pilots could face; the airplane develops insufficient lift to remain flying and unless the situation is immediately corrected it will almost certainly crash. If this airplane was indeed about to stall, as the first officer had told the captain, continuing the flight would have meant almost certain catastrophe. Given the airplane's close proximity to the ground there was little or no possibility that the captain could have taken the necessary actions to avoid a stall. However, because of the airplane's high speed and heavy takeoff weight, and the limited runway distance remaining, attempting to land the airplane would also have meant an almost certain accident.

The captain's decision to land clearly led to the accident. However, because the first officer had erroneously interpreted the stall warning and told the captain that the airplane was about to stall, in the limited time available the captain's ability to effectively assess the situation, difficult at best, was almost impossible to achieve. As a result, he gave more weight to the first officer's pronouncement then he would likely have given otherwise. The captain's inaccurate situation awareness about an impending stall, albeit an awareness largely influenced by the erroneous assessment of another team member, led to the decision to attempt to land.

Decision making quality versus quality of the decision

The difficulty of examining errors in naturalistic decision making can be attributed, in part, to difficulties in distinguishing between the quality of the decision making process and the quality of the decision itself. The two are similar but different, and the quality of a decision should not be used to gauge the quality of the process used to reach that decision. Applying good decision making techniques, such as systematically obtaining, soliciting, and comprehending available system information, does not guarantee that decisions will be effective; poor decisions can follow good decision making.

For example, investigators may conclude that an operator properly interpreted the available information, effectively solicited information about the system and its operating environment, and still made a decision that later proved to be ineffective or worse, led to an accident. In addition, circumstances in complex systems may be so dynamic that the critical information changes after an operator initially obtained situation awareness. Although a systematic process is required for a "good" decision, decisions will only be as good as the information upon which they are based, and upon the circumstances being encountered.

Case study

A 1989 accident that involved a Boeing 737-400 that crashed just short of the runway near Kegworth, Leicestershire, illustrates the effects of deficient situation awareness on operator decision making (Air Accidents Investigation Branch, 1990). About 13 minutes after takeoff, the pilots felt what investigators termed "moderate to severe vibration and a smell of fire." The flight data recorder (FDR) showed that, at that time, the left engine was vibrating severely and exhibiting other anomalies. According to the report,

> The commander took control of the aircraft and disengaged the autopilot. He later stated that he looked at the engine instruments but did not gain from them any clear indication of the source of the problem. He also later stated that he thought that the smoke and fumes were coming forward from the passenger cabin, which, from his appreciation of the aircraft air conditioning

system, led him to suspect the No. 2 (right) engine. The first officer also said that he monitored the engine instruments and, when asked by the commander which engine was causing the trouble, he said "It's the le...It's the right one," to which the commander responded by saying "Okay, throttle it back." The first officer later said that he had no recollection of what it was he saw on the engine instruments that led him to make his assessment. The commander's instruction to throttle back was given some 19 seconds after the onset of the vibration when, according to the FDR, the No. 2 engine was operating with steady engine indications. (p. 5)

Forty-three seconds after the onset of the vibrations, the commander ordered the first officer to "shut it down," referring to the right engine. Investigators found that, although the left engine of the two-engine airplane sustained substantial internal damage, damage that had caused the vibrations that the pilots observed, they incorrectly shut down the right engine in the mistaken belief that it was the one that had failed. That engine was later found to have been undamaged before the accident. Rather, the left engine, the one pilots believed to have been operating effectively, had been damaged. The pilots recognized this only moments before the accident, when it was too late to restart the right engine and avoid the impact.

The circumstances of this accident were substantially different from the 1982 accident that occurred in Washington, D.C., although both involved a Boeing 737. Although similar in many ways, the British operated aircraft was a 737-400, an updated version of the 737-200 model that had been involved in the Washington accident, one with different engines and, more important for situation awareness, different displays. In the Washington accident, the crew had about 30 seconds to assess and respond to a complex scenario, one that was unlike any that either pilot had previously experienced. By contrast, the crew in the Kegworth accident had over 20 minutes from the first indication of engine difficulty to just before the accident, sufficient time to accurately assess the situation and respond appropriately.

Moreover, airline pilots repeatedly encounter engine failures in training and they are regularly tested on their ability to correctly diagnose and respond to an engine failure. Given the circumstances of this accident, the pilots' errors in 1) failing to properly identify the damaged engine and 2) shutting down the functioning engine before properly assessing the situation, are difficult to understand. Investigators sought to explain how the crew failed to obtain situation awareness with regard to the engine that had failed, despite the presence of engine status cues and sufficient time to comprehend the given information.

Information available

Investigators described the situation the pilots encountered–severe engine vibrations–and examined the amount of time that was available to assess the situation, decide what to do, and act. They documented the information available to the pilots on the actual state of both engines, and identified the information they had used to diagnose engine status. They also examined the pilots' training in recognizing and responding to engine anomalies, and evaluated the quality of their situation assessment and subsequent decision making.

Three cues were available to the pilots on the source of the engine vibrations–

- Aircraft motion into the direction of the damaged engine, after the pilots had disengaged the autopilot
- Diminished vibration and smell of fire after they first reduced engine power to both engines and then shut down the right engine
- Digital displays that presented engine-vibration information, in place of the analog displays used on the Boeing 737 involved in the Washington, D.C. accident.

Aircraft motion Neither pilot recognized that the airplane turned after the autopilot had been disengaged. The turn into the direction of the damaged engine, indicating loss of engine power, is a basic cue of engine failure that is taught to pilots first learning to operate multi-engine aircraft.

Vibration and fire smell After the pilots first reduced power to both engines, the cues that had alerted them to the engine problem, i.e., vibration and smell of fire, diminished. Their perceptions corroborated their initial identification of the damaged engine, and supported their belief in the correctness of the actions that they had taken in response. As the report notes,

> Because the decision to shut it [the No. 2 or right engine] down was made after its throttle had been closed, having failed to confirm its normal operation by comparison with the No. 1 engine instruments, the crew could

no longer confirm its normal operation by comparison with the No. 1 engine instruments. Indeed, it appears that they were so sure that they had contained the situation that the commander engaged in lengthy communications with BMA [British Midlands Airways] Operations just after the No. 2 throttle had been closed. Moreover, as the commander also said later, the clearance from the flight deck of the smell of fire powerfully reinforced their conviction that they had taken the correct action. (p. 91)

Engine instrumentation The airplane was equipped with an accurate and reliable display of engine vibration data. Investigators concluded that the pilots' "incorrect diagnosis of the problem must, therefore, be attributed to their too rapid reaction and not to any failure of the engine instrument system to display the correct indications" (p. 88).

Unlike displays on earlier 737 models, such as the one involved in the Washington, D.C., accident, the model in this accident used an electronic instrument system that digitally presented critical engine-related information, such as engine vibration, more reliably and accurately than had the earlier electro-mechanical displays. Many pilots, including a majority of the pilots surveyed at the airline, had not known that the electronic displays were more reliable than the older displays. Rather, they believed that it was more difficult to perceive information on electronic displays than on the electro-mechanical displays. The bulk of the captain's experience had been with the electro-mechanical displays.

The airline had informed its pilots, including the pilots of the accident airplane, of the greater reliability and accuracy of the electronic engine vibration displays on the –400 model. However, the flight simulators that the airline had used to train its pilots were equipped with electro-mechanical rather than electronic displays. As a result, the pilots had no experience before this flight in obtaining information from electronic engine vibration displays. Their initial experience with the electronic vibration displays took place when they flew the 737-400 for the first time, in revenue passenger service, where they would have had little reason to refer to them during the uneventful flight.

Although the pilots had the necessary information on engine vibration available, they had failed to attend to the information. Investigators proposed two explanations for this failure, the captain's extensive experience on the earlier 737 models and his relative inexperience on the newer models, and his lack of training in a model equipped with the more reliable displays. Between the two he had little exposure to and dependence upon the reliable electronic displays.

Investigators also believed that the captain should have reengaged the autopilot, or delegate aircraft control back to the automation, after manually controlling the airplane. By failing to do so, he increased both his and the first officer's workload when it was already high. This further limited their ability to gain situation awareness. Not only did they have to maintain aircraft control during this period, but they also had to diagnose and respond to the engine anomaly, communicate with air traffic control and with their company, and help prepare the cabin crew and passengers for the emergency landing. Delegating aircraft control to the autopilot would have relieved them of a major activity, and allowed them to devote more attention to diagnosis.

Therefore, it could be seen that several factors led to their decision making error, despite the availability of sufficient time to effectively assess the situation. Their initially incorrect diagnosis, with the subsequent cessation of symptoms of the engine anomaly after shutting down the functioning engine, the high workload, and their limited experience with the electronic displays, led to their failure to attend to the abnormally high reading of vibrations on the No. 1 engine.

Bias

This accident also illustrates a decision making bias. The pilots' failed to alter their initial, incorrect, situation assessment, despite having sufficient time to revisit the initial assessment. Their unwillingness to seek subsequent information after their initial assessment also demonstrates confirmation bias; they did not solicit, and actually ignored evidence that failed to support their initial identification of the damaged engine.

Further, the pilots' shutting down the engine instead of reducing engine power demonstrates how operators can alter the circumstances that elicited their initial decision by their subsequent actions and decisions. When they were within sight of the airport and needed additional engine thrust, they had insufficient time to restart the engine that they had shut down. Their decisions to, 1) act on the "good" rather than the "bad" engine, and 2) shut the engine down, changed the subsequent circumstances and reduced the number of options available.

The accident also illustrates a type of error antecedent found in multi-operator systems, as discussed in Chapter 6. In ambiguous circumstances, in this case when the engine vibrations became perceptible, one operator's erroneous input can harm the other's situation assessment. The recorded crew conversations show that the captain's erroneous identification of the damaged engine quickly followed, and was influenced by, the first officer's misidentification of the source of the engine vibrations. Finally, the report illustrates how ineffective situation awareness, misidentifying the damaged engine, led to deficient decision making.

In summary, this accident demonstrates that–

- Despite the availability of necessary information, and sufficient time to analyze the information, operators can fail to gain situation awareness.
- Deficient situation awareness can lead to ineffective decision making
- Poor decisions can alter subsequent events and harm subsequent decision making.
- An initial assessment can be difficult to alter, despite the presence of "disconfirming" cues.

Summary

Operators perform situation assessment to understand the system state and its operating environment. Situation awareness is the understanding operators have of the system and its environment at any one time. Equipment factors, such as display interpretability, operator factors, such as experience, knowledge, and skills, and company factors, such as training, affect situation awareness quality. The quality of situation awareness directly affects the quality of subsequent decision making.

In general, operators use one of two types of decision making processes. One, classical decision making, is applied primarily to relatively static situations and the other, naturalistic decision making, is applied primarily to dynamic situations. In classical decision making the decision maker generates options based on the nature of the situation, evaluates the costs and benefits of the options, and selects the one with the greatest benefits for the least cost. In naturalistic decision making, the decision maker quickly makes a decision by first recognizing the situation and then selecting an option that seems to work for that situation, even if it is not necessarily the "best" option that could follow a more thorough analysis. Decision making biases influence the quality of decisions made through either process.

Documenting situation awareness and decision making

Situation awareness

- Identify the information that the operator used or, if the operator is unavailable, was likely to have used to obtain situation awareness.
- Document equipment, operator, and company antecedents that could have affected the operator's understanding of the event.
- Document the system state from recorded data, operating manuals, personnel interviews, and other relevant data sources.
- Observe system operations if possible to determine the information upon which the operators relied.
- Interview operators, both critical and non-critical to the event, to learn of the techniques they use to understand the state of the system and its operating environment.
- Document the sources of information available to the operator, using the methods described in the preceding chapters.
- Identify the operator's previous encounters with similar scenarios in similar systems.
- Document the time the operator first perceived the critical situation and the time he or she responded.
- Compare the operator's perceptions of the events with actual system state.

Decision making

- Document the tasks that the operator performed, and the amount of time available to complete the tasks.
- Determine the information available, and the information that the operator used.
- Identify the operator's decisions and actions.
- Evaluate the effectiveness of the decisions in terms of their consequences as well as the decision making process used.
- Examine training programs and procedures to identify deficiencies that could have led to adverse outcomes.
- Examine the circumstances the operator encountered and the extent to which they changed between the time a decision was made and the time it was implemented.

14 Automation

"David, I'm afraid."

Hal the computer to astronaut David Poole as he was removing Hal's higher cognitive powers, in Stanley Kubrick's film, *2001: A Space Odyssey*[5]

Introduction

Although much of the technological innovations that Stanley Kubrick had envisioned in his landmark 1968 film, *2001: A Space Odyssey,* have not been realized, dramatic changes have nonetheless taken place in complex systems since then. Unlike Hal, the omniscient computer, automation today does not exercise absolute control over complex systems and the people who operate them. People still control complex systems, although their role has changed as automation has increased and grown more sophisticated.

Automated subsystems now perform an ever-larger share of the manual and cognitive tasks that operators had previously performed themselves. The increased role of automation in systems has enhanced many aspects of system operations, but it has also led to unique antecedents to errors, errors that have led to incidents and accidents.

Two aircraft incidents, involving what today would be considered relatively simple automation, illustrate the type of operator errors that could result from the application of automation to complex systems. In each, the aircraft sustained substantial damage but the pilots were able to land safely. In 1979 a DC-10 experienced an aerodynamic stall and lost over 10,000 feet of altitude before the pilots recovered. They had inadvertently commanded a control mode through the airplane's autopilot that called for a constant speed climb, but during the climb they did not realize that the airspeed had decreased below the stall speed (NTSB, 1980b).

---

[5] The quote, taken from the film, was not in the Arthur C. Clarke novel upon which the film was based.

As discussed in Chapter 2, an aircraft experiencing an aerodynamic stall develops insufficient lift to maintain flight. Unless pilots respond quickly the aircraft will almost certainly crash. In this accident the pilots had engaged an automated flight mode that maintained the pilot selected climb rate. However, with no other changes in aircraft control, a climbing aircraft can only maintain a constant climb rate at the expense of its forward airspeed. At some point, the airspeed will be insufficient to develop lift and the airplane will stall.

The pilots had delegated airplane control to the autopilot, but did not effectively monitor the aircraft's performance thereafter. Instead, they relied on it to perform accurately and reliably, but did not notice that the airplane's airspeed had decreased below the required minimum. Despite three sources of data, presented visually, aurally, and tactually, informing them of their insufficient airspeed and the stall, none recognized that the airplane had experienced a stall.

Several years later a Boeing 747 lost power on an outboard engine while in cruise flight (NTSB, 1986). Should an engine on an aircraft with four engines fail, the two engines on the other wing would generate about twice the thrust as the remaining engine. Unless the pilots took corrective action, the airplane would swing or "yaw" to the side of the failed engine.

An engine failure is not a catastrophic event, so long as the pilots perform maneuvers that all pilots are trained to perform to maintain aircraft control. However, these pilots did not respond to the engine failure and did not perform the necessary actions to correct the yaw. The autopilot continued to counteract the yaw in order to maintain the selected flight path. However, after several minutes, it could no longer maintain the heading and it automatically disengaged from controlling the airplane. The airplane entered a steep dive and lost over 30,000 feet before it was recovered. The pilots neither recognized nor responded effectively to the situation until the airplane had reached the end of the dive.

In both instances, what today would be considered relatively primitive types of aircraft automation performed precisely as designed. The DC-10 pilots failed to monitor the actions of the automation mode that they had selected, and the Boeing 747 pilots did not disengage the automation and manually control the airplane when necessary. Neither of the two teams of pilots seemed to recognize that the automation, which had performed so reliably in the past, could also lead to catastrophe if not monitored.

Since then the application of automation to complex systems has increased, and more sophisticated types of automation applied, but operators have continued to make errors interacting with the automation.

For example, a highly automated aircraft that was introduced in the late 1980s and operated by different airlines, each with its own operating procedures, was involved in a number of fatal accidents due, at least in part, to operator errors in dealing with the automation. The relatively high number of accidents of this airplane type illustrates a phenomenon that seems to occur after technologically advanced systems have begun service, a lengthy initial period in which managers and regulators come to recognize how the new technology requires changes in the way operators deal with the system. Training programs and procedures are then modified in response to the effects of the technological advances. As Amalberti writes (1998),

> Any new technology calls for a period of adaptation to eliminate residual problems and to allow users to adapt to it. The major reason for this long adaptive process is the need for harmonization between the new design on one hand and the policies, procedures, and moreover the mentalities of the...system on the other hand. (p. 173)

To better understand how automation can affect operator performance, the nature of automation itself will be examined, and effects of automation on system operations reviewed.

Automation

Automation can mean many things to many people. Billings (1996) defines automation as the replacement of tasks that humans had previously performed by machines. Moray, Inagaki, and Itoh (2000) define automation as "any sensing, detection, information-processing, decision making, or control action that could be performed by humans but is actually performed by machine" (p. 44).

Automated systems can perform a wide range of both manual and cognitive tasks, ranging from minimal to complete system control. Indeed, when planning complex systems, designers decide on the level of automation to bring to the system. Parasuraman (2000), and Parasuraman, Sheridan, and Wickens (2000) describe up to ten levels of automated control that designers can incorporate into a system, from the absence of automation to complete automated system control. In the lowest level, the operator performs all tasks, and in the highest level the automation makes all decisions and takes all actions independent of, and without communicating with, the operator. The levels in between range from automated sensing and detection, to offering operators decision alternatives, to deciding for the operator, to the highest level, complete control. They recommend that designers consider the level of automation that is optimum for the operator tasks they wish to automate, and the effects of the automation level on the operator's ability to perform the requisite tasks.

Others argue that the severity and immediacy of error consequences should dictate the level of automation implemented. Moray, Inagaki, and Itoh (2000) believe that the optimal level of automation depends on such elements as the complexity of the system, the risk of a fault and the dynamics of an event. They suggest that an immediate response to a system fault is needed when an automated response will be superior to a human one. However, to avoid unnecessary and quite costly system shutdowns in situations that are not time critical, they suggest that operators, not the automation, retain ultimate control of the system.

Today, after extensive research into automation's effects on operator performance has been carried out and several automation-related events have occurred, many recognize that automation has led to many positive and negative effects on operator performance.

Automation advantages and disadvantages

Benefits

There is little question that automation has brought many beneficial changes to complex systems. Wiener and Curry (1980), and Wiener (1988), examining the effects of automation in the aviation environment, believe that these were believed to have resulted from a combination of technological, economic, and safety factors, not all of which have been realized.

They suggest that designers have argued that technological advances reduce the role of the human operator, thereby leading to a reduction in operator errors or reduced consequences from operator errors. Because automation can perform many cognitively demanding tasks faster and more accurately than could operators, designers have also believed that assigning cognitively demanding tasks to machines reduces operator workload, enabling operators to attend to "higher level" activities, such as system monitoring and troubleshooting. By reducing workload, automation can also raise the productivity of each operator, decreasing the number of operators needed and lowering operating costs.

Modern systems also offer flexibility to the design of both displays and controls. This enhances safety by displaying highly interpretable and accurate system-related information, benefiting situation awareness and increasing operators' abilities to recognize and respond effectively to system anomalies. Digital displays can integrate and present data with fewer gauges, and in a more interpretable manner than could be done with analog gauges, and controls can be designed to better match the needs of operators than in older, non-automated systems.

Shortcomings

Automation has also brought about shortcomings that, on occasion, have adversely affected operator performance and increased opportunities for error. These derive from several factors.

User interface Some automation applications have altered sources of data that operators had depended upon for system performance feedback, thereby reducing operator's awareness of the system state (e.g., Norman, 1991; Billings, 1997). Feedback alteration is evident in several highly automated aircraft types. Two interconnected pilot control columns that pilots had used to control the flight path also enabled each to observe the other's control column movements through corresponding movement in their own controls. These have been replaced by control sticks with no corresponding movement. Moving one does not move the other. Pilots using these controls cannot rely on tactile and visual feedback from control column movement to recognize the other pilot's inputs as they could on older models. Rather, they must focus on flight displays and interpret the data to recognize the results of changes to aircraft controls.

Similarly, in older aircraft pilots move throttles or control levers forward or back to increase or decrease engine thrust. On aircraft equipped with autothrottles, engine thrust is automatically maintained, varying in response to pilot selected performance parameters, environmental conditions, design limitations, and operating phase. On most autothrottle-equipped aircraft, pilots have two sources of information to inform them of autothrottle commanded changes in engine thrust: forward and aft throttle movement and engine-related data displays. However, on some advanced aircraft stationary throttles have replaced moving throttles, thus eliminating visual and tactile cues of throttle movement that pilots had relied upon to detect engine thrust changes. This has reduced the available sources of information on engine thrust changes to one source, visually-presented information from engine displays. Worse, with changes to both controls pilots have been forced to rely on their foveal or central vision to learn of changes, rather than their peripheral vision. Because peripheral vision is more sensitive to changes in movement than central vision, control changes have become even less detectable than they had been before.

Automation has also changed the design of system controls by making extensive use of computer keyboards or similar controls, rather than the larger and more defined controls that are often found in older systems. In routine situations in which operator workload is predictable, controlling the system through keyboard entries will likely not affect operator performance. However, in non-routine situations, when operator workload is likely to be high, interacting with the automated controls can be cognitively demanding, increasing operator workload further, in the most inopportune circumstances.

For example, in automated cockpits the operators, the pilots, can program a complete flight path through a small keyboard, potentially reducing pilot workload because further control inputs would not necessarily be needed during the flight so long as the programmed flight path does not change. However, should the flight path be changed, pilots will have to execute numerous keystrokes. Operators must then attend to the keyboard and the keystrokes, steps that can increase workload substantially over the steps that would be required in non-automated cockpits. Further, these actions are often performed at points in the operating cycle, departing or approaching the airport environment, when pilot workload is already high, and they are least able to accommodate workload increases.

Opacity Few operators are aware of the design or logic of the software and the databases that guide the automation of the systems they operate. As many software users do, rather than understanding a program's underlying design, operators strive to become sufficiently familiar with its application, either through formal training, experience, or both, to operate it as needed. In most circumstances, this lack of understanding automation logic, what Woods, Johannesen, Cook, and Sarter (1994), describe as the "opaque" nature of automation, will not adversely affect operator performance. However, in the event of a system anomaly, operators' unawareness of the reasons for the actions of the automation, or the inability to predict its next actions degrades their ability to diagnose and respond. As Billings (1997) notes, "regardless of the cause, the net effect [of this] is diminished awareness of the situation, a serious problem in a dynamic environment" (p. 188).

Further, automation opacity makes operators reluctant to intervene should they become uncertain of the automation outcomes to expect. Sarter and Woods (2000) found that when pilots were faced with unexpected automation actions, they hesitated to become more involved in the system's operation. Instead, most persisted in attempting to understand the nature of the error, even to the point of not monitoring the airplane's operation and allowing it to enter potentially dangerous conditions.

Moreover, in some systems the automation is sufficiently independent that it can engage one of multiple operating modes of a single control without operator input or guidance. Each operating mode offers capabilities specific to the needs of the various operating phases, but the system may not effectively inform operators of the identity of the mode that is engaged. Several researchers have found that operators were often unaware of the system's operating mode, a potentially critical element of situation awareness (e.g., Degani, Shafto, and Kirlik, 1999; Sarter & Woods, 1995, 1997, 2000).

Sarter and Woods (1997) characterize mode changes and related phenomena that operators do not expect as "automation surprises," which,

> Begin with misassessments and miscommunications between the automation and the operator(s), which lead to a gap between the operator's understanding of what the automated systems are set up to do and how the automated systems are or will be handling the underlying process(es). (p. 554)

They suggest that automation surprises are based on poor operator mental models of automation, as well as low system observability and highly dynamic or nonroutine situations. By itself the loss of mode awareness can create opportunities for error. However, in combination with automation opacity, loss of mode awareness can considerably reduce operator situation awareness and enhance opportunities for error.

The effects of several of these automation effects are evident in the December 1995 accident involving a Boeing 757 that crashed near Cali, Colombia (Aeronautica Civil, 1996). The crew was using the airplane's automated flight management system to control the flight. The captain misinterpreted an air traffic controller's clearance to Cali and reprogrammed the aircraft automation to fly directly to the Cali radio navigation beacon rather than to waypoints located short of the field, as the approach procedure had required. When told to report passing over a waypoint in between, both pilots were unaware that they had inadvertently deleted the critical waypoint and all intermediate waypoints from the automated flight path control by establishing the direct course to the Cali beacon.

After repeated, unsuccessful attempts to locate the critical waypoint through the automation, they decided to fly to a waypoint just short of the field, again by reprogramming the automation to fly the new flight path. However, they were unfamiliar with the designation of navigation data stored in the airplane's navigation database, and inadvertently established a course away from Cali. After the crew had recognized their error and they turned back to Cali, the airplane struck a mountain.

Monitoring, vigilance and situation awareness Automation has helped to distance the operator from many system-related cues. Norman (1981, 1988) believes that in automated systems operators may no longer directly observe the system, hear its sounds, or feel its movement. Instead they monitor the data that automated sensors detect and display; which may or may not effectively convey the needed information. This diminished their mode awareness and decreased their ability to respond effectively to unexpected system states.

Further, monitoring displays over extended periods is fatiguing. Operators lose the ability to accurately detect and respond to system anomalies after prolonged periods of monitoring (e.g., Wiener and Curry, 1980; Molloy and Parasuraman, 1996; Parasuraman, Mouloua, Molloy, and Hillburn, 1996).

Researchers have obtained considerable evidence demonstrating that increasing automation and decreasing operator involvement in system control reduces operator ability to maintain awareness of the system and its operating states. Endsley and Kaber (1999) found that among various levels of automation, people perform best when actively involved in system operation. Endsley and Kiris (1995) term the reduced operator involvement in system control in highly automated systems the "out-of-the-loop performance problem." They attribute reduced operator ability to recognize system anomalies in automated systems to three factors, 1) reduced vigilance and increased complacency from monitoring instead of active system control, 2) passive receipt of information rather than active information acquisition, and 3) loss or modification of feedback concerning system state.

The findings of the investigation of a 1997 accident involving a highly automated turboprop aircraft, an Embraer Brasilia, support these conclusions (NTSB, 1998c). The pilots did not recognize that the wings of their aircraft had become contaminated by ice, degrading their aerodynamic characteristics. The autopilot, a sophisticated flight management system, attempted to maintain the selected flight path of the increasingly unstable aircraft.

Because the pilots were not directly controlling the airplane they had no tactile feedback from the movement of the control column. Only two sources of visual information were available to inform them of the airplane's increasing loss of lift, an airplane attitude display and the autopilot-induced control column movements, which corresponded to what would have been pilot-induced control column movements. The pilots did not perceive these cues and so did not recognize that the airplane was about to stall.

The autopilot reached the limit of its control ability and disengaged. The airplane quickly went into a turn and then dive, but the pilots were unable to regain aircraft control. Had they been controlling the airplane manually, the tactile cues of the control column forces would have been far more perceptible than were the visual cues of the displays, enabling them to recognize that the airplane was approaching a stall. With that information they would have likely responded in sufficient time to avoid the accident.

Workload redistribution Automation has generally reduced operator workload; but it has often done so during already low-workload operating phases, and it has increased it during already high-workload phases. Wiener (1989) has described this redistribution of workload as "clumsy automation" (also Woods, 1996; Kantowitz and Campbell, 1996), a phenomenon that increases rather than decreases opportunities for operator errors.

Yet even simply reducing workload can also degrade operator performance, if this occurs during already low workload periods. Excessively reduced workload over extended periods can increase boredom and increase operator difficulty in maintaining vigilance (O'Hanlon, 1981). As noted in Chapter 7, operator alertness decreases over extended periods of relative inactivity, increasing the subsequent effort needed to detect system anomalies.

Trust, bias, and skill degradation Automation performs so well that operators' interactions with the automation change. As system automation increases, the number of tasks that are performed more accurately and reliably than could operators, grows. This has increased operator trust in the automation's ability to perform those tasks. Yet, as this trust grows, their confidence in their own abilities to perform the same tasks manually may decrease (e.g., Lee and Moray, 1992).

Researchers have explored the relationship between automation and operator trust. Parasuraman and Riley (1997) found that, over time, as operator trust in the automation grows, they increasingly delegate responsibility for system monitoring to the automation. At the same time, their vigilance and ability to recognize system faults may decrease because their expectation of, and preparedness for, system faults decreases with their growing trust in the automation.

Moray, Inagaki, and Itoh (2000) note that operator trust in a system depends primarily on system reliability. Below about 90 percent reliability, trust falls off considerably. By contrast, operators' self-confidence in their own ability to operate the system depends not on the system but on their experiences with the system. Paradoxically, the high reliability and accuracy of automation make it more, rather than less, likely that operators will fail to effectively monitor automated systems as they come to rely on it more and more, and on themselves less and less.

Mosier and Skitka (1996) term the excessive trust and reliance on automation "automation bias." They suggest that it can lead operators to overlook problems that the automation fails to detect, or unquestioningly follow the guidance that automation offers, even when the guidance is inappropriate. Operators can over-rely on the automation in highly automated systems, much as team members can over-rely on other multi-operator team members.

Bainbridge (1987) and Billings (1997) point out that reliance on automation for monitoring and decision making can erode operator skills, increasing the likelihood of error in the event of a system fault. Bainbridge terms this an "irony of automation" because,

> When manual takeover [of a system] is needed there is likely to be something wrong with the process, so that unusual actions will be needed to control it, and one can argue that the operator needs to be more rather than less skilled, and less rather than more [task] loaded, than average. (p. 272)

An accident that occurred in Columbus, Ohio, in 1994, in which a Jetstream J-41, a highly automated turboprop airplane, crashed just short of the runway, illustrates how insufficient operator self confidence and excessive trust in automation can lead to critical errors (NTSB, 1994e). At the time of the accident, the weather was poor and visibility substantially reduced, conditions that are often quite demanding, thus increasing pilot workload. Each pilot had reason to lack confidence in his own operating skills. The first officer, with little experience operating highly automated aircraft, had only recently been hired. The captain, though experienced in the aircraft, had demonstrated deficiencies in several failed check or examination flights.

The captain had programmed the airplane's flight management computer (FMC) and engaged it to fly the precise flight path to an approach and landing. However, although the FMC could accurately fly a preprogrammed three-dimensional flight path, it exercises more limited airplane control than does comparable automation of other aircraft. On this airplane, the pilots and not the automation monitor and control the aircraft's airspeed.

The captain had delegated flight path control to the automation, but then failed to effectively monitor the airspeed. The airplane flew precisely along the flight path, until its airspeed decayed and it experienced an aerodynamic stall. The pilots were unable to recover the airplane. The captain's history of piloting deficiencies contributed to his reliance on the automation. With apparently greater confidence in the airplane's automation than in his own abilities, he delegated flight path control to the flight management computers. Although this was not in itself an error, the evidence suggests that he then monitored only a portion of the airplane flight path rather than the airspeed, an essential element of the flight path, and this failure led to the accident.

The captain's actions on this flight are consistent with Riley's (1996) observations that the reliability of automation itself influences an operator's decision on task assignment. As he observed,

> If the operator had more confidence in his or her own ability to do that task than trust in the automation, the operator was likely to do the task manually, whereas if the operator's trust in the automation was higher than the operator's self-confidence, the operator was likely to rely on the automation. (p. 20)

Team performance Researchers have suggested that automation can be considered to be a member of a multi-operator team, altering the role of the team members. Scerbo (1996) suggests that an automated subsystem can coordinate activities, be guided by a coach, perform functions without causing harm, provide necessary information when needed, and otherwise perform the types of tasks that human operators typically perform. Paris, Salas, and Cannon-Bowers (2000) contend that automation can replace all or part of team functions, leading to restructured teams and redefined team member roles. As Woods (1996) notes, "introducing automated and intelligent agents into a larger system in effect changes the team composition. It changes how human supervisors coordinate their activities with those of the machine agents" (p. 4).

Automation-related errors

New technology can engender changes in complex systems that, using Reason's (1990, 1997) terms, lead to latent errors or latent conditions that, in turn, create antecedents to operator errors. Although automation is still evolving, and both operators and companies learn to adapt to automation effects, certain commonalities in automation-related errors have emerged. Operators committing automation-related errors often fail to effectively monitor the systems, or to understand the effects of their actions or those of the automation.

These types of errors were seen in several previously described accidents. In the 1972 accident discussed in Chapter 7, involving the Lockheed L-1011 that crashed in the Everglades, the pilots engaged the automation to maintain a flight path at a prescribed altitude (NTSB, 1973). Several minutes later they inadvertently disengaged the altitude hold feature and the airplane began to descend, but they were unaware of this. After delegating flight path control to the automation, they attended to a system anomaly and no longer monitored the flight path. They did not realize that the automation had ceased maintaining the selected altitude.

Similarly, in a 1992 accident involving an Airbus A-320 that crashed while on approach to Strasbourg, France, (Commission of Investigation, 1994), the pilots established a 3,300-foot per minute descent rate, several times faster than a standard descent rate. However, the evidence suggests that they had actually intended to establish a 3.3^0 descent angle; a flight path angle that would have corresponded to the actual descent path called for in the approach, unlike the one the aircraft actually flew. As with the L-1011 accident, after programming the flight path, the crew failed to monitor a critical aspect of the aircraft's performance, the increasingly rapid descent rate. Although they had established the descent rate through their actions, they did not recognize it and did not attempt to reduce it before the accident.

Case study

On June 10, 1995, the cruise ship Royal Majesty, en route from Bermuda to Boston, Massachusetts, grounded off the United States coast, causing over $7 million in damages to the vessel (NTSB, 1997e).

The navigation system

Early in the voyage a navigator tested the ship's navigational equipment, a system that included a GPS (global positioning satellite) antenna and receiver, and assured that the ship was following the correct course. The GPS system receives signals from a series of satellites and uses them to derive highly accurate position information.

The vessel was also equipped with an integrated bridge system that combined GPS data with other navigation information to steer the vessel along a preprogrammed course, while compensating for wind, current and sea state. The integrated bridge system displayed the ship's derived position on a video screen in grid coordinates. The operators were confident that the displayed, GPS-derived position was accurate.

The system was designed to automatically default to dead reckoning navigation, a method that did not compensate for wind, current, and sea state, when GPS satellite signals became unavailable. Because it lacked the accuracy of the GPS, dead reckoning required much crew attention to ensure that the ship was maintaining the desired course, unlike GPS-based navigation. In the event that the system defaulted to dead reckoning, the integrated bridge system would emit a series of aural chirps for one second. It would also display on the video screen "DR" for dead reckoning, and "SOL" for solution. The font sizes used for DR and SOL were considerably smaller than those used for the position coordinates.

The crewmembers who used the integrated bridge system, the master, the chief officer, the second officer, and the navigator, had not used this type of system before their assignment to the Royal Majesty, and the cruise line had not formally trained them in its use. The ship's officers learned to operate the system by reading the relevant manuals and receiving on-the-job training from an officer experienced in the system.

The accident

The sequence of occurrences that led to the accident began after the ship departed Bermuda, when the cable between the GPS antenna and the receiver separated. As a result, the integrated bridge system could not receive GPS signals and it defaulted to dead reckoning navigation, as designed. It then continued to navigate and steer the vessel in this mode, but its course began to deviate from the intended one, until the vessel grounded 17 miles off course.

Investigators identified several errors that the watch officers, responsible for monitoring the vessel and its course, had committed. The officers did not understand the "DR" and "SOL" messages that the system displayed, and had not attempted to learn their meaning. Therefore, they did not recognize that the system had ceased to receive GPS data for navigation and course control, and were unaware that it had defaulted to the less accurate dead reckoning method. Although they had regularly checked the bridge system's display to confirm that the vessel was following the programmed course, they did not verify that the course that was displayed corresponded to the programmed one.

If the system had been navigating by GPS, the programmed and the actual course would have matched. However, because of the limitations of dead reckoning, without crew intervention the courses were much less likely to match when the system used that navigation method, and the vessel increasingly deviated from its intended course.

Investigators determined that several aspects of the crew's use of the automation led to their errors, and that the automation had fundamentally affected the crewmember roles. As they conclude (NTSB, 1997e),

> Bridge automation has also changed the role of the watch officer on the ship. The watch officer, who previously was active in obtaining information about the environment and used this information for controlling the ship, is now "out of the control loop." The watch officer is relegated to passively monitoring the status and performance of the automated systems. As a result...the crewmembers of the Royal Majesty missed numerous opportunities to recognize that the GPS was transmitting in DR mode and that the ship had deviated from its intended track.

> [Further,] the watch officers on the Royal Majesty may have believed that because the GPS had demonstrated sufficient reliability for 3½ years, the traditional practice of using at least two independent sources of position information was not necessary.

> Notwithstanding the merits of advanced systems for high-technology navigation, the Safety Board does not consider the automation of a bridge navigation system as the exclusive means of navigating a ship, nor does the Board believe that electronic displays should replace visually verifiable

navigation aids and landmarks. *The human operator must have the primary responsibility for the navigation*; he must oversee the automation and exercise his informed judgment about when to intervene manually. (Emphasis added, pp. 34 & 35)

Summary

Automation, the replacement of tasks by automated system components that operators had previously performed themselves, has both enhanced and degraded system safety. Many aspects of automation have affected the role of the operator, and some have created antecedents to error. Automation's high reliability and accuracy can lead operators to excessively rely on it, degrading their vigilance and system monitoring skills. As operators repeatedly experience the beneficial aspects of automation, they may delegate tasks to it without proper monitoring to ensure that the system performs as directed.

Some operators have demonstrated greater trust in the abilities of the automation to control the system than in their own abilities. This may lead to their unquestioning acceptance of automation guidance, or to overlook problems that the automation has failed to detect.

Documenting automation-related errors

- Evaluate automated system displays and controls in accordance with criteria listed in Chapter 3.
- Describe the specific functions the automated system, its capabilities in system monitoring and control, and the nature of its presentation of system-related data.
- Document the tasks the automation performs, its information sources, the results of its information processing, and the level of operator input and control over these tasks.
- Record operator actions and decisions involving automation, and the type of automation-related error committed.
- Determine the tasks that the operators delegated to the automation, and the extent to which the operators monitored critical system parameters.
- Examine the company's training and procedures in automation use, and interview and observe operators, if possible, to learn the practices that they employed with regard to automation-related interactions.

Part V
Applying the Data

15 Case Study

Introduction

Many aspects of errors have been examined and numerous accidents cited. One accident will illustrate several additional points, describe challenges that investigators could face, and demonstrate the data gathering and analysis processes used to identify critical errors and the antecedents that led to the errors, and recommendations to remediate system deficiencies.

The accident

The accident, which occurred in May 1996, was introduced in Chapter 1 (NTSB, 1997a). Investigators were told that a DC-9 had crashed in the Florida Everglades a large, swamp-like area of fresh water in the southern part of Florida, 17 minutes after the accident. Air traffic controllers had been informed of the aircraft's plight when the pilots reported "smoke in the cockpit." Within minutes, after the airplane had disappeared from radar, controllers alerted investigative authorities. In addition, eyewitnesses in the area had informed law enforcement officials of the accident as well. The NTSB assembled a team of investigators to dispatch to Miami, about one-hour's drive from the accident site. In addition to other specialists, the team included a human performance investigator, an operations investigator, and maintenance specialists.

When investigators arrived on scene, they were unable to see the wreckage; none of it was visible because the water and silt of the Everglades covered it. Dressed in full protective gear to prevent contamination by jet fuel, human remains, poisonous snakes, and other hazards, they located the wreckage shortly after arriving on scene, by covering the area on foot and poking sticks into the silt to detect solid objects. Within a few days they located the cockpit voice and flight data recorders. Cockpit voice recorder data showed that a fire had erupted in the cabin and quickly spread.

Airplane loading documents indicated that prohibited items, listed as "Oxy Cannisters (sic)-'Empty,'" canisters of chemical oxygen generators, had been loaded into the cargo compartment in Miami. Investigators suspected that the fire and the canister shipment were related.

Courtesy National Transportation Safety Board

Figure 15.1 The accident site in the Florida Everglades

This evidence helped focus the investigation onto the errors that operators, primarily maintenance personnel, committed in loading prohibited, and potentially flammable items, onto the airplane. Although the errors would not be officially identified until later, this information helped to guide the fact gathering process and the search for the critical errors.

The errors

Several days after the accident, investigators obtained physical evidence from the wreckage site, components from the forward part of the airplane fuselage. The components demonstrated that the airplane had been substantially burned. Investigators determined that the canisters of oxygen caused the fire. They supplied the heat necessary to ignite the fire in the airtight cargo hold into which they had been placed, and the oxygen needed to sustain it with sufficient intensity to penetrate the compartment's fire resistant lining and enter the cabin.

Written documentation associated with the cargo, particularly the shipping documents describing empty chemical oxygen generators, and physical evidence of the burned generators, led investigators to focus on activities at SabreTech, the maintenance facility contracted by the airline, ValuJet, to overhaul several of its aircraft, to learn how the canisters had been loaded onto the airplane. After examining maintenance records at SabreTech and interviewing its personnel, investigators identified several errors.

Courtesy National Transportation Safety Board

Figure 15. 2 Burned oxygen generator retrieved from the wreckage site, adjacent to unburned, unexpended canister

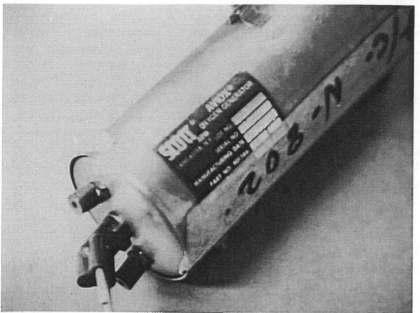

Courtesy National Transportation Safety Board

Figure 15. 3 Unexpended, unburned chemical oxygen generator

In March 1996, two months before the accident, SabreTech technicians removed the canisters from two airplanes that the airline had acquired, because the canisters were either approaching or had passed their expiration dates. At that point, the canisters were to have been disabled and disposed of.

Investigators also examined the role of two additional organizations in the accident, the airline and the regulator. They focused on the airline, ValuJet, to determine its role in the maintenance errors, and on the regulator, the FAA, to determine the extent to which it was, or should have been, aware of the quality of maintenance that SabreTech performed for ValuJet.

Placing the errors that permitted the canisters to be loaded onto the airplane in chronological order, from first to last, closest to the accident in descending order to furthest from the accident–

- Permitting the mislabeled boxes to be placed onto the aircraft.
- Labeling the boxes as "COMAT" or company material
- Signing the maintenance work cards indicating that the canisters had been disposed of, disabled, or expended when they had not been
- Placing green "repairable tags" on the canisters, instead of red tags that SabreTech required for components that were to be discarded
- Storing the canisters loosely in cardboard boxes rather than in protected containers
- Failing to properly dispose of, disable, or expend the canisters.

Because technicians at SabreTech committed most of these errors, SabreTech and its operations will be examined first.

The maintenance facility

At the time SabreTech personnel removed the chemical oxygen generators from the two ValuJet aircraft, the company had been facing substantial pressure to complete its work on the aircraft. Its contract with the ValuJet required it to credit the airline $2500 per aircraft, for each day's delay returning the aircraft to the airline, past the agreed upon deadlines. SabreTech had been encountering delays in completing the maintenance on the two aircraft.

Investigators found that SabreTech personnel had intensely focused on returning the aircraft to the airline as quickly as possible. To expedite the remaining maintenance, SabreTech canceled vacations of its maintenance technicians and required them to work seven days a week, 12 hours a day, until its work on the airplanes was complete.[6]

SabreTech directly employed less than half of the maintenance technicians who had worked on the ValuJet contract. It obtained the services of technicians from six contractors, as needed. Investigators estimated that 57 percent of the technicians who worked on the ValuJet aircraft were contractor personnel, not SabreTech employees, at the time the oxygen canisters had been removed from the two airplanes.

SabreTech, like most maintenance facilities, used work cards that delineated the steps to be taken to perform maintenance tasks. Each of the

---

[6] One airplane was delivered one day beyond the deadline and the other, 13 days beyond.

work cards had unique numbers associated with them and the particular actions required. The steps associated with removing and disposing of the generators were enumerated on the work card designated number 0069.

The procedures on work card 0069 called for either disabling the canisters with locking caps, or expending their contents by initiating the oxygen generation process. However, the facility did not have the necessary locking mechanisms available and therefore, technicians were unable to disable the canisters. The evidence suggests that SabreTech personnel did not recognize that the locking caps would be needed until they were about to perform the procedures on work card 0069.

Mechanics gave investigators conflicting information about the locking caps. One reported that his supervisor had told him that the caps were not available. Another indicated that he and others had discussed placing caps from the new generators onto the expired generators, but they did not actually do this. One supervisor indicated that no one had discussed the need for the caps with him.

Rather than locking or expending them, maintenance technicians improvised several techniques. One tied the strings that helped initiate the oxygen generation process around the canisters to prevent them from inadvertently actuating. Another cut the strings and placed the canisters into the packing containers that had housed the new generators.

SabreTech records showed that 72 maintenance technicians had worked 910 hours to remove the canisters from the two aircraft. They obtained 144 canisters in all, placing them in five cardboard boxes. After the accident only six of the canisters were found in SabreTech's facility. Investigators believed that the rest had been loaded onto the accident aircraft.

SabreTech procedures called for attaching colored tags to components, according to their value and the subsequent actions that needed to be performed. Green tags signified components that needed further repairs or testing, white tags, components that were to be reinstalled, and red tags, condemned or rejected components.

Nevertheless, all but one of the technicians at SabreTech who had worked on the canisters applied green colored tags to the removed canisters, not red tags, as their procedures had required. One mechanic reported that he had applied first green tags and then white tags to the components after the facility had run out of green tags. Maintenance personnel wrote, on the "reason for removal" section of the tag, that the oxygen generators had expired or were out of date.

When technicians completed the steps on work card 0069, they were to include certain information to verify that the steps had been performed. They were to sign their names in a block on the card, write their employee numbers and the date that the steps had been completed. Mechanics who signed work cards 0069, indicating that the canisters had been disposed of or disabled, gave investigators conflicting accounts of their actions. One interpreted his supervisor's instruction to "go out there and sell this job" to mean that he was to sign the card without attending to the subsequent required actions to complete the work on the canisters. Another knew that the canisters had neither been expended nor disabled and discussed this with his supervisor. He signed the card after being told that technicians in the shipping, receiving, and storage department would discard the canisters. Of the four mechanics that had signed work card 0069, all but one reported to investigators of having been unaware of the need for locking caps.

Several days later, one of the maintenance technicians placed three of the five boxes of canisters in SabreTech's shipping, receiving, and storage department, near shelves that contained ValuJet components. Investigators were not able to determine how the other two boxes had arrived at that location. Clerks in the storage section put the boxes in a hold area that contained the other two boxes of canisters and other ValuJet material. The company did not have procedures in place to inform shipping, receiving, and storage personnel when they were being given hazardous material. The technician who had brought the three boxes to the department did not inform its personnel of the nature of the boxes' contents.

Several weeks later, a potential customer was scheduled to inspect the SabreTech's facility. The supervisor of the shipping, receiving, and storage department directed personnel to clean the hold area, because another customer had earlier found the area to be dirty. The supervisor told a stock clerk that he expected a ValuJet representative to decide how to dispose of its components.

The stock clerk suggested to the supervisor that he prepare the boxes containing the canisters for return to the airline, and the supervisor agreed. The clerk then redistributed the canisters, placed them on their sides, end to end along the length of the box, and wrapped each one with plastic bubble wrap–a potent source of fuel when burned. He attached a blank ValuJet "COMAT" (company material) label to the boxes and wrote "aircraft parts" on each. The COMAT label informs cargo handlers and airline personnel that the contents are company documents or material to be returned to the airline.

On May 9, the shipping and receiving clerk asked another clerk to prepare a shipping ticket for the five boxes of canisters. The first clerk gave the other clerk a shipping ticket and asked him to write "Oxygen Canisters-Empty" on it. The receiving clerk complied, (shortening one of the words) and added the date, May 10, 1996. The clerk then asked a driver to take the boxes to the ramp but the driver was unable to do so. He asked again the next day and this time the driver complied.

The driver brought the five boxes of canisters, three tires and their wheels, all labeled COMAT, to flight 592. The airline's ramp agent and flight 592's first officer reviewed the shipping ticket that accompanied the material. Neither objected to loading the material onto the airplane. Ramp personnel placed the boxes in the cargo bin with passenger luggage.

The antecedents

Operators

Investigators focused on the actions of maintenance technicians and those of shipping and receiving personnel, who committed the bulk of the errors that led to the accident, to identify potential error antecedents. They examined the activities of those who had removed the oxygen generators from the two aircraft, signed the two work cards, put the labels on the canisters and boxes containing the canisters, and prepared the boxes for shipping. They also assessed the first officer's actions in approving the boxes of oxygen generators for loading onto the airplane.

Investigators did not identify behavioral or physiological antecedents among the technicians or shipping and receiving personnel. However, investigators found a common element among the actions of many of the maintenance personnel—they either were unaware of or misunderstood the consequences of mishandling chemical oxygen generators. As will be discussed shortly, this deficiency was attributed not to the operators but to their superiors.

Equipment

Investigators reviewed the maintenance activities pertaining to the oxygen canisters' removal, storage, and preparation for shipping. They examined the tools and the work cards that the operators used, but did not identify flaws in the tool designs, card layouts, or operating environment. They did find fault with information contained on work card number 0069, pertaining to oxygen generator removal. As the regulator required, the airplane manufacturer, McDonnell-Douglas,[7] had developed procedures for removing the oxygen generators, and incorporated them in the aircraft's master maintenance manual. ValuJet had adopted the manufacturer's procedures, obtained FAA approval for its maintenance program, and then gave the procedures to SabreTech to follow when performing maintenance on ValuJet aircraft. By regulation, SabreTech was to adhere to those procedures, on the airline's behalf, when maintaining its aircraft.

The steps of the airline and the manufacturer were almost identical with regards to the canister removal, except that the airline listed seven steps for the task, one less than the manufacturer had listed. The additional manufacturer's step called for technicians to: "Store or dispose of oxygen generator (Ref. paragraph 2.C. or 2.D.)." Paragraph 2.C. required the installation of locking caps on the canisters. After the caps had been installed, the canisters were to be stored in a safe environment, protected from exposure to heat or other potential hazards. Paragraph 2.D. included a full description of the method of expending the generators. Both the airline and the manufacturer's procedures warned that the canisters would generate intense heat when expended. However, the airline's work card did not state that unexpended generators needed special care and that out of date generators needed to be expended or discarded.

Investigators also compared ValuJet's procedures for removing the canisters to another airline's procedures for maintaining the same aircraft. Unlike ValuJet, the other airline required its maintenance personnel to expend the generators, label the expended canisters as hazardous waste, retain them at the location at which they were removed, and then immediately notify its environmental affairs manager of the presence of the canisters.

Investigators cited the airline for omitting substantive information on chemical oxygen generator disposal; an omission they believed influenced the errors of the maintenance personnel. They note,

> Although work card 0069 warned about the high temperatures produced by an activated generator, it did not mention that unexpended generators required special handling for storage or disposal, that out-of-date generators should be expended and then disposed of, or that the generators contained hazardous substances/waste even after being expended; further the work card was not required to contain such information. Thus, the mechanics who

---

[7] The Boeing Corporation has since acquired McDonnell-Douglas Corporation.

removed the oxygen generators from the MD-80s were not made fully aware, by reading only work card 0069, of the hazardous nature of the generators or of the existence of an approved, uncomplicated procedure for expending the generators that required no unusual equipment. (NTSB, 1997a; pp. 113 & 114)

Investigators identified the lack of information about the canister removal on the work card as a deficiency that led to the failure to lock or expend the generators. However, identifying this antecedent does not sufficiently explain why the maintenance personnel committed the errors, because several errors were involved, such as using incorrectly colored tags and mislabeling the canisters. Although deficiencies in the work cards can be considered to be antecedents to errors, other errors were involved as well.

Multi-operator teams

Multi-operator teams perform most major maintenance tasks because the operators who begin the tasks may not necessarily be the ones that complete them, and because many of the tasks require several operators to perform them. These tasks are susceptible to multi-operator team errors if technicians ineffectively communicate to their colleagues critical information about the tasks to be performed, the components associated with those tasks, and related information.

Investigators believed that maintenance technicians at SabreTech ineffectively communicated the hazards associated with unexpended oxygen generators to their colleagues. Because of its role in developing, implementing, and overseeing communications among team members, investigators considered SabreTech responsible for the antecedents to this communication error. SabreTech had not developed or implemented procedures requiring maintenance personnel to brief those on incoming or outgoing shifts about hazardous materials, or to track the progress of specific tasks performed during each shift. Consequently, although some technicians who had removed the canisters of oxygen generators from the two aircraft were aware of the hazards of the unexpended oxygen generators, others were not. Some attempted to disable the canisters and others did not. None of the personnel in shipping and receiving was aware of these hazards and as a result, they improperly stored the material and prepared it to be loaded onto a passenger carrying aircraft.

The company

Investigators identified three organizations whose policies and practices either caused or contributed to the accident. One was SabreTech, whose personnel committed the errors that led to loading the chemical oxygen generators aboard the accident flight. The second was ValuJet, the company that had contracted with SabreTech to perform its maintenance, and was responsible for ensuring that SabreTech performed the maintenance properly. The third was the FAA, the regulator that approved the maintenance procedures, and was required to ensure that both ValuJet and SabreTech complied with them.

The maintenance facility Investigators identified numerous deficiencies in SabreTech's maintenance that served as antecedents to the errors that caused the accident. These included–

- Inattention to required procedures
- Ineffective communications among maintenance personnel
- Inadequate training
- Inadequate planning for and stocking of needed components.

These deficiencies led to the errors in disposing of the canisters. If SabreTech's procedures, communication, training, and parts acquisition had been effective, the maintenance technicians would have been aware of the need to properly disable or discard the oxygen generators, the needed parts would have been available, and the accident would not have occurred.

The evidence indicated that many SabreTech maintenance personnel paid little attention to, and were likely unaware of the potential hazards associated with unexpended, uncapped, chemical oxygen generators. Many antecedents could account for this. Given the pressure placed on supervisors and maintenance personnel to complete the work on the two aircraft to be delivered to the airline, statements of several supervisors and technicians suggest that maintenance activities at SabreTech were geared to completing the remaining work on the aircraft, not to handling components removed from those aircraft. Close attention to canister disposal would not have hastened completing the maintenance on the two aircraft, but it would have reduced the likelihood that technicians would commit the errors that led to the accident.

SabreTech's inattention to procedures was also evident in the tags that technicians attached to the canisters. After removing the canisters from the two aircraft, several of the boxes containing the canisters were placed in SabreTech's shipping and receiving department at night, when no one from that department was present. The only information available to shipping and receiving personnel about the contents of the boxes was conveyed by colors of the tags attached to some of the canisters. The tag colors conveyed the wrong information–that they were to be reused. When shipping and receiving personnel reported for work the next morning, they saw the tags and believed that the canisters were to be retained. Had technicians attached the correctly colored tags, the arriving personnel would have realized that the canisters had no value and therefore, would not have had a reason to return them to the airline, and the accident would likely have been avoided.

Because misinterpreting or misunderstanding instructions is an antecedent to error, the need for enhanced communications is clear. Investigators cited this deficiency and concluded that its absence led to technicians improperly signing the step on work card 0069, indicating that the oxygen canisters had been replaced and disposed of properly, without verifying that the necessary steps had been carried out.

Investigators also cited SabreTech for its failure to implement procedures requiring maintenance personnel to explicitly inform shipping and receiving personnel of the contents of components they conveyed to them, and for not employing a system to track hazardous materials. Had these procedures been in place, technicians would have likely learned the true nature of the contents of the boxes instead of relying on the tag colors for the information, and would have been unlikely to load the unexpended generators onto the airplane.

Investigators cited deficiencies in SabreTech's maintenance technician training in canister disposal. The company provided two hours of instruction in ValuJet policies and procedures to its own personnel, with some receiving an additional two hours of instruction on the airline's inspection procedures, and others an additional 40 hours on MD-80 familiarization and 40 hours on DC-9 and MD-80 differences. SabreTech also provided an undetermined number of its personnel training in hazardous material handling. However, SabreTech contractor personnel, who comprised the majority of the technicians working on the canisters, received no SabreTech training. SabreTech required temporary personnel to have appropriate licenses and experience, but did not train them. Without this training the temporary personnel were likely unaware of how SabreTech or ValuJet wanted the procedures to be applied, or other more subtle aspects of SabreTech's application of ValuJet's maintenance procedures.

Investigators also criticized SabreTech for not stocking the locking caps required to disable the unexpended oxygen generators. SabreTech's contract with ValuJet called for the airline to purchase "peculiar expendables," parts not regularly needed for maintenance of the airline's aircraft, but neither SabreTech nor ValuJet anticipated the need for locking caps. The parts were unavailable when the oxygen generators had been removed from the two aircraft.

The totality of evidence indicates that neither SabreTech supervisors nor its maintenance personnel understood the full implications of improperly disposing of or expending chemical oxygen generators. This failure may have resulted from the influence of the antecedents cited on the technicians' performance, or of other, unidentified antecedents, acting alone or in combination with each other. Regardless, their lack of understanding led SabreTech supervisors to fail to properly oversee the work of the technicians. In this way the company helped to create the antecedents that led to the errors of its maintenance personnel.

Although the number of errors and antecedents to those errors precludes establishing a one to one relationship between each antecedent and each error, one can identify errors that SabreTech technicians committed and the antecedents that preceded them, and relate one to the other to help understand the relationship between antecedents and errors. Figure 15.4 illustrates the relationship between antecedents and errors.

Maintenance facility common elements Two common elements, organizational antecedents of the maintenance facility, influenced operator performance, albeit more subtly than did the other organizational antecedents. SabreTech's efforts to contain costs and its pressure to hasten the remaining maintenance tasks degraded the maintenance that its technicians' performed.

SabreTech's efforts to contain expenses were evident in its method of obtaining the services of maintenance personnel. By contracting with other companies, they avoided the expense of employing full-time personnel during relatively low activity periods. The practice saved them money, but it also hampered their ability to develop a "culture" or "climate" of organizational maintenance practices, as discussed in Chapter 8. Over time, employees adopt company norms and apply them to such activities as interpreting procedures and regulations, and determining acceptable standards of performance. Although the absence of norms among its employees may itself not have been an antecedent to error, the lack of norms meant that nothing was in place to counter the adverse effects of the other common element, the pressure placed on supervisors and technicians to rapidly complete the maintenance activities. Norms of strict and thorough adherence to maintenance practices could have encouraged more meticulous adherence to the required canister disposal procedures, in the face of pressure to do the opposite.

SabreTech antecedents
- Inattention to required procedures
- Ineffective communications among maintenance personnel
- Inadequate technician training
- Inadequate planning for and stocking of needed components.

SabreTech operator errors-failed to
- Properly lock or dispose of the generators
- Place correctly colored white and green tags on the canisters instead of red tags
- Properly store the cardboard boxes containing the canisters
- Correctly indicate on the work cards that the oxygen generator disposal process had been completed.

Figure 15.4 Relationship between SabreTech antecedents and SabreTech personnel errors

In short, the pressure on maintenance technicians to rapidly complete maintenance on the ValuJet aircraft, with the lack of organizational norms, adversely affected disposal of the oxygen generators by–

- Heightening the importance of completing work on the two airplanes, to the detriment of properly processing components removed from those aircraft

- Increasing the importance of signing the work cards, to the detriment of assuring that all steps in the work cards had been completed
- Forcing supervisors and technicians to focus on the pace of maintenance tasks rather than the quality of those tasks.

The airline The contractual relationship between ValuJet and SabreTech included regulatory as well as financial obligations. In agreeing to maintain ValuJet's aircraft, SabreTech was to adhere to FAA regulations governing its maintenance activities, although the regulations placed ultimate responsibility on ValuJet to assure that SabreTech maintained its aircraft in accordance with the airline's procedures. Investigators concluded that the airline did not meet its regulatory obligations. As they write,

> As an air carrier choosing to subcontract its heavy maintenance functions to SabreTech (among other contractors), ValuJet should have overseen and ensured that it understood the activities of SabreTech to the same extent that it would oversee its in-house maintenance functions and employees. Although ValuJet conducted an initial inspection and a subsequent audit of SabreTech, and assigned three technical representatives to the facility, there was limited ongoing oversight of the actual work SabreTech was performing for ValuJet.

> ValuJet failed to provide significant on-site quality assurance at SabreTech's Miami facility. As a result, ValuJet failed to recognize the need for and coordinate the acquisition of oxygen generator locking caps and failed to discover the improper maintenance signoffs indicating that locking caps had been installed. ValuJet also did not recognize and correct SabreTech's use of the wrong parts tags on the expired oxygen generators or ensure that SabreTech employees were trained on ValuJet's hazardous materials practices and policies. Further, ValuJet failed to recognize and possibly accepted SabreTech's lack of procedures for communicating the hazardous nature of aircraft items left in the shipping and stores area and failed to identify these inadequacies in SabreTech's procedures during its audits and oversight of SabreTech. (NTSB, 1997a; p. 123)

ValuJet assigned three technical representatives to SabreTech to oversee SabreTech's maintenance of its aircraft. Of the three, only one was a permanent ValuJet employee; two worked for contractors to ValuJet. As SabreTech had done, the airline had retained contract employees to oversee critical maintenance programs, personnel who would not be as familiar with its procedures as would its own employees. Further, these representatives were only present at SabreTech during the day and not at night, when much of the maintenance was performed because of the need to expeditiously complete the maintenance on the ValuJet aircraft. Therefore, they could not have monitored much of the maintenance that the facility was performing on its aircraft, a finding that became evident after the accident. None of the technical representatives could recall discussing with ValuJet or SabreTech personnel either procedures for disposing of the canisters, or the need to install locking caps on them.

Although organizations can contract out many of their activities–as ValuJet and SabreTech had done–and still effectively oversee those activities, the airline's oversight of the maintenance facilities activities were ineffective because of two factors. One, which corresponded to a SabreTech antecedent, was its lack of a corporate "culture" that is found among stable and long-term work forces, and the other was the dilution of ultimate oversight responsibility of the maintenance. As investigators conclude,

> The Safety Board recognizes that air carriers can successfully subcontract many of the functional areas of their operations; however, it is the Safety Board's position that air carriers engaging in subcontracting remain responsible for the safety of their operations and the airworthiness of their airplanes, and therefore must properly oversee their outside contractors...An air carrier cannot delegate its responsibility for the safety of its operations and maintenance to its subcontractors (NTSB, 1997a; pp. 122-123).

ValuJet's technical representatives should have recognized that technicians at SabreTech focused on the pace and timeliness of the maintenance rather than on its quality, and did not appear to recognize that the resulting maintenance was inferior and potentially unsafe. This was due, in part, to the fact that two of ValuJet's three supervisors were not ValuJet employees but contract employees. As a new airline, with all major maintenance performed at contractor facilities, there was no opportunity for it to develop and inculcate in its personnel norms that conveyed commitment to thorough and meticulous maintenance. With contractor maintenance, overseen by contractor personnel who were absent for much of the maintenance activities, the lack of such norms was a critical antecedent. Had the maintenance been overseen by employees of a single organization that developed and oversaw its own maintenance procedures, employed and trained the needed personnel, and was responsible for acquiring critical parts, the errors that led to this accident may not have occurred.

ValuJet may also have been responsible for introducing the antecedent that influenced the final error that led to the accident, the first officer's approving loading the boxes of canisters onto the aircraft. He should have recognized that depleted canisters of chemical oxygen generators, as the shipping label had erroneously indicated, were worthless and thus had no reason to be returned to the airline. His failure to do so was the final error that led to the accident. However, investigators did not determine the origin of the antecedent to this error.

His failure to reject the shipment may have resulted from unfamiliarity with the potential dangers of chemical oxygen generators. ValuJet may not have ensured that its pilots were aware of these potential hazards and the prohibition against loading unprotected and unexpended generators on aircraft. On the other hand, the airline may have provided the necessary information, but he may have forgotten it. Investigators did not identify the antecedent of this error. It may have been due to airline deficiencies or shortcomings with the first officer. Without more information, one cannot make that determination.

Figure 15.5 diagrams the SabreTech errors with their ValuJet antecedents.

The regulator Investigators cited the regulator, the FAA, primarily for its failure to require fire detection and suppression systems in below deck cargo compartments. As the regulator responsible for approving the aircraft's design, the FAA had the authority and investigators believed, the justification from a previous incident, to mandate their installation. Investigators argued that had the cargo compartment on the accident aircraft been so equipped, the fire could have been suppressed, or at worst, the pilots would have been alerted to it before it could penetrate the passenger cabin, and would have had enough time to land before it could endanger the passengers and crew. Because the FAA did not mandate this change before the accident–it did so afterwards–despite evidence of this need, investigators determined that this was a cause of the accident.

Investigators cite other FAA antecedents that relate more directly to the operator errors under discussion, although they did not cite them as having caused the accident. These are the errors in handling the chemical oxygen generators after they had been removed from the two airplanes. As the regulator, the FAA establishes the rules governing maintenance procedures and oversees compliance with them. Investigators believed that the FAA's failure to monitor compliance with its rules allowed the antecedents to lead to errors that caused the accident.

Investigators learned that, about three months before the accident, FAA personnel responsible for overseeing the airline's operations and maintenance had became alarmed by the airline's rapid expansion, and by a series of non-fatal accidents it had experienced. They asked their superiors at the FAA's headquarters to immediately review the airline's operations and maintenance, going so far as to propose that they consider withdrawing its approval of the airline's fitness to operate, a recommendation that would have led to the airline's cessation of operations. Although FAA supervisory personnel did not approve this recommendation, it did order an increase in its oversight of the airline, and, about two months before the accident, it began a 120-day intensive inspection of the carrier. This inspection was being carried out on the day of the accident.

ValuJet antecedents-failed to
- Train, or ensure that SabreTech employees were trained to handle hazardous materials
- Anticipate the need for and acquire locking caps for the oxygen generators
- Correct SabreTech's use of incorrectly colored tags on the chemical oxygen generators instead of red tags
- Correct SabreTech's improper storage of the chemical oxygen generators after they had been removed from the airplanes.

SabreTech operator errors-failed to
- Properly lock or dispose of the generators
- Place correctly colored white and green tags on the canisters instead of red tags
- Properly store the cardboard boxes containing the generators
- Correctly indicate on the work cards that the oxygen generator disposal process had been completed
- Properly designate the boxes instead of designating them COMAT.

Figure 15.5 Relationship between ValuJet antecedents and SabreTech personnel errors

Investigators concluded that the FAA's oversight of SabreTech and ValuJet was flawed. Before the accident no FAA inspector involved in overseeing the airline's maintenance had visited the SabreTech facility. After the accident, FAA personnel inspected the airline and its contract maintenance facilities and obtained sufficient evidence of unsafe practices to warrant asking the airline to cease operations until could demonstrate that it could safely resume. On June 18, 1996, the airline ceased operations.[8]

The errors The regulator's antecedents to error are straightforward. The FAA creates regulations governing aircraft maintenance that, if followed, should provide an acceptable level of safety. SabreTech personnel did not comply with those rules, but FAA personnel were unaware of this because they failed to properly oversee SabreTech's maintenance. As a result, it failed to realize that neither the airline nor the maintenance facility was complying with maintenance rules.

Investigators cited several flaws in the FAA's surveillance of the airline and the maintenance facility. Although FAA inspectors based in Atlanta had the responsibility to oversee the airline's operations and maintenance, airline personnel did not actually perform the maintenance. FAA inspectors nearest the facilities that the airline had contracted with to perform its maintenance, who were able to travel to and inspect the maintenance performed at those locations, were largely unfamiliar with the airline's maintenance program.

Investigators also found that the FAA had an insufficient number of inspectors near the airline's Atlanta, Georgia, headquarters, to oversee the airline's maintenance. Before the accident, the manager of the FAA's Atlanta office had asked for additional personnel to cope with inspection demands generated by the carrier's growth; however, the request was denied. Consequently, even if the airline had maintained its aircraft at its own facility, it is doubtful that the FAA would have had a sufficient number of inspectors available to effectively oversee the maintenance.

In addition, communication among FAA personnel was found to have been deficient, adversely affecting FAA's oversight of ValuJet. Senior FAA personnel, who made staffing and other decisions concerning the airline's oversight, were unaware that lower level personnel with regular contact with the airline had serious reservations about the airline's continued ability to operate safely. Investigators contended that if internal

---

[8] It resumed operations on September 30, 1996, on a considerably smaller scale than before the accident.

FAA communication had been better, decision makers in the FAA would have known of the challenges its Atlanta personnel faced and would have approved the request for more personnel.

One can conclude therefore, that had the FAA conducted effective oversight of the airline it would have learned far more than it did before the accident, including information that—

- ValuJet representatives were only present at SabreTech during the day and did not monitor maintenance performed at night.
- Most of the SabreTech personnel who worked on the ValuJet aircraft were not employed by SabreTech, and had not been trained in either the airline's maintenance procedures or the maintenance facility's policies.
- Technicians at SabreTech did not follow the facility's own policies on the use of color-coded tags.
- Technicians at SabreTech performed critical maintenance activities called for on work card 0069 without requisite components—the locking caps.
- SabreTech had no procedures governing communication between shifts of maintenance technicians, and between maintenance personnel and those at shipping and receiving.
- Neither technicians nor their supervisors understood the hazards associated with unexpended chemical oxygen generators.
- SabreTech management encountered and exerted substantial pressure on its mechanics and supervisors to hasten the pace of maintenance being performed on the airline's aircraft.

Because the regulator had not detected these deficiencies, it did not prevent airline and maintenance facility personnel from creating antecedents that adversely influenced operator performance. As investigators conclude,

> Before the accident, the FAA's oversight of ValuJet did not include any significant oversight of its heavy maintenance functions. This is especially disturbing given that by February 1996 the FAA had determined that there were problems serious enough at ValuJet to warrant more than the normal level of surveillance. Had the FAA subjected the Miami facility of SabreTech to the same level of surveillance as it did ValuJet itself, it might have discovered the deficiencies later uncovered in the special FAA inspection of that facility after the accident, which led to the surrender of the facility's operating certificate. (NTSB, 1997a; pp. 124-125)

The difficulty that the FAA encountered overseeing the airline and its maintenance facility's activities may be attributed, in part, to the novelty of the airline's maintenance program and its relative inexperience with such approaches to operations. FAA policies on maintenance surveillance had been developed to oversee "traditional" airlines, with maintenance procedures they developed to meet their own needs, for maintenance that they performed on their own aircraft. ValuJet, however, followed a different approach, with which the regulator had little previous experience. The airline contracted out much of what had traditionally formed the core of airline operations, pilot training and aircraft maintenance.

As required of all airlines, ValuJet developed maintenance procedures for the aircraft it operated, but unlike traditional airlines, it then contracted with others to perform all heavy maintenance. Although it followed the "letter" of the procedures that the regulator had approved, because it did not actually perform its own maintenance and did not directly employ those who did, impermanence among both maintenance technicians and the supervisors of those performing the airline's maintenance was the norm.

Technicians with little or no familiarity with the airline's "culture of maintenance" maintained the aircraft at locations far from airline personnel, under the supervision of managers with little or no experience with the airline, and with little or no opportunity to directly interact with those who were knowledgeable and experienced in the airline's way of "doing things." Therefore, incorporation of "norms of maintenance" and subtle interpretations of maintenance procedures were absent from those who performed the maintenance and their supervisors.

With "traditional" airlines with which the regulator was familiar, inspectors based at the airline's headquarters could visit the maintenance facility as needed, with little effort and expense. The proximity between the regulator and the airline, and the relative permanence of the workforce in each, allowed each to learn and appreciate the other's expectations and way of doing things. Phone calls and e-mails could clarify ambiguity and answer questions each may have had. However, with a "non-traditional" airline this was not possible. Instead, the regulator was required to expend considerable resources to perform minimal maintenance oversight, to a degree that it had not recognized.

In listing the regulator's errors and antecedents, it could be seen that its error was its inadequate oversight of both the airline and the maintenance facility. Three antecedents appear to have led to this error, insufficient personnel, inadequate internal communication, and inadequate recognition and comprehension of the nontraditional aspects of the airline's major maintenance activities. Figure 15.6 diagrams the antecedents with this error, illustrating the relationship between the two.

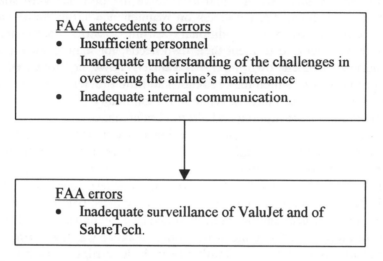

Figure 15.6 Relationship between FAA antecedents and FAA personnel errors

Antecedents and errors

Two questions, to determine whether relationships proposed between antecedent, error, and the event under consideration meet standards of acceptability, were described in Chapter 14. These were, 1) would the error have occurred if the antecedent that preceded it had not been present, and 2) would the accident have occurred if the error that preceded it had not been committed? As an additional check, three criteria were proposed to determine the value of relationships between antecedents and errors. These require the relationships to be simple, logical, and superior to other possible relationships.

Relationships between antecedents and errors

Had both the maintenance facility and the airline understood the potential hazards of unexpended oxygen generators, it is highly likely that they would have had locking caps available when the maintenance was performed, or would have ensured that the generators were expended. Had the maintenance facility's work been effectively overseen, technicians at the facility would likely have labeled the canisters properly. Proper labeling would have effectively communicated their hazards, even to those who had no knowledge of their contents, such as the shipping, receiving, and storage clerks. Alternatively, had better internal communications taken place within the maintenance facility, shipping and receiving clerks would have learned the true nature of the canisters, even if they had been mislabeled. The relationships cited are simple, logical, and superior to others. Little effort is needed to understand them, and their influence on other aspects of the accident.

Common elements

SabreTech Had the common elements of SabreTech's extensive cost reduction efforts and pressure to quickly complete the maintenance on the two ValuJet aircraft not been present, the antecedents noted would likely have been absent as well. The maintenance facility might have focused needed attention on properly discarding the canisters as well as on completing the remaining maintenance on the two aircraft. Instead, ill-trained personnel, with incomplete understanding of the disposal process, gave the canisters little attention and allowed them to be placed on a passenger carrying aircraft.

The common elements relate simply to the antecedents, the antecedents relate simply and logically to the errors, and the errors relate directly to the accident. If one of the errors had not been committed, the accident would almost certainly not have occurred.

ValuJet As SabreTech, the common element of the airline's cost reduction efforts created conditions that allowed the error antecedents to adversely affect operator performance. It relied on the maintenance facility to oversee its own maintenance, but ineffectively oversaw the maintenance. The antecedents and errors associated with ValuJet are simple, logical and most important, necessary for the subsequent outcome, error or accident, to have occurred.

The FAA The regulator failed to effectively monitor the maintenance performed at the maintenance facility on behalf of the airline. However, although the regulator's error played a part in the accident, common elements to the antecedents to the error could not be identified.

Terminating the search for antecedents

Chapter 14 addressed the point at which the search for antecedents should be stopped. One can go back seemingly indefinitely to antecedents that may have influenced the errors, but at some point one would reach a point of diminishing returns and the additional search would not be worth the effort. In this accident, that search terminated at the FAA management level that made decisions affecting the quality of its oversight of the airline's and maintenance facility's maintenance. Searching for antecedents beyond this level would dilute the importance of the antecedents that are closest to the critical errors leading to the accident.

Recommendations

Investigators issued 27 recommendations to address deficiencies they identified in this accident. Many addressed issues regarding flight crew, cargo compartment fire protection, and other issues not directly related to the errors discussed presently.

Several recommendations dealt with the antecedents to errors discussed presently (NTSB, 1997a). These were addressed to the FAA rather than to the airline or the maintenance facility, so that the recommended changes would be applied to all airlines across the board. Investigators asked the FAA to–

> Require that routine work cards used during maintenance of Part 121 [i.e., major airlines] aircraft (a) provide, for those work cards that call for the removal of any component containing hazardous materials, instructions for disposal of the hazardous materials or a direct reference to the maintenance manual provision containing those instructions and (b) include an inspector's signature block on any work card that calls for handling a component containing hazardous materials. (p. 139)

> Require all air carriers to develop and implement programs to ensure that other aircraft components that are hazardous are properly identified and that effective procedures are established to safely handle those components after they are removed from aircraft. (p. 139)

> Develop and implement a system requiring items delivered to shipping and receiving and stores areas of the facility to be properly identified and classified as hazardous or non-hazardous, and procedures for tracking the handling and disposition of hazardous materials. (p. 139)

Require air carriers to ensure that maintenance facility personnel, including mechanics, shipping, receiving, and storage personnel, at air carrier-operated or subcontractor facilities, are provided initial and recurrent training in hazardous materials recognition, and in proper labeling, packaging, and shipment procedures with respect to the specific items of hazardous materials that are handled by the air carrier's maintenance functions. (p. 140)

Ensure that Part 121 air carrier's maintenance functions receive the same level of Federal Aviation Administration surveillance, regardless of whether those functions are performed in house or by a contract maintenance facility. (p. 140)

Review the volume and nature of the work requirements of principal maintenance inspectors assigned to Part 145 contract repair stations [contract maintenance facilities] that perform maintenance for Part 121 air carriers, and ensure that these inspectors have adequate time and resources to perform surveillance. (p. 140)

The recommendations propose strategies that, if implemented, would effectively address many of the deficiencies that investigators identified. Although one could suggest additional recommendations, these effectively addressed many of the antecedents that led to the critical errors. If implemented, similar errors would likely not recur.

Investigators did not focus exclusively on the errors that led to the accident, but also examined technical, design, and certification issues as well. Given the scope of the investigation, the recommendations go a long way to enhancing the safety of maintenance procedures.

Summary

An accident involving a DC-9 that crashed into the Florida Everglades in May 1996 after a fire broke out in the cabin, was examined in detail. The critical error, loading prohibited canisters of chemical oxygen generators into the airplane's below deck cargo compartment, was preceded by several errors that maintenance personnel committed two months before the accident, while performing maintenance on two aircraft that the airline had acquired. Investigators determined that the canisters, which become very hot when the oxygen generation process is initiated, ignited adjacent material in the cargo compartment. The generators provided a ready source of oxygen in the airtight compartment, which led to an intensely hot fire that burned through the fire resistant cargo liners and into the cabin. The generators had been removed from two aircraft that the airline had acquired, in preparation for operation in regular service.

Investigators found that maintenance personnel committed five errors in sequence, and ramp personnel and the first officer a sixth error in allowing the containers to be loaded onto the airplane. The maintenance errors involved improper disposal of the canisters, improper storage, tagging, and labeling; and improper signing of a maintenance work card indicating that the canisters had been properly disposed of.

The airline had developed procedures for maintaining its aircraft, and contracted with several maintenance facilities to perform the maintenance. The facility that maintained the two aircraft that provided the canisters, as part of the maintenance, removed and replaced components from the airplanes that had passed or were approaching their expiration dates, such as the oxygen generators.

The maintenance facility was encountering delays in completing its work on the two aircraft, and if faced potentially large financial penalties because of the delays. Its managers exerted substantial pressure on maintenance personnel to complete the maintenance.

Both the airline and the maintenance facility used contractors to provide personnel to perform important functions. Three airline personnel, two of whom worked for contractors, oversaw the maintenance facility's work on the aircraft. Over half of the maintenance facility's personnel who worked on the oxygen generators were not employees of the facility but were employed by contractors to the facility. They would not have integrated corporate cultural norms relating to maintenance procedures, norms that may otherwise have contributed to an appreciation of the need for more careful attention to required maintenance actions.

Investigators also considered the regulator's oversight of both the airline and the maintenance facility to be deficient. The regulator had an insufficient number of inspectors to oversee the airline's maintenance, was aware of the need for additional oversight, but did not provide the personnel needed to carry out the oversight. Consequently, regulator personnel responsible for overseeing the airline's maintenance had not visited the maintenance facility before the accident. In addition, the regulator was unfamiliar with, and unprepared to respond to the type of maintenance that the airline had undertaken, where those from outside the company performed all but a small portion of its total maintenance activities.

16 Final Thoughts

The text has reviewed the nature of error in complex systems, presented methods of error investigation, illustrated the application of the methods with case studies of events, and discussed issues in error in complex systems. However, notwithstanding the importance of understanding the context of error in complex systems, much as changed in our view of these systems since the September 11, 2001, terrorist attacks on the World Trade Center and the Pentagon. Terrorists studied a system readily accessible to the public—commercial aviation—discovered security vulnerabilities, and used these to bring harm to innocent men, women, and children.

The deliberate use of complex system vulnerabilities to bring about destruction on the unprecedented scale of September 11, 2001, underscores the need to assess and minimize complex system vulnerabilities. Although the focus of this text has been on unintended actions, errors, and their antecedents, and although law enforcement expertise has traditionally been called upon to respond to security matters, the methods used to identify security vulnerabilities are similar to those used to identify safety deficiencies. Much as one investigates incidents of error in order to reduce future opportunities for error, acts of sabotage and terrorism can be investigated in order to reduce system vulnerabilities.

It should be remembered however, that the post-September 11, 2001, need to examine security vulnerabilities in complex systems, should not be carried out at the expense of the need to focus on the safety of those systems. Both security and safety are necessary for the continued effective operation of complex systems, and many of the lessons and methods of error investigations apply equally to security as well.

Proactive investigations

Most investigations are carried out after an event has occurred. But the search to reduce opportunities for error or vulnerabilities to sabotage should be ongoing, even in the absence of an accident or security breach.

System managers, administrators, operators, regulators, and others involved in operating complex systems need to be vigilant in the search for system deficiencies that could lead to errors and accidents. This is proactive and in the best interests of safety.

Given the daily pressures of those involved in system operations, one could be expected to encounter difficulties conducting proactive investigations in the absence of an incident or accident (e.g., Carroll, Rudolph, Hatakenaka, Wiederhold, and Boldrini, 2001). Few operators, managers, or regulators have the time available for the data gathering and analysis activities that are needed to recognize and suggest remediation strategies to reduce system deficiencies and vulnerabilities.

Reason (1997) offers several techniques to improve the "safety culture" of complex systems. He argues that safety cultures are designed to reduce opportunities for error in complex systems, and actions can be taken before the fact to improve the safety of many aspects of system operations, from maintenance, to regulation, to daily operations, if the necessary data have been collected and disseminated. As he writes,

> In the absence of bad outcomes, the best way–perhaps the only way–to sustain a state of intelligent and respectful wariness is to gather the right kinds of data. This means creating a safety information system that collects, analyses and disseminates information from incidents and near misses as well as from regular proactive checks on the system's vital signs. All of these activities can be said to make up an informed culture–one in which those who manage and operate the system have current knowledge about the human, technical, organizational and environmental factors that determine the safety of the system as a whole. In most important respects, an informed culture is a safety culture. (p. 195)

Managers, administrators, regulators, and others hoping to obtain "the right kinds of data" can accomplish this in several ways. Reason suggests developing and implementing a self-reporting system in which employees can report safety deficiencies in a non-punitive environment. A self-reporting system should encourage learning about safety deficiencies, and security vulnerabilities, before they lead to potentially severe consequences.

Companies can also conduct proactive investigations in response to minor events. These investigations may highlight previously unknown safety- and security-related information, and improve investigative skills as well.

Investigative proficiency

Conducting safety reviews and proactive investigations also help maintain and enhance investigative proficiency, as well as provide information to enhance safety and security. The environment in which proactive incident investigations are conducted, in the absence of a major event, is also likely to be free of the stresses that often follow major events, and therefore, likely to be a supportive environment for novice investigators.

Criteria

Because of routine operational needs, managers and administrators may be reluctant to divert potentially valuable resources from operational duties to conduct incident investigations, notwithstanding their likely long-term safety and security benefits. Rather than recognizing the potential benefits, they may instead focus on the personnel and resource expenditures needed to conduct proactive investigations.

Investigators can help managers and administrators select events that warrant investigations by developing criteria to evaluate the need for a proactive investigation. The criteria that follow are applicable to nearly all complex systems–

- Type and frequency of errors committed and severity of their consequences
- Frequency and severity of recent incidents
- Length of interval since most recent investigation
- Amount and value of other system safety data.

The greater the number of operator errors in the incident, the more serious their consequences, the more frequent the recent incidents, and the less the amount and value of available system safety data available, the more a proactive investigation is warranted.

An incident in which many errors were committed has a greater need for an investigation than one with just a few. A system that has experienced a relatively high number of incidents in a short period of time also would benefit from a proactive investigation. These suggest the presence of safety deficiencies that could otherwise lead to a major accident, and that could lead to effective recommendations to address the deficiencies. On the other hand, a system with a substantial amount of safety data available may not benefit from a proactive investigation. The cost of collecting additional safety-related data may not be outweighed by the potential benefits, assuming the data provide information about the presence of system safety deficiencies.

Models of error, investigations, and research

Moray (1994; 2000) and Reason's (1990; 1997) models of error have guided much of the process outlined in this text. These models have had considerable value in helping to understand error, and substantial influence on the insights of students of error. Both models have helped to bridge the gap that often exists between human performance theories and their application to error investigations.

Models help researchers and investigators understand the data they have gathered and guide their analytical efforts. However, models that guide can also hamper activities, if investigators rigidly adhere to them to the detriment of other, more applicable investigative approaches. No single error model is equally applicable to all circumstances; each may have shortcomings that are applicable to particular circumstances.

As with empirical research, one needs to follow what the data describe rather than the models or theories used to explain them. This means allowing the data to determine the relationships between antecedents and errors and between errors and the events under investigation. Assuming that investigators have obtained the appropriate data, the model or theory that best explains the relationships of interest should be applied to the investigation. Although this text has adopted Moray and Reason's models to illustrate investigative technique and methodology, others may be better suited to the needs of the investigation of the event. So long as the fundamental rules of logic and research are followed, the derived relationships and explanations will be sound.

Research and investigations

Both research studies and accident investigations can provide data that explain behavior in complex systems. For example, as discussed, the extensive research that has been conducted on decision making in "real world" dynamic environments has led to findings that are directly relevant to investigations of many events, helping investigators understand the nature of the operator decisions and thus, assisting in the development of remediation strategies to prevent similar occurrences. Information from accident investigations has also helped to focus research needs and activities by revealing operator actions in real world settings. Knowledge of the findings of both research and investigations can assist both the researcher and the investigator to better understand the issues being examined.

However, investigators may encounter events where few relevant research studies and previous investigations have been conducted. Circumstances in which relatively unexplored issues play major roles in accidents occasionally occur and, while the efforts to investigate them may be substantial, the derived information may have substantial value to a variety of settings. For example, investigators of the 1996 explosion of the Boeing 747 over Long Island (NTSB, 2000d), focused on a rarely encountered scenario, an in-flight explosion caused by fuel tank vapors, with which little pertinent information was available.

Investigators conducted original research to obtain fundamental information regarding fuel volatility and ignition to understand the phenomenon. Although it is rare for researchers to conduct original research in the context of an accident investigation, the needs of the investigation may require that. In the investigation of that Boeing 747 accident, the information obtained from the investigation will help aircraft designers, regulators, and the aviation industry improve aviation safety for years to come.

Quick solutions

Operators, managers, regulators–as well as investigators–may seek quick or facile solutions to address a recognized safety deficiency or vulnerability. Frequently, quick solutions are needed and appropriate. However, the complexity of modern systems and the relationships among antecedents and errors within them often call for complex and time consuming solutions to provide effective mitigation techniques. Those involved in system operations need to be prepared to implement long-term, potentially difficult strategies to improve system safety. The methods may be expensive and/or difficult to implement, but the objective of improving system safety will warrant it.

Conclusions

When beginning an investigation the task may seem arduous and the frustrations overwhelming, but the benefits to be gained from systematic and thorough investigations will make the efforts worthwhile. One has only to examine the steady improvements in system safety since the ValuJet and Three Mile Island accidents to appreciate the benefits to be gained. In the period since the Three Mile Island nuclear accident, there has been only one major civilian nuclear accident, at the former Soviet reactor in Chernobyl. Similarly, the rate of civilian air transport accidents has continued to decline, despite considerable increase in worldwide operations in environments that had once been considered to be primitive and relatively unsafe. Although the events of September 11, 2001, have highlighted security vulnerabilities in complex systems, over time methodical improvements in security should match the methodical improvements seen in system safety.

The potential for human error, and, unfortunately, the desire to destroy, will not be eliminated. However, investigators have demonstrated that opportunities for both can be effectively reduced. Complex systems are likely to increase in their complexity and, as Perrow (1999) has argued, this will increase the likelihood of "normal accidents." But even Perrow would argue that applying the lessons of error investigations reduces their likelihood. The objective of this text has been to provide the knowledge and skills investigators need to accomplish this. The benefits of doing so will continue to make the efforts worthwhile.

References

Abbott, T. S. (2000). Task-oriented display design: The case of an engine-monitoring display. In N. B. Sarter and R. Amalberti (Eds.), *Cognitive engineering in the aviation domain* (pp. 133-152). Mahwah, New Jersey: Lawrence Erlbaum Associates.

Accident Investigation Commission. (1996). *Informe Finale, Accidente de la Aeronave Boeing 757-200, Operada por La Empresa de Transporte Aereo Del Peru S. A., Aeroperu, Ocurrido el Dia 02 de Octubre de 1996* [Final report, Accident of the Boeing 757-200, operated by the transport company AeroPeru, on October 2, 1996]. Lima, Peru.

Adams, M. J., Tenney, Y. J., and Pew, R. W. (1995). Situation awareness and the cognitive measurement of complex systems. *Human Factors, 37,* 85-104.

Aeronautica Civil of the Government of Colombia. (1996). *Aircraft accident report, controlled flight into terrain, American Airlines flight 965, Boeing 757-223, N651AA, near Cali, Colombia, December 20, 1995.* Bogotá, Colombia.

Air Accidents Investigation Branch, (1990). *Report on the accident to Boeing 737-400, G-OBME, near Kegworth, Leicestershire, on 8 January, 1989.* Aircraft Accident Report No. 4/90 (EW/C1095). London: Department of Transport.

Air Accidents Investigation Branch, (1992). *Report on the accident to BAC One-Eleven, G-BJRT over Didcot, Oxfordshire, on 10 June, 1990.* Aircraft Accident Report No. 1/92 (EW/C1165). London. Department of Transport.

Alcov, R. A., Borowsky, M. S., and Gaynor, J. A. (1982). Stress coping and the U.S. Navy aircrew factor mishap. *Aviation, Space, and Environmental Medicine, 53,* 1112-1115.

Allen, J., Rankin, B. and Sargent, B. (1998). Human factors process for reducing maintenance errors. *Aero, 3,* 28-33.

Amalberti, R. R. (1998). Automation in aviation: A human factors perspective. In D. J. Garland, J. A. Wise, and V. D. Hopkin, (Eds.), *Handbook of aviation human factors* (pp. 173-192). Mahwah, New Jersey: Lawrence Erlbaum Associates.

Anderson, T., and Twining, W. (1991). *Analysis of evidence: How to do things with facts based on Wigmore's science of judicial proof.* Evanston, Illinois: Northwestern University Press.

Annett, J., and Stanton, N. A., (2000). Editorial. *Ergonomics, 43,* 1045-1051.

Bainbridge, L. (1987). Ironies of automation. In J. Rasmussen, K. Duncan and J. Leplat (Eds.), *New technology and human error* (pp. 271-283). New York: John Wiley and Son.

Banbury, S. P., Macken, W. J., Tremblay, S., and Jones, D. M. (2001). Auditory distraction and short-term memory: Phenomena and practical implications. *Human Factors, 43,* 12-29.

Belz, S. M., Robinson, G. S., and Casali, J. G. (1999). A new class of auditory warning signals for complex systems: Auditory icons. *Human Factors, 41,* 608-618.

Billings, C. E. (1997). *Aviation automation: The search for a human-centered approach.* Mahwah, New Jersey: Lawrence Erlbaum Associates.

Brenner, C. (1964). Parapraxes and wit. In W. Haddon, Jr., E. Suchman, and D. Klein (Eds.), *Accident research: Methods and approaches* (pp. 292-295). New York: Harper and Row.

Bowers, C. A., Oser, R. L., Salas, E., and Cannon-Bowers, J. A. (1996). Team performance in automated systems. In R. Parasuraman and M. Mouloua (Eds.), *Automation and human performance: Theory and applications* (pp. 243-263). Mahwah, New Jersey: Lawrence Erlbaum Associates.

Brown, M. T. (1999). Marine voyage recorders. *Proceedings of the International Symposium on Transportation Recorders* (pp. 47-60). Washington, DC: National Transportation Safety Board.

Buckhout, R. (1974). Eyewitness testimony. *Scientific American, 231,* 23-31.

Cara, F., and LaGrange, V. (1999). Emerging expertise in process control. *Ergonomics, 42,* 1418-1430.

Carley, W. M., and Pasztor, A. (1999). Korean Air confronts dismal safety record rooted in its culture, *The Wall Street Journal,* July 7, 1999.

Carroll, J. S., Rudolph, J. W., Hatakenaka, S., Wiederhold, T. L., and Boldrini, M. (2001). Learning in the context of incident investigation: Team diagnoses and organizational decisions at four nuclear power plants (pp. 349-365). In E. Salas and G. Klein (Eds.). *Learning expertise and naturalistic decision making.* Mahwah, New Jersey: Lawrence Erlbaum Associates.

Chapanis, A. (1996). *Human factors in system engineering.* New York: John Wiley and Sons.

Commission of Investigation. (1994). *Final report of the investigation commission into the accident that occurred on 20 January 1992, near Mont Sainte-Odile (Bas-Rhin), to Airbus A-320, Registration F-GGED, operated by Air Inter.* Paris, France: Minister of Equipment, Transport and Tourism.

Corlett, E. N., and Clark, T. S. (1995). *The ergonomics of workspaces and machines* (2nd ed.). London: Taylor and Francis.

Costa, G. (1998). Fatigue and biological rhythms. In D. J. Garland, J. A. Wise, and V. D. Hopkin (Eds.), *Handbook of aviation human factors* (pp. 235-255). Mahwah, New Jersey: Lawrence Erlbaum Associates.

Dawson, D., and Fletcher, A. (2001). A qualitative model of work-related fatigue: background and definition. *Ergonomics, 44,* 144-163.

Dawson, D., and Reid, K. (1997a). Fatigue, alcohol and performance impairment. *Nature, 388,* 235.

Dawson, D., and Reid, K. (1997b). Equating the performance impairment associated with sustained wakefulness and alcohol intoxication. *Journal of the Centre for Sleep Research, 2,* 1-8.

Degani, A., Shafto, M., and Kirlik, A. (1997). Modes in human-machine systems: Constructs, representation, and classification. *International Journal of Aviation Psychology, 9,* 125-138.

Dobranetski, E., and Case, D. (1999). Proactive use of recorded data for accident prevention. *Proceedings of the International Symposium on Transportation Recorders.* (pp. 99-120). Washington, DC: National Transportation Safety Board.

Drury, C. G. (1998). Human factors in aviation maintenance. In D. J. Garland, J. A. Wise, and V. D. Hopkin (Eds.), *Handbook of aviation human factors* (pp. 591-606). Mahwah, New Jersey: Lawrence Erlbaum Associates.

Dyer, J. L. (1984). Team research and team training: A state-of-the-art review. In F. A. Muckler (Ed.), *Human factors review: 1984* (pp. 285-323). Santa Monica, California: Human Factors Society.

Edworth, J., Loxley, S., and Dennis, I. (1991). Improving auditory warning design: Relationship between warning sound parameters and perceived urgency. *Human Factors, 33,* 205-231.

Ellis, H. D. (1982). The effects of cold on the performance of serial choice reaction time and various discrete tasks. *Human Factors, 24,* 589-598.

Endsley, M. R. (1995). Toward a theory of situation awareness. *Human Factors, 37*, 32-64.

Endsley, M. R. (2000). Theoretical underpinnings of situation awareness: A critical review. In M. R. Endsley and D. J. Garland (Eds.), *Situation awareness: Analysis and measurement* (pp. 3-32). Mahwah, New Jersey: Lawrence Erlbaum Associates.

Endsley, M. R., and Kaber, D. B. (1999). Level of automation effects on performance, situation awareness, and workload in a dynamic control task. *Ergonomics, 42*, 462-492.

Endsley, M. R., and Kiris, E. O. (1995). The out-of-the-loop performance problem and level of control in automation. *Human Factors, 37*, 381-394.

Federico, P. A. (1995). Expert and novice recognition of similar situations. *Human Factors, 37*, 105-122.

Fenwick, L., (1999). Security of recorded information. *Proceedings of the International Symposium on Transportation Recorders.* (pp. 145-151). Washington, DC: National Transportation Safety Board.

Fisher, R. P., and Geiselman, R. E. (1992). *Memory-enhancing techniques for investigative interviewing: The cognitive interview.* Springfield, Illinois: Charles C. Thomas.

Flach, J. M., and Rasmussen, J. (2000). Cognitive engineering: Designing for situation awareness. In N. B. Sarter and R. Amalberti (Eds.), *Cognitive engineering in the aviation domain* (pp. 153-179). Mahwah, New Jersey: Lawrence Erlbaum Associates.

Fletcher, A., and Dawson, D. (2001). A quantitative model of work-related fatigue: empirical evaluations. *Ergonomics, 44*, 475-488.

Foushee, H. C. (1984). Dyads and triads at 35,000 feet. *American Psychologist, 39*, 885-393.

Foushee, H. C., and Helmreich, R. L. (1988). Group interaction and flight crew performance. In E. L. Wiener and D.C. Nagel (Eds.), *Human factors in aviation* (pp. 189-227). San Diego, California: Academic Press.

French, H. W. (1999). Under pressure, Japanese nuclear workers were lax, report says. *The New York Times*. October 4, 1999.

French, H. W. (2000). Accident makes Japan reexamine A-plants. *The New York Times*. January 13, 2000.

Gander, P. H., Rosekind, M. R., and Gregory, K. B. (1998). Flight crew fatigue VI: A synthesis. *Aviation, Space, and Environmental Medicine, 69, Section II*, B49 – B60.

Grosjean, V., and Terrier, P. (1999). Temporal awareness: Pivotal in performance? *Ergonomics, 42*, 1443-1456.

Haber, R. N., and Haber, L. (2000). Experiencing, remembering and reporting events. *Psychology, Public Policy, and Law. 6*, 1057-1097.

Halberstam, D. (2000). Maybe I remember DiMaggio's kick. *New York Times*, October 21, 2000, Op Ed Page.

Hancock, P. A., and Warm, J. S. (1989). A dynamic model of stress and sustained attention. *Human Factors, 31*, 519-538.

Harris, R. J. (1975). *A primer of multivariate statistics*. New York: Academic Press.

Helmreich, R. L., and Foushee, H. C. (1993). Why crew resource management: Empirical and theoretical bases of human factors training in aviation. In E. Wiener, B. Kanki and R. Helmreich (Eds.), *Cockpit resource management* (pp. 1-45). San Diego, California: Academic Press.

Helmreich, R. L., and Merritt, A. C. (1998). *Culture at work in aviation and medicine: National organizational, and professional influences*. Aldershot, England: Ashgate.

Helmreich, R. L., Merritt, A. C., and Wilhelm, H. A. (1999). The evolution of crew resource management training in commercial aviation. *The International Journal Of Aviation Psychology, 9,* 19-32.

Helmreich, R. L., Wilhelm, J. A., Klinect, J. R., and Merritt, A. C. (2001). Culture, error, and crew resource management. In E. Salas, C. A. Bowers, and E. Edens (Eds.), *Improving teamwork in organizations: Applications of resource management training* (pp. 305-331). Mahwah, New Jersey: Lawrence Erlbaum Associates.

His Majesty's Government of Nepal. (1993). *Report on the accident of Thai Airways International A310, flight TG 311 (HS-TID), on 31 July 1991.* Katmandu, Nepal.

Hofstede, G. (1980). *Culture's consequences: International differences in work-related values.* Beverly Hills, California: Sage.

Hofstede, G. (1991). *Cultures and organizations: Software of the mind.* New York: McGraw-Hill.

Hollnagel, E. (1993). *Human reliability analysis: Context and control.* San Diego, California, Academic Press.

Hyman, I. E. (1999). Creating false autobiographical memories: Why people believe their memory errors. In E. Winograd, R. Fivush, and W. Hirst (Eds.), *Ecological approaches to cognition: Essays in honor of Ulric Neisser* (pp. 229-252). Mahwah, New Jersey: Lawrence Erlbaum Associates.

Ilgen, D. R. (1999). Teams embedded in organizations: Some implications. *American Psychologist, 54,* 129-139.

International Civil Aviation Organization. (1970). *Manual of aircraft accident investigation* (4th ed.). Montreal, Province Quebec, Canada.

International Civil Aviation Organization (1993). *Human factors digest No. 7: Investigation of human factors in accidents and incidents.* (ICAO Circular 240-AN/144). Montreal, Province Quebec, Canada.

Ivergard, T. (1999). Design of information devices and control. In W. Karwowski and W. S. Marras (Eds.), *The occupational ergonomics handbook*. Boca Raton, Florida: CRC Press.

Janis, I. L. (1982). *Groupthink: Psychological studies of policy decisions and fiascoes*. Boston: Houghton Mifflin.

Jentsch, F., Barnett, J., Bowers, C. A., and Salas, E. (1999). Who is flying this plane anyway? What mishaps tell us about crew member role assignment and air crew situation awareness. *Human Factors, 41*, 1-14.

Jones, D. G. (1997). Reducing situation awareness errors in air traffic control. In *Proceedings of the Human Factors and Ergonomics Society 41ˢᵗ Annual Meeting*. Santa Monica, California: Human Factors and Ergonomics Society.

Jones, D. G., and Endsley, M. R. (1996). Sources of situation awareness errors in aviation. *Aviation, Space and Environmental Medicine, 67*, 507-512.

Jones, D. G., and Endsley, M. R. (2000). Overcoming representational errors in complex environments. *Human Factors, 42*, 367-378.

Jordan, P. (2001). This line will not be crossed. *The New York Times Magazine*, December 23, 2001.

Kahan, J. P. (1999). Safety Board methodology. *Proceedings of the Second World Congress on Safety of Transportation, 18-20 February 1998*. Delft, Netherlands: Delft University Press.

Kantowitz, B. H., and Campbell, J. L. (1996). Pilot workload and flightdeck automation. In R. Parasuraman and M. Mouloua (Eds.), *Automation and human performance: Theory and applications* (pp. 117-136). Mahwah, New Jersey: Lawrence Erlbaum Associates.

Karwowski, W., and Marras, W. S. (1999). *The occupational ergonomics handbook*. Boca Raton, Florida: CRC Press.

Kemeny, J. G. (1979). *The need for change: The legacy of TMI.* Report of The President's Commission on the accident at Three Mile Island. Washington, DC: Government Printing Office.

Kerlinger, F. N. (1973). *Foundations of behavioral research* (2nd ed.). New York: Holt, Rinehart and Winston.

Klein, G. (1993a). A recognition-primed decision (RPD) model of rapid decision making. In G. A. Klein, J. Orasanu, R. Calderwood, and C. E. Zsambok (Eds.), *Decision making in action: Models and methods* (pp.138-147). Norwood, New Jersey: Ablex.

Klein, G. (1993b). *Naturalistic decision making: Implications for design.* Wright-Patterson Air Force Base, Ohio: Crew System Ergonomics Information Center.

Klein, G. (1999). Applied decision making. In P.A. Hancock (Ed.), *Human performance and ergonomics* (pp. 87-107). San Diego, California: Academic Press.

Langewiesche, W. (1998). The lessons of ValuJet 592. *The Atlantic Monthly,* March 1998, 81-98.

Lawton, R., and Parker, D. (1998). Individual differences in accident liability: A review and integrative approach. *Human Factors, 40,* 655-671.

Leach, J., and Morris, P. E. (1998). Cognitive factors in the close visual and magnetic particle inspections of welds underwater. *Human Factors, 40,* 187-197.

Leary, W. E. (2000). Poor management by NASA is blamed for Mars failure. *The New York Times,* March 29, 2000.

Lee, J. D., Forsythe, A. M., and Rothblum, A. M. (2000). *The use of crew size evaluation method to examine the effect of operational factors on crew needs* (Report No. UDI-16(1)). Seattle, Washington: Battelle Seattle Research Center.

Lee, J., and Moray, N. (1992). Trust, control strategies and allocation of function in human-machine systems. *Ergonomics, 35,* 1243-1270.

Loftus, E. F. (1997), Creating false memories. *Scientific American,* September, 70-75.

Logan, G. D. (1988). Automaticity, resources, and memory: Theoretical controversies and practical implications. *Human Factors, 30,* 583-598.

Maurino, D. E. (1994). Crosscultural perspectives in human factors training: Lessons from the ICAO human factors program. *The International Journal of Aviation Psychology, 4,* 173-181.

Maurino, D. E. (2000). Human factors and aviation safety: What the industry has, what the industry needs. *Ergonomics, 43,* 952-959.

McFadden, K. L. (1997). Policy improvements for prevention of alcohol misuse by airline pilots. *Human Factors, 39,* 1-8.

Menges, R. J. (1975). Assessing readiness for professional practice. *Review of Educational Research, 45,* 173-208.

Meister, D. (1999). *The history of human factors and ergonomics.* Mahwah, New Jersey: Lawrence Erlbaum Associates.

Miller, C. O. (2000). Resolving "action failure." *The ISASI Forum,* April-June 2000, 14-16.

Miller, R. J., and Penningroth, S. (1997). The effects of response format and other variables on comparisons of digital and dial displays. *Human Factors, 39,* 417-424.

Mitler, M. M., and Miller, J. C. (1996). Methods of testing for sleeplessness. *Behavioral Medicine, 21,* 171-183.

Molloy, R., and Parasuraman, R. (1996). Monitoring an automated system for a single failure: Vigilance and task complexity effects. *Human Factors, 38,* 311-322.

Monk, T. H., Folkard, S., and Wedderburn, A. I. (1996). Maintaining safety and high performance on shiftwork. *Applied Ergonomics, 27,* 17-23.

Moray, N. (1994). Error reduction as a systems problem. In M. S. Bogner, (Ed.), *Human error in medicine* (pp. 67-91). Hillsdale, New Jersey: Lawrence Erlbaum Associates.

Moray, N. (2000). Culture, politics and ergonomics. *Ergonomics, 43,* 858-868.

Moray, N., Inagaki, T., and Itoh, M. (2000). Adaptive automation, trust, and self-confidence in fault management of time-critical tasks. *Journal of Experimental Psychology: Applied, 6,* 44-58.

Moroney, W. F., and Moroney, B. W. (1998). Flight simulation. In D. J. Garland, J. A. Wise, and V. D. Hopkin, (Eds.), *Handbook of aviation human factors* (pp. 355-388). Mahwah, New Jersey: Lawrence Erlbaum Associates.

Mosier, K. L., and Skitka, L. J. (1996). Human decision makers and automated decision aids: Made for each other? In R. Parasuraman and M. Mouloua (Eds.), *Automation and human performance: Theory and applications* (pp. 201-220). Mahwah, New Jersey: Lawrence Erlbaum Associates.

Mumaw, R. J., Roth, E. M., Vicente, K. J., and Burns, C. M. (2000). There is more to monitoring a nuclear power plant than meets the eye. *Human Factors, 42,* 36-55.

National Institute on Drug Abuse. (1999). *Cocaine Abuse and Addiction.* (National Institutes of Health Publication No. 99-4342). Bethesda, Maryland.

National Transportation Safety Board. (1973). *Aircraft Accident Report, Eastern Air Lines, Inc., L-1011, N310EA, Miami, Florida, December 29, 1972.* (Report Number: AAR-73-14). Washington, DC.

National Transportation Safety Board. (1979). *Aircraft Accident Report, Japan Airlines Company, Ltd., JA 8054, Anchorage, Alaska, January 13, 1977.* (Report Number: AAR-78-07). Washington, DC.

National Transportation Safety Board. (1980a). *Special Investigation Report, Design induced landing gear retraction accidents in Beechcraft Baron, Bonanza, and other light aircraft.* (Report Number: SR-80-01). Washington, DC.

National Transportation Safety Board. (1980b*). Aircraft Accident Report, Aeromexico DC-10-30, XA-DUH, over Luxembourg, Europe, November 11, 1979.* (Report Number: AAR-80-10). Washington, DC.

National Transportation Safety Board. (1982). *Aircraft Accident Report, Air Florida, Inc., Boeing 737-222, N62AF, Collision with 14th Street Bridge, near Washington National Airport, Washington, DC, January, 13, 1982.* (Report Number: AAR-82-08). Washington, DC.

National Transportation Safety Board. (1986). *Aircraft Accident Report, China Airlines Boeing 747-SP, N4522V, 300 nautical miles northwest of San Francisco, California, February 19, 1985.* (Report Number: AAR-86-03). Washington, DC.

National Transportation Safety Board. (1987*). Aircraft Accident Report, Piper PA-23-150, N2185P and Pan American World Airways, Boeing 727-235, N4743, Tampa, Florida, November 6, 1986.* (Report Number: AAR-87-06). Washington, DC.

National Transportation Safety Board. (1988a). *Railroad Accident Report, Rear-end collision of Amtrak Passenger train 94, The Colonial, and Consolidated Rail Corporation Freight Train ENS-121, on the Northeast Corridor, Chase, Maryland, January 4, 1987.* (Report Number: RAR-88-01). Washington, DC.

National Transportation Safety Board. (1988b). *Aircraft Accident Report, Northwest Airlines, Inc., McDonnell Douglas DC-9-82, N312RC, Detroit Metropolitan Wayne County Airport, Romulus, Michigan, August 16, 1987.* (Report Number: AAR-88-05). Washington, DC.

National Transportation Safety Board. (1989). *Aircraft Accident Report, Trans-Colorado Airlines, Inc., flight 2286, Fairchild Metro III, SA227AC, N68TC, Bayfield, Colorado, 1988.* (Report Number: AAR-89-01). Washington, DC.

National Transportation Safety Board. (1990a). *Aircraft Accident Report, United Airlines flight 232, McDonnell Douglas DC-10-10, Sioux Gateway Airport, Sioux City, Iowa, July 19, 1989.* (Report Number: AAR-90-06). Washington, DC.

National Transportation Safety Board. (1990b). *Marine Accident Report, Grounding of U.S. tankship Exxon Valdez on Bligh Reef, Prince William Sound, Near Valdez, Alaska, March 24, 1989.* (Report Number: MAR-90-04). Washington, DC.

National Transportation Safety Board. (1991a). *Aircraft Accident Report, Northwest Airlines, Inc., Flights 1482 and 299, runway incursion and collision, Detroit Metropolitan/Wayne County Airport Romulus, Michigan, December 3, 1990.* (Report Number: AAR-91-05). Washington, DC.

National Transportation Safety Board. (1991b). *Aircraft Accident Report, Grand Canyon Airlines, flight Canyon 5, De Havilland Twin Otter, DHC-6-300, N75GC, Grand Canyon National Park Airport, Tusayan, Arizona, September 27, 1989.* (Report Number: AAR-91-01). Washington, DC.

National Transportation Safety Board. (1993). *Aircraft Accident Report, Aborted takeoff shortly after liftoff, Trans World Airlines flight 843, Lockheed L-1011, N11002, John F. Kennedy International Airport Jamaica, New York July 30, 1992.* (Report Number: AAR-93-04). Washington, DC.

National Transportation Safety Board. (1994a). *Aircraft Accident Report, Uncontrolled collision with terrain, American International Airways flight 8808, Douglas DC-8-61, N814CK, U.S. Naval Air Station in Guantanamo Bay, Cuba, August 18, 1993.* (Report Number: AAR- 94-04). Washington, DC.

National Transportation Safety Board. (1994b). *Aircraft Accident Report, Controlled flight into terrain, Federal Aviation Administration, Beech Super King Air 300/F, N82, Front Royal, Virginia, October 26, 1993.* (Report Number: AAR-94-03). Washington, DC.

National Transportation Safety Board. (1994c). *Special Investigation Report, Maintenance anomaly resulting in dragged engine during landing rollout, Northwest Airlines flight 18, Boeing 747-251b, N637US, New Tokyo International Airport, Narita, Japan, March 1, 1994.* (Report Number: SIR-94-02). Washington, DC.

National Transportation Safety Board. (1994d). *Special Study, A review of flightcrew-involved, major accidents of U.S. air carriers, 1978 through 1990.* (Report Number: SS-94-01). Washington, DC.

National Transportation Safety Board. (1994e). *Aircraft Accident Report, Stall and loss of control on final approach, Atlantic Coast Airlines, Inc. United Express flight 6291 Jetstream 4101, N304UE Columbus, Ohio January 7, 1994.* (Report Number: AAR-94-07). Washington, DC.

National Transportation Safety Board. (1996). *Railroad Accident Report, Collision of Washington Metropolitan Area Transit Authority Train T-111 with Standing Train at Shady Grove Passenger Station, Gaithersburg, Maryland January 6, 1996.* (Report Number: RAR-96-04). Washington, DC.

National Transportation Safety Board. (1997a). *Aircraft Accident Report, In-flight fire and impact with terrain, ValuJet Airlines, flight 592, DC-9-32, N904VJ, Everglades, Near Miami, Florida, May 11, 1996.* (Report Number: AAR-97-06). Washington, DC.

National Transportation Safety Board. (1997b). *Railroad Accident Report, Near head-on collision and derailment of two New Jersey Transit commuter trains, near Secaucus, New Jersey, February 9, 1996.* (Report Number: RAR-97-01). Washington, DC.

National Transportation Safety Board. (1997c). *Aircraft Accident Report, Descent below visual glidepath and collision with terrain, Delta Air Lines flight 554, McDonnell Douglas MD-88, N914DL, LaGuardia Airport, New York, October 19, 1996.* (Report Number: AAR-97-03). Washington, DC.

National Transportation Safety Board. (1997d). *Aircraft Accident Report, Wheels-Up Landing, Continental Airlines flight 1943, Douglas DC-9, N10556, Houston, Texas, February 19, 1996.* (Report Number: AAR-97-01). Washington, DC.

National Transportation Safety Board. (1997e). *Marine Accident Report, Grounding of the Panamanian passenger ship Royal Majesty on Rose and Crown Shoal near Nantucket, Massachusetts, June 10, 1995.* (Report Number: MAR-97-01). Washington, DC.

National Transportation Safety Board. (1998a). *Aircraft Accident Report, Uncontained engine failure, Delta Airlines flight 1288, McDonnell Douglas MD-88, N927DA, Pensacola, Florida, July 6, 1996.* (Report Number: AAR-98-01). Washington, DC.

National Transportation Safety Board. (1998b). *Railroad Accident Report, Derailment of Amtrak Train 4, Southwest Chief, on the Burlington Northern Santa Fe Railway, near Kingman, Arizona, August 9, 1997.* (Report Number: RAR-98-03). Washington, DC.

National Transportation Safety Board. (1998c). *Aircraft Accident Report, In-flight icing encounter and uncontrolled collision with terrain, Comair flight 3272, Embraer EMB-120RT, N265CA, Monroe, Michigan, January 9, 1997.* (Report Number: AAR-98-04). Washington, DC.

National Transportation Safety Board. (1999a). *Safety Report, Evaluation of U.S. Department of Transportation efforts in the 1990s to address operator fatigue.* (Report Number: SR-99/02). Washington, DC.

National Transportation Safety Board. (1999b). *Aircraft Accident Report, Controlled flight into terrain, Korean Air, flight 801, Boeing 747-300, HL7468, Nimitz Hill, Guam, August 6, 1997.* (Report Number: AAR-99-02). Washington, DC.

National Transportation Safety Board. (1999c). *Aircraft Accident Report, Uncontrolled descent and collision with terrain, USAir flight 427, Boeing 737-300, N513AU, Near Aliquippa, Pennsylvania, September 8, 1994.* (Report Number: AAR-99-01). Washington, DC.

National Transportation Safety Board. (2000a). *Safety Recommendations I-00-1–I-00-4*, January 13, 2000. Washington, DC.

National Transportation Safety Board. (2000b). *Highway Accident Report, Collision of Greyhound Lines, Inc. motorcoach with tractor semi-trailers on the Pennsylvania Turnpike, Burnt Cabins, Pennsylvania, June 20, 1998*. (Report Number: HAR-00-01). Washington, DC.

National Transportation Safety Board. (2000c). *Safety Recommendations A-00-30–A-00-31*, April 11, 2000, Washington, DC.

National Transportation Safety Board. (2000d). *In-flight Breakup Over the Atlantic Ocean, Trans World Airlines flight 800, Boeing 747-131, N93119, near East Moriches, New York, July 17, 1996*. (Report Number AAR-00-03). Washington, DC.

Nickerson, R. S. (1999). Engineering psychology and ergonomics. In P.A. Hancock (Ed.), *Human performance and ergonomics* (pp. 1-45). San Diego, California: Academic Press.

Norman, D. A. (1981). Categorization of action slips. *Psychological Review, 88*, 1-15.

Norman, D. A. (1988). *The psychology of everyday things*. New York: Basic Books.

O'Hanlon, J. F. (1981). Boredom: Practical consequences and a theory. *Acta Psychologica, 49*, 53-82.

O'Hare, D. (2000). The 'Wheel of Misfortune': A taxonomic approach to human factors in accident investigation and analysis in aviation and other complex systems. *Ergonomics, 43*, 2001-2019.

Orasanu, J. M. (1993). Decision-making in the cockpit. In E. L. Wiener, B. G. Kanki, and R. L. Helmreich (Eds.), *Cockpit resource management* (pp. 137-172). New York: Academic Press.

Orasanu, J., Fischer, U., and Davison, J. (1997). Cross-culture barriers to effective communication in aviation. In C. S. Granrose and S. Oskamp (Eds.), *Cross-cultural work groups*. Thousand Oaks, California: Sage Publications.

Orasanu, J. M., Martin, L., and Davison, J. (1998), Errors in aviation decision making: Bad decisions or bad luck. Paper presented at the Fourth Conference on Naturalistic Decision Making, Warrenton, Virginia, May 29-31.

Orasanu, J. M., Martin, L., and Davison, J. (2001), Cognitive and contextual factors in aviation accidents: Decision errors. In E. Salas and G. Klein (Eds.), *Linking expertise and naturalistic decision making* (pp. 209-225). Mahwah, New Jersey: Lawrence Erlbaum Associates.

Packer Engineering. (2000). *Report submitted to Special Commission on the 1999 bonfire*. Naperville, Illinois: Packer Engineering.

Parasuraman, R. (2000). Designing automation for human use: Empirical studies and quantitative models. *Ergonomics, 43,* 931-951.

Parasuraman, R., Mouloua, M., Molloy, R., and Hilburn, B. (1996). Monitoring of automated systems. In R. Parasuraman and M. Mouloua (Eds.), *Automation and human performance: Theory and applications*. Mahwah, New Jersey: Lawrence Erlbaum Associates.

Parasuraman, R., and Riley, V. (1997). Humans and automation: Use, misuse, disuse and abuse. *Human Factors, 39,* 230-253.

Parasuraman, R., Sheridan, T. B., and Wickens, C. D. (2000). A model for types and levels of human interaction with automation. *IEEE Transactions on Systems, Man, and Cybernetics–Part A: Systems and Humans. 30,* 286-297.

Paries, J., and Amalberti, R. Aviation safety paradigms and training implications. In N. B. Sarter and R. Amalberti (Eds.), *Cognitive engineering in the aviation domain* (pp. 253-286). Mahwah, New Jersey: Lawrence Erlbaum Associates.

Paris, C. R., Salas, E., and Cannon-Bowers, J. A. (1999). Human performance in multi-operator systems. In P. A. Hancock (Ed.), *Human performance and ergonomics* (pp. 329-386). San Diego, California: Academic Press.

Paris, C. R., Salas, E., and Cannon-Bowers, J. A. (2000). Teamwork in multi-person systems: A review and analysis. *Ergonomics, 43,* 1052-1075.

Parsons, S. O., Seminara, J. L., and Wogalter, M. S. (1999). A summary of warnings research. *Ergonomics in Design,* January 1999, 21-31.

Patterson, R. D. (1990). Auditory warning sounds in the work environment. *Philosophical Transactions of the Royal Society of London, 327,* 485-492.

Perrow, C. (1999). *Normal accidents: Living with high-risk technologies* (2nd ed.). Princeton, New Jersey: Princeton University Press.

Rasmussen, J. (1983). Skill, rules, and knowledge; Signals, signs and symbols, and other distinctions in human performance models. *IEEE Transactions on Systems, Man and Cybernetics, 13,* 257-266.

Rasmussen, J., Pejtersen, A. M., and Goodstein, L. P. (1994). *Cognitive systems engineering.* New York: John Wiley and Sons.

Rasmussen, J., and Vicente, K. J. (1989). Coping with human errors through system design: Implications for ecological interface design. *International Journal of Man-Machine Studies, 31,* 517-534.

Reason, J. T. (1990). *Human Error.* New York: Cambridge University Press.

Reason, J. T. (1997). *Managing the risks of organizational accidents.* Aldershot, England: Ashgate Publishing.

Riley, V. (1996). Operator reliance on automation: Theory and data. In R. Parasuraman and M. Mouloua (Eds.), *Automation and human performance: Theory and applications* (pp. 19-35). Mahwah, New Jersey: Lawrence Erlbaum Associates.

Rochlin, G. I. (1999). Safety operation as a social construct. *Ergonomics, 42*, 1549-1560.

Rodgers, M. D., and Blanchard, R.E. (1993). *Accident proneness: A research review.* (DOT/FAA/AM Report No. 93/9). Washington, DC: The Federal Aviation Administration, Office of Aviation Medicine.

Rosekind, M. R., Gander, P. H., Miller, D. L., Gregory, K. B., Smith, R. M., Weldon, K. J., Co, E. L., McNally, K. L., and Lebacqz, V. (1994). Fatigue in operational settings: Examples from the aviation environment. *Human Factors, 36*, 327-338.

Ross, L. E., and Mundt, J. C. (1988). Multiattribute modeling analysis of the effects of a low blood alcohol level on pilot performance. *Human Factors, 30*, 293-304.

Ruffell-Smith, H. P. (1979). *A simulator study of the interaction of pilot workload with errors, vigilance, and decisions.* (NASA Technical Memorandum 78482). Moffett Field, California: NASA-Ames Research Center.

Sanders, M. S., and McCormick, E. J. (1993). *Human factors in engineering and design* (7th ed.). New York: McGraw-Hill.

Salas, E., Driskell, J. E., and Hughes, S. (1996). Introduction: The study of stress and human performance. In J. E. Driskell and E. Salas (Eds.) *Stress and human performance* (pp. 1-45). Mahwah, New Jersey: Lawrence Erlbaum Associates.

Sarter, N. B. (2000). The need for multisensory interfaces in support of effective attention allocation in highly dynamic event-driven domains: The case of cockpit automation. *International Journal of Aviation Psychology. 10*, 231-245.

Sarter, N. B., and Woods, D. D. (1995). How in the world did we ever get into that mode? Mode error and awareness in supervisory control. *Human Factors, 37*, 5-19.

Sarter, N. B., and Woods, D. D. (1997). Team play with a powerful and independent agent: Operational experiences and automation surprises on the Airbus A-320. *Human Factors, 39,* 553-569.

Sarter, N. B., and Woods, D. D. (2000). Team play with a powerful and independent agent: A full-mission simulation study. *Human Factors, 42,* 390-402.

Scerbo, M. W. (1996). Theoretical perspectives on adaptive automation. In R. Parasuraman and M. Mouloua (Eds.), *Automation and human performance: Theory and applications* (pp. 37-63). Mahwah, New Jersey: Lawrence Erlbaum Associates.

Schein, E. H. (1990). Organizational culture. *American Psychologist, 45,* 109-119.

Schein, E. H. (1996). Culture: The missing concept in organizational studies. *Administrative Science Quarterly, 41,* 229-240.

Senders, J. W., and Moray, N. P. (1991). *Human error: Cause, prediction, and reduction.* Hillsdale, New Jersey: Lawrence Erlbaum Associates.

Shappell, S. A., and Wiegmann, D. A. (1997). A human error approach to accident investigation: The taxonomy of unsafe operations. *The International Journal of Aviation Psychology, 7,* 269-292.

Shappell, S. A., and Wiegmann, D.A. (2001). Human factors analysis and classification system. *Flight Safety Digest, February 2001,* 15-25.

Sheridan, T. B., and Parasuraman, R. (2000). Human versus automation in responding to failures: An expected-value analysis. *Human Factors, 42,* 403-407.

Sklar, A. E., and Sarter, N. B. (1999). Good vibrations: Tactile feedback in support of attention allocation and human-automation coordination in event driven domains. *Human Factors, 41,* 543-552.

Smith, A. P. (1990). Respiratory virus infections and performance. *Philosophical Transactions of the Royal Society of London, 327,* 519-528.

Smith, L., Folkard, S., and Poole, C. J. M. (1994). Increased injuries on night shift. *Lancet, 344,* 1137-1139.

Soeters, J. L., and Boer, P. C. (2000). Culture and flight safety in military aviation. *The International Journal of Aviation Psychology, 10,* 111-133.

Sorkin, R. D. (1988). Why are people turning off our alarms? *Journal of the Acoustical Society of America, 84,* 1107-1108.

Special Commission on the 1999 Texas A & M Bonfire. (2000). *Final report.* College Station, Texas: Texas A & M University.

Stern, S. E., Mullennix, J. W., Dyson, C., and Wilson, S. J. (1999). The persuasiveness of synthetic speech versus human speech. *Human Factors, 41,* 588-595.

Sundstrom, E., De Meuse, K. P. and Futrell, D. (1990). Work teams: Applications and effectiveness. *American Psychologist, 45,* 120-133.

Sutcliffe, A., and Rugg, G. (1998). A taxonomy of error types for failure analysis and risk assessment. *International Journal of Human-Computer Interaction, 10,* 381-405.

Tiffany, S. T. (1999). Cognitive concepts of craving. *Alcohol Research and Health, 23,* 215-224.

Tilley, A. J., Wilkinson, R. T., Warren, P. S. G., Watson, B., and Drud, M. (1982). The sleep and performance of shift workers. *Human Factors, 24,* 629-643.

Tuchman, B. (1962). *The guns of August.* New York: Macmillan.

Tversky, A., and Kahneman, D. (1974). Judgment under uncertainty: Heuristics and biases. *Science, 185,* 1124-1131.

United States Navy. (2001). Transcripts of the Court of Inquiry into the Collision of the USS Greenville and the Ehime Maru, February 19, 2001. *http://www.cpf.navy.mil/cpfnews/coidownloadtranscripts.html.* August 1, 2001.

Van Orden, K. F., Benoit, S. L., and Osga, G. A. (1996). Effects of cold air stress on the performance of a command and control task. *Human Factors, 38,* 130-141.

Vaughan, D. (1996). *The Challenger launch decision: Risky technology, culture, and deviance at NASA.* Chicago: The University of Chicago Press.

Vicente, K. J. (1997). Heeding the legacy of Meister, Brunswik, and Gibson: Toward a broader view of human factors research. *Human Factors, 39,* 323-328.

Vicente, K. J. (1999). *Cognitive work analysis: Toward safe, productive, and healthy computer-based work.* Mahwah, New Jersey: Lawrence Erlbaum Associates.

Wald, M. (1999a). Experts say lapses led to Japan's A-plant failure. *The New York Times,* October 23, 1999.

Wald, M. (1999b). Secret witness to car crashes in black boxes. *The New York Times,* May 30, 1999.

Weiler, J. M., Bloomfield, J. R., Woodworth, G. G., Grant, A. R., Layton, T. A., Brown, T. L., McKenzie, D. R., Baker, T. W., and Watson, G. S. (2000). Effects of fexofenadine, diphenhydramine, and alcohol on driving performance: A randomized, placebo-controlled study in the Iowa driving simulator. *Annals of Internal Medicine, 132,* 354-363.

Wells, G. L., Malpass, R. S., Lindsay, R. C. L., Fisher, R. P., Turtle, J. W., and Fulero, S.M. (2000). From the lab to the police station: A successful application of eyewitness research. *American Psychologist, 55,* 581-598.

Westrum, R., and Adamski, A. J. (1998). Organizational factors associated with safety and mission success in aviation environments. In D. J. Garland, J. A. Wise, and V. D. Hopkin, (Eds.), *Handbook of Aviation Human Factors* (pp. 67-104). Mahwah, New Jersey: Lawrence Erlbaum Associates.

Wickens, C. D., and Carswell, C. M. (1995). The proximity compatibility principle: Its psychological foundation and relevance to display design. *Human Factors, 37,* 473-494.

Wickens, C. D., and Hollands, J. G. (2000). *Engineering psychology and human performance* (3rd ed.). Upper Saddle River, New Jersey: Prentice Hall.

Wiener, E. (1988). Cockpit automation, in E. L. Wiener and D. C. Nagel (Eds.), *Human factors in aviation* (pp. 433-461). San Diego, California: Academic Press.

Wiener, E. L. (1989). *Human factors of advanced technology ("glass cockpit") transport aircraft* (NASA Technical Report 117528). Moffett Field, California: NASA-Ames Research Center.

Wiener E. L., and Curry, R. E. (1980). *Flight-deck automation: Promises and problems.* (NASA Technical Memorandum 81206). Moffett Field, California: NASA-Ames Research Center.

Wiegmann, D. A., and Shappell, S. A. (1999). Human error and crew resource management failures in naval aviation mishaps: A review of U.S. Naval Safety Center data, 1990-96. *Aviation, Space, and Environmental Medicine. 70,* 1147-1151.

Woods, D. D. (1995). Toward a theoretical base for representation design in the computer medium: Ecological perception and aiding human cognition. In J. Flach, P. Hancock, J. Caird, and K. Vicente (Eds.), *Global perspectives on the ecology of human-machine systems* (pp. 157-188). Hillsdale, New Jersey: Lawrence Erlbaum Associates.

Woods, D. D. (1996). Decomposing automation: Apparent simplicity, real complexity. In R. Parasuraman and M. Mouloua (Eds.), *Automation and human performance: Theory and applications* (pp. 3-17). Mahwah, New Jersey: Lawrence Erlbaum Associates.

Woods, D. D., Johannesen, L. J., Cook, R. I., Sarter, N. B. (1994). *Behind human error: Cognitive systems, computers, and hindsight.* Wright-Patterson Air Force Base, Ohio: Crew Systems Ergonomics Information Analysis Center.

Wyon, D. P., Wyon, I., and Norin, F. (1996). Effects of moderate heat stress on driver vigilance in a moving vehicle. *Ergonomics, 39,* 61-75.

Index